EFFICIENCY ISSUES IN TRANSITIONAL ECONOMIES

For CT

Efficiency Issues in Transitional Economies

An application to Hungary

Jenifer Piesse
Birkbeck College
University of London

Ashgate

Aldershot • Brookfield USA • Singapore • Sydney

Published by
Ashgate Publishing Ltd
Gower House
Croft Road
Aldershot
Hants GU11 3HR
England

Ashgate Publishing Company
Old Post Road
Brookfield
Vermont 05036
USA

British Library Cataloguing in Publication Data
Piesse, Jenifer
    Efficiency issues in transitional economies : an
    application to Hungary
    1. Production (Economic theory) 2. Industrial efficiency -
    Hungary 3. Hungary - Economic conditions
    I. Title
    338'.06'09439

Library of Congress Catalog Card Number: 98-74444

ISBN 1 84014 979 5

Printed in Great Britain by The Book Company, Suffolk

Contents

List of Tables

List of Figures

Acknowledgements

I would like to thank Saul Estrin (London Business School) and Paul Hare (Herriot Watt University) for allowing me to use the data. The sample is part of a multi-country dataset associated with the project *Transition to a Market Economy: Competitiveness, Ownership and Regulation, ESRC Grant no: R3009/25/3007*. Although I have complained about its inadequacies repeatedly, I am grateful to have been given the opportunity to work with it.

I would also like to thank the following: Derek Bailey, George Battese, David Begg, Alison Booth, David Hadley, Yogesh Khatri, Sarah-Kay McDonald, Paul Mosley, Ron Smith, Lena Takla, Colin Thirtle and Rob Townsend.

Introduction

National income accounting has become a well accepted tool for keeping track of economic changes in the western countries, but in Central and Eastern Europe (CEE) the variations in the aggregate statistics available from different sources are huge, as the next chapter will explain. This study offers an alternative means of following the progress of the economic transitions in CEE. A range of techniques for measuring the efficiency of production are applied to a large sample of firm-level data for Hungary over the period 1985 to 1991. The industries chosen are agriculture, light manufacturing and services. This allows discussion of the structural transformation and inferences on the changing positions of the primary, secondary and tertiary sectors during the early years of the transition, which has attracted little prior attention. The range of techniques allow for different producer objectives, which is particularly necessary when an economic system is undergoing a series of changes in its fundamental institutions, on which the productive activity is based, such as occurs during periods of political and economic transition.

In such a context, it is important that a rigorous approach to performance measurement exists in order to develop and implement national economic policy. We have every reason to believe that nation states with a clear accounting system do better than those without. Indeed, one of the reasons commonly given for the failure of economic development in African economies is poor policy, frequently the result of a lack of information and effective measurement - we simply do not know what is going on (Lipton, 1989).

By comparison, for the transitional economies of Central and Eastern Europe (CEE) there are national income accounting statistics from various sources as well as national and international attempts to measure productivity, but the variation in the final figures is so huge that it is difficult to believe that any of these aggregate statistics should be taken seriously. In many cases it is not possible even to know if the reforms in these countries are resulting in an increase or a decrease in industrial output and productivity, or to make the kind of international comparisons that would be necessary to determine the likely effects of major organisational change.

This book seeks to address this measurement problem in the following manner. Part I provides the background, sets out the relevant theory and describes the data. Chapter 1 begins by explaining why valid measures of efficiency in production are important in the context of transitional economies and outlines the contribution of the book. Chapter 2 reviews the transition literature to provide a framework for the subsequent analysis. The approach to performance measurement leans heavily on established methodologies in the production economics literature, and the theory behind these approaches is outlined in Chapter 3. The volume of work in this area is vast and, more recently, merges with applied methods of econometric analysis where data is incomplete or unreliable. Econometric modelling and nonparametric programming methods are included in this chapter, as are the accounting techniques and index number theory which will be used in total factor productivity (TFP) measurement. Innovations in techniques of efficiency frontier construction and the use of panel data have also progressed, although details of these developments are omitted from Chapter 3 and are left to the empirical chapters themselves. An analysis of the emergence of an information-based accounting system from the pre-reform socialist reporting procedures is discussed in Chapter 4. This chapter also describes the available data in detail, discusses the reconciliation of the accounting definitions, and provides a rationale for the series used and the choice of the industrial sectors and enterprises that have been included in the analysis that follows.

Part II is the kernel of the research, as it is the estimation and results section.[1] Chapter 5 estimates the output elasticities of the firms and compares the changing relative importance of inputs in the industries as well as considering the effect of a new ownership structure on the individual enterprises. Chapter 6 constructs firm-specific technical efficiency

---

[1] Much of this analysis is very output intensive. Most of the results are summarised in the chapters and some is included in short appendices. However, full results are available from the author.

2

measures for the industries and reports their performance over the seven year period. Chapter 7 considers the scale of production and discusses the effect of size of firm on the transition process. Difficulties in the adjustment of current value data to a form appropriate for time series analysis are addressed in Chapter 8 and a number of panel data models are estimated. This is an attempt to introduce some inter-temporal factors into the analysis while confronting the problems of working with time series data where prices are not known or not reliable. Having established that the lack of good price data is not a fatal limitation, the analysis becomes more interesting, as it uses index techniques, which are easier to follow and illustrated in a specific application.

Thus, Part III begins with Chapter 9, where TFP indices are constructed to compare productivity measures within and between the sectors. This is followed in Chapter 10 by an examination of the relative progress of the three sectors as the economy experienced the beginnings of transition. It suggests that agricultural productivity recovers relatively quickly, so that agriculture could be the leading sector in the transition, and the normal relative decline of agriculture may be temporarily reversed. In the course of this analysis, the TFP is decomposed into measures of efficiency and technical change, which completes the analysis of the Hungarian economy. Both elements are found to be important, with the average efficiency levels of less than 80% in two of the three industries studied, but this result is dominated by the very substantial technological regression in all three industries.

The conclusion summarises the previous chapters, noting what they attempted and what the major results were. These are then discussed in the context of the recent literature, which shows that these data do corroborate the conclusions that are being reached by more qualitative methods. Throughout this summary there are two strands to the discussion; the first is what has actually been discovered about Hungary and the transition process more generally; the second is an assessment of the limitations of the data and the reliability of the results.

The conclusions on the data are not what was expected ex ante. The lack of firm-specific price information was thought to be the most crippling limitation of the dataset, but the results were less sensitive to the choice of deflators than was expected. However, the total lack of information on the firms, and especially the farms, proved to be much more damaging than was expected a priori. Not knowing the type of enterprise (grain, intensive animal raising, horticulture, viniculture, etc.) meant that the agricultural dataset, which appeared to be the jewel in the crown, could

3

not even be used to solve the farm size issue. This problem is not specific to this study: in the general case, numbers alone, no matter how many or how good, are not adequate without a considerable amount of qualitative information. The problem becomes glaringly obvious when the fumbling interpretation of the Hungarian results falls short of a comparable study completed earlier (Piesse et al (1996)). This illustrates one of the main conclusions here: taking data collected by others, with insufficient background information and no contact to solve problems, is dangerous. Griliches (1986) warnings on situations where the collectors and users of data differ need to be heeded and the data constraint (Griliches, 1994) will not easily be lessened in transitional economies.

PART I:
THE TRANSITION, PRODUCTION THEORY, HUNGARIAN ACCOUNTING AND DATA

1 Measurement in Periods of Transition

Introduction

Much of the current literature on transitional economies discusses the order and speed of liberalization and transformation. But I would claim that a precondition for doing any empirical analysis of the order of events in the transition, or the speed at which it should be pushed forward, is the ability to measure changes in efficiency and productivity. Aggregate analysis fails to provide consistent measures of national performance, with the difficulties arising from two main areas. Firstly, real differences exist in the method of compiling national accounting data between the CEE countries and those in the West. And secondly, distorted prices and exchange rates, and the inherent political accounting biases, such as the ambiguous incentives of those reporting directly from the firm, make it difficult to construct consistent values at an aggregate level.

An interest in alternative models of the firm, and in the special difficulties facing the countries of Central and Eastern Europe, and other regions of political and social transition, has led economic restructuring and transition to become a major area of research. A theoretical consensus has evolved about the process, although some debate exists about the speed and sequencing of the reform. Added to this are the studies measuring the economic efficiency and performance of firms operating within various organisational arrangements, often comparing the growth and development of firms in transition economies with those in Western Europe and the USA.

National policy formulation, especially that concerned with increasing integration into a wider economic community, requires reliable information on performance at the industry level. Examination of relative performance in different sectors shows that the transitional economies are sufficiently different from the developing countries that many aspects of national industrial policy are not readily transferable between countries, an issue of considerable importance to international funding agencies. The stages of growth and structural transformation literatures[2] suggest that during the development process agriculture declines in importance relative to industry and later the service sector. However, for much of this century in the countries of CEE under communist control, industrialization was a central feature of the strategic plan. The relative decline of agriculture in preference to industry, and without the support of a necessary service sector, was forced prematurely by policy. The results in Chapter 10 suggest that liberalization and reliance on market forces may temporarily reverse the normal direction of the structural transformation until the establishment of markets in all sectors is complete.

The analysis of many policy issues depends heavily on consistent performance indicators. For the transition economies, full liberalization and market transformation is directly linked to European integration. With the European Union at the centre of this integration, full membership will be the objective of most reforming economies. The impact of this is of importance to all member states, particularly with respect to those states retaining a relatively large agricultural sector, measured in terms of proportion of GDP. With the current state of knowledge, it is scarcely possible to compare countries that similar ideological histories. Useful comparisons between the other aspiring member countries and the current incumbents seem even more elusive.

Given an opportunity to analyze an extensive multi-sector, firm level data set, it is possible to construct some more meaningful measures of productivity and efficiency, and hence to derive some performance indicators. These allow intertemporal, and within and between industry comparisons, all of which are superior to the existing aggregate measurement. In this study, enterprise-level data for a large sample of Hungarian firms for the period 1985-1991 allows the measurement of productive efficiency during a period which coincides with the starting point

---

[2] Originally introduced by the German Historical School, for example, Friedrich List (1841), this was developed further by Fisher in the 1930's, Clark (1940) and more recently Rostow (1971).

of significant economic and structural change.[3] This presents a chance to develop an understanding of productivity in an economy which has begun to slowly enter the process of transition, but where the precise direction of some of the institutional arrangements are still under review, and certain policies have yet to be implemented fully. Also, as is common. in the majority of transition economies, Hungary is subject to reasonably high inflation during the period under review.

In terms of subject area and empirical background this study draws on the literature on the CEE transition and tries to address some of the problems associated with the newly reordered enterprises. The methods used are from the production economics literature, specifically production function estimation using pooled data, deterministic and stochastic, parametric and nonparametric frontiers and productivity indices. The third strand of literature is that of socialist accounting and the process of transforming the accounting data into a production dataset.

The Characteristics of Economies in Transition

The re-establishment of a market economy presents quite different challenges from the process of development in newly industrialised countries. Historically, the development of modern economies has been assisted by the evolution of an institutional framework capable of securing the scale and structure of investment necessary to create an advanced industrial economy. But the countries of CEE Europe were already fully industrialised and run by large, bureaucratic, and highly interventionist states. Therefore, the peculiar problem faced by the transitional economies has been the dismantling of the state operations and redundant structures of over-industrialization, and the simultaneous construction of a new state with market institutions capable of generating a new economic base, able to compete in world markets.

Overshadowing the transition process has been the problem of which market model to follow. There was a danger that new market systems would be imported from the west, where they had taken centuries

---

[3] The beginning of the transition in the countries of Central and Eastern Europe has been defined as the year in which there was a large decline in industrial production. This is 1990 for Hungary, Poland and Bulgaria, and 1991 for the Czech Republic and Slovakia (Blanchard, 1996).

to develop, without due consideration of how appropriate they may be. Traditionally, national economic systems and institutions have evolved from political and social experience, with the result that a range of quite different conventions and organisational arrangements exist. Corbett and Mayer (1991) argue that the Anglo-American model, with its emphasis on capital markets and equity ownership, and the associated tendency toward short-termism, is a less effective financial structure than one with a greater involvement of the banking sector and cross-company ownership, such as that in Japan and to a lesser extent, Germany. The high levels of long term investment required in the transition economies may imply the latter is the more suitable model.

Clearly, many of the aspects of transition are a function of macroeconomic policy and institution building, including the growth of markets, but it also depends on the organisation of corporate decision making and a transparent and unambiguous structure of incentives. It is also necessary to ensure efficiency in the allocation of funds at the national level and in the use of resources in production and in the distribution of subsequent output at the firm level. In the welfare economics literature (for example, Bator (1957)), the theoretical framework encompasses efficiency in consumption, efficiency in production (both technical and allocative) and arriving at the right product mix that gives the optimum. The primary concern of this study is the measurement of the technical efficiency in production of individual firms although data availability limits even the extent to which this can be fully analyzed. As will be seen in later chapters where it is formally defined, technical efficiency is a more easily measured concept, given the nature of the data, than allocative efficiency.[4]

Both technical and allocative efficiency raise some important issues specific to the transition economies. It requires little imagination to think of producers operating in a conventional market environment pursuing conventional economic objectives under budgetary or resource constraints. But this does not easily extend with equal force to CEE producers, perhaps operating in regulated or otherwise restricted markets, or in markets with newly established and still imperfect institutions, or pursuing objectives other than the usually assumed goal of profit maximisation. Thus models must be carefully chosen, often specifically to minimise the number of

---

[4] Schmidt (1988) provides an important result in this context (see Chapter 8).

necessary behavioural assumptions, such as those provided in the programming framework.

Why Measuring Efficiency in Production is Worthwhile

It is generally recognised within the western economies that in the long run increased productivity resulting from technical change is the primary explanation of growth (Solow, 1957). Recently, the new growth models support this view, suggesting that externalities in some inputs such as education and technology are major sources of endogenous growth (Barros, 1993). The same may well be true for the transition economies in the long run, but in the transition improving economic efficiency may be more important than technical change. Indeed, Myint (1971) argued that moving towards the production possibility frontier, rather than shifting it outwards can be the major source of growth for developing countries in the short term. Thus, the approaches taken in this study include some emphasis on separating efficiency and technological change.

Much of this book is concerned with the nature and measurement of technical efficiency and the contribution this may make to the development and growth of the transforming economies. Intuitively, the notion of technical efficiency refers to the achievement of maximum output from a given set of resources: the greater the output relative to the inputs, the higher the level of efficiency. Growth that follows from an increase in the amounts of available physical inputs is understandable and frequently predictable. However, sometimes growth can occur without any increase in the measured physical inputs and this can only be explained by an improvement in use of individual inputs.

The relationship between inputs and outputs can be measured within the context of the production function, although this restricts the analysis to technical efficiency only. The other component of economic efficiency requires the right mix of products implied by consumer tastes. This includes the effect of relative prices and is best captured in a profit function. Unfortunately, this option is not successful in the present study, due to the absence of reliable price data, although this is not the only reason why the measurement of full economic efficiency is not an appropriate aim here. Competitive markets and profit maximising behaviour on the part of decision takers are also prerequisites in the neo-classical model of economic efficiency.

But there are insufficient grounds for such assumptions to be made in the emerging economies of CEE, particularly very early in their transformation, such as the period represented by the current data for Hungary. Indeed, while there is no difficulty in stating that production is technically inefficient if it is possible to produce a given output with less of at least one input and no more of another, firms may be operating in the non-economic region. This may be the situation for many organisations undergoing restructuring prior to privatisation, or for those remaining in the public sector. Particular examples of firms producing outside the economic region are those operating in a regulatory environment that restricts input usage, such as a required rate of return or output supply, conservation protection or the cultural remnants of a command economy model. The point is that in many cases the behavioural assumptions are not known, and hence should not be imposed.[5]

Regardless of the nature of the underlying economic system, there exists a common objective of efficiency in the use of resources in production and the nature of economic production models raises a number of compelling questions. For example, it is important to know whether technologically efficient production is characterised by economies of scale or scope, whether cost efficient production is sub-additive by nature and whether economies of scale or scope that may accompany a natural monopoly are present. Then there is the issue of frontier (or best practice) versus average performance. The structure of economic frontiers can be different from the structure of average practice economic functions constructed from the same data, since while best practice is not just better than average practice, it may also be structurally different. Therefore it is important to know whether and in what way the structure of fully efficient production differs from the structure of average production. Best practice may be better than average practice precisely because it exploits available substitution possibilities or scale opportunities that average practice does not, or is excluded from. Or perhaps because their control systems are

---

[5] Note the difference between the successful pursuit of an unconventional objective and the failure to achieve a mis-specified conventional objective, such as the numerous examples of cooperatives, the labour managed Illyrian firm, or the profit constrained-revenue maximising firms described by Baumol (1959) and Williamson (1963). All of these models are worthy of consideration and only a very narrow view of the organisation of productive activity would exclude any of them.

better.   If there are production constraints or barriers, perhaps technological, physical (second best location) or informational (managerial competence and skills) these need to be identified, and policy directed towards removing or reversing them.

The distance between production frontiers and observed producers is obviously of interest in policy formation, particularly in those economies that are in the process of institutional reform. Public policy and institution-building based on the structure of best practice frontiers may be very different from that based on the structure of average practice functions, and in welfare terms, the average may be more appropriate for a broader effect. It is important to know how inefficient observed production is on average, and how costly is the inefficiency, both to the firm and to society at large. It is also important to know what types of producers are most efficient and least efficient, the causes of their inefficiency and which type of inefficiency is most prevalent.

An early study of the distance between best practice and average practice was work by Salter (1966). Using labour productivity as the performance measure,[6] Salter found the ratio of best to average practice can result in labour productivity being unity for some industries and very large for others. Primary, secondary and tertiary industries use labour in selectively different ways, and the gap between best and average practice is not the same across industrial sectors. Therefore sectors grow at different absolute and relative rates, with the leading sector changing over time.

This study uses data from Hungary, and although it is clear the transition economies cannot be treated as a homogeneous group, there are similarities between them.   The choice of Hungary for the empirical analysis was partly a function of the accessibility of firm level data, but also because Hungary is interesting for research of this kind. One reason is that it was one of the first economies to introduce a programme of reform. In the past, there had been attempts to move away from the strictly Soviet-type central planning, and an experiment with an alternative market system

---

[6] Productivity may be defined as the ratio of a measure of output to a measure of one or more of the inputs, but some artificial unit of measurement must be used for consistency from the base year to t (Easterfield, 1959).

13

resulted in the interim step of market socialism, begun in 1968.[7] Another factor is that, in the past, Hungarian economic performance was superior to that in many of the other socialist states. Clark (1940) reported that the level of GDP per capita for Hungary was 70-90 per cent of that of Austria during the inter-war period, and similar, or higher, than that of Greece, Finland and Italy. The estimates by Good (1994) using proxy indicators of GDP per capita, place Hungary ahead of the peripheral economies of Southern and Western Europe. But by the mid 1980's, this had declined to around 50 percent of the average in Western Europe and had fallen behind many of the previously non-industrial European countries. Identifying and accounting for this relative decline is an objective of the book.

Conclusion: The Contribution of this Study

This study consists of an analysis and interpretation of financial accounting data at the firm level for Hungary, for 1985 to 1991. The period represents the years immediately prior to the introduction of reforms to begin the transition from a centrally planned to a market economy, and the first few years of that transformation.

Three main objectives are achieved. The first is the reconciliation of data prepared under the socialist system of accounting to an equivalent set of identifiable balance sheet and profit and loss statements and hence a production dataset. Secondly, established methods of panel data econometrics and programming techniques are used to construct measures of efficiency in production at the firm level for three industrial sectors; primary, secondary and tertiary. Modelling productivity at the firm level has previously been exclusive to market economies, with proxy samples of co-operatives operating in otherwise orthodox market systems, although more recently, Chinese enterprises have also been the subject of analysis. Also measurement is inherently more interesting as an indication of progress or regress over several periods rather than an evaluation at a single point in time. In particular, the growth or decline in productivity has been

---

[7] Swain (1992) explains the period of market socialism in some detail, although Stiglitz (1994) suggests that political considerations, particularly in the mid and late 1970's, limited the extent to which this model could be implemented.

especially difficult to model because of a lack of time series data. Given the most common reporting practice in centrally planned economies was values rather than separated quantities and prices, the difficulty in acquiring a unique set of price indices makes the construction of a constant series of prices a serious problem. Therefore the productivity indices produced here, with high levels of consistency across the various technical approaches, provides a valuable addition to performance measurement.

Finally, this study contributes to the debate concerning industrial transformation policy. The decomposition of productivity change into its constituent parts provides valuable information to inform strategic decisions. If the nature of the inefficiency is known, resources can be allocated to address the specific deficiency directly, with more benefits gained from the higher degree of disaggregation. Therefore these techniques are used to demonstrate the distinction between a lack of growth due to technological regress (for example, technological obsolescence) and that resulting from managerial incompetence, a derelict capital base or a lack of skilled labour.

2 The Economics of Transition

Introduction

This chapter reviews the literature on transition, beginning with a general overview and then briefly considers some country-specific questions. It then goes on to discuss a number of papers which compare different organisational models and the various attempts that have been made to measure the relative productive efficiency of each. The final section on industrial policy, provides a context and a rationale for performance measurement and presents a case for the use of this information in determining growth strategies in the future. This section provides the context for interpreting the empirical results that begin in Part II.

An Overview of the Process of Reform

There is a growing literature on the nature and progress of the reforms in Central and Eastern Europe, as well as other countries in Africa and the Far East, that are in the process of moving from a planned economy to a market-based system. There is considerable consensus on most issues, with the principal controversy centred around the speed and the sequencing of the transition.

A formal analysis of the transition identifies the tasks at the centre of reform (see Sachs, (1996) and Fischer (1996)). The first is systematic transformation, which encompasses the institutional change to support the move from state ownership and central planning to private ownership and market allocation of resources. This includes the establishment of legal, administrative and political systems, and the reform of the enterprises. The second is structural adjustment, and is concerned with the reallocation of resources within the economy, and is developed in this literature in terms of the de-industrialization which is a necessary prerequisite to the re-industrialization.

The other two major areas are the creation of macroeconomic stability and the conditions for long-term growth. The first of these is the objective of financial stabilization. This represents the elimination of high pre-reform monetary overhang, the lowering of inflation and the reduction of large fiscal deficits. This is the long-term objective of governments in both the transitional and developing countries and will build a framework to promote rapid economic growth. Clearly there is a strong interaction between economic reforms, macroeconomic policy and sector and enterprise level restructuring. Economic reform measures enable the development of institutions and the implementation of industrial restructuring programmes, but there is a mutual dependence between the two as both reply on the other for a real improvement of trading performance to take place. However, it is within the firms themselves that changes are required, particularly in the approach to manufacturing and production and the identification of product markets, especially their internal organisation and management.

The debate about the speed of the transition has focused on the choice between a *big bang*, or a more *gradualist* approach (see Aghion and Blanchard (1994) for a formal analysis), although those favouring a rapid transition often base their arguments on politics rather than economics. Two main political arguments relating to privatisation are presented. The first concerns the redistributive effects, where the workers expected their share to be larger than that of the population at large, and the whole privatisation programme could be blocked if this was not the case. In some cases, privatisation proposals were blocked, for example Poland, while accepted by others, for example the Czech Republic. Similarly the degree of acceptance of restitution varies across countries. The second, and more serious, political issue relate to restructuring. Roland (1994) states this in terms of modern incentive theory, defining socialism to be a regime with low incentives and high insurance, and due to the former, incomes are low. Conversely, capitalism is a regime with high incentives and low insurance, and again due to the former, incomes are high. But during the early stages of the transition, uncertainty is high but incentives are not sufficiently established to be effective. Thus, apart from the expectation of a massive shift from heavy industry to services (see Bolton and Roland, 1992) no clear indications exist about which enterprises are likely to survive.

One of the central factors in the transition is the privatisation of state enterprises. Should one privatise before or after restructuring, or should they proceed simultaneously? The argument supporting the radical reform programme is based on the claim that the breaking up of large operations may be easier to accomplish quickly than the establishment of a new private sector. Then the task of restructuring is left to the owners of the newly privatised firms. Likewise it is suggested that macroeconomic stabilization and microeconomic liberalization respond more readily to a radical programme (see Frydman and Rapaczynshi (1991), Blanchard et al (1991) and Sachs, (1993)).

But even those who favour a speedy transition acknowledge the importance of determining the details of the new legal framework, especially the introduction of laws concerning bankruptcy and contracts. Stiglitz (1994) notes it is vital that institutional changes, once agreed upon, are put in place with the relevant information widely disseminated, as uncertainties impede the economy as a whole. However this aspect of the transition programme needs to be approached with caution, given the problems associated with changing the legal and constitutional rules of any economy, since there are sunk costs associated with establishing rules, which having been set, are difficult to change.

Writers in favour of a more gradualist approach to transition (see for example, Klaus, (1994) and Kornai (1993)) base their argument on three principal areas. The first emphasises the political commitment required to ensure that the reforms are not reversed in the future. If change is not considered to be permanent, investors in particular, will not feel sufficiently secure to participant, which in turn, will block the creation of an active capital market. A more gradual reform programme has the advantage that potential growth areas in the economy can be identified and risks more easily assessed, leading to more attractive investment opportunities.

The second centres on education, and learning by doing. This allows individuals and organisations to become familiar with the new economic and political environment, to learn the technology and business practices and to progress incrementally with their learning and experience in parallel, so that decisions can be made effectively in the light of easily understood and useful market information.

Finally, a gradual transition avoids the loss of information that occurs when organisations are dismantled and institutions destroyed, as is inevitable when there is rapid change. Stiglitz (1994, p 265) claims this evolutionary approach is superior to the revolutionary one. Since organisations embody information about the relative ability of individuals,

18

reallocating effort because the necessary tasks have changed is done more efficiently when there are some known comparative advantages than when there are none. Thus if credibility can be sustained, a gradual transition may be smoother, and has more direction, than a radical one. Whether this applies to Hungary remains unclear.

The question of the sequencing of reform can only rationally be discussed in the context of the initial starting point, and the transition economies did not begin with a single set of conditions. Fischer and Gelb (1991) separate the major differences in terms of the extent of macroeconomic imbalance, both internal and external, and the degree of centralization of economic management including the extent of the use of product markets over central planning in the past. Those countries with a decentralised economy prior to the transition, such as Hungary, Poland and the former Yugoslavia, were at an advantage and able to undertake reforms more easily. In these cases, there was more familiarity with internal and export markets, and the ability to respond to incentives based on competitive pressures already existed at some level. These economies also experienced more structural change early in the transition period, (pre-1989) and the quality gap between their products and those of western producers was fairly small. The disadvantage is that it is often more difficult to exert new regulations on firms that have become accustomed to a degree of autonomy.

In contrast, Czechoslovakia, Bulgaria and the former GDR had a high degree of economic centralization. This was characterised by the delayed and muted response to the changing external economic environment, which had implications for the nature of trade relations within CMEA (see van Brabant (1987)). Historically, these strong market ties provided a shield against major structural changes in the world economy, a protection that is now no longer there.

The extent of structural reform required is a function of the degree of macroeconomic imbalance. Countries better placed in this respect, and Fischer and Gelb include Czechoslovakia and Hungary[1], were able to concentrate on structural reforms leading to a market system. On the other hand, Poland and the former Yugoslavia required urgent stabilization policy.

---

[1] Perhaps Hungary less so, given the crippling amount of outstanding external debt.

Another very important difference in the starting positions was the degree of indebtedness. For example, Bulgaria, Hungary and Poland had high levels of external debt (measured against hard-currency exports, as well as GDP) without adequate collateral in terms of real or financial assets, whereas Czechoslovakia had relatively low levels of foreign debt, reflecting the balanced state budget of a more centralised economic system.

In general, domestic macro-imbalances pre-reform resulted from soft budget constraints in state enterprises, involving open inflation in some cases or the involuntary accumulation of financial assets (financial overhang), where private assets were restricted, as well as the extensive rationing of many goods. In either case, structural reform would be ineffective without controls on aggregate demand and inflation. The problems posed by inflation forced many reforming economies to focus their attention on macroeconomic stability. McKinnon (1991) emphasizes that, in the early stages of transition, state finances are eroded, as the difference between the producer prices (production costs) and consumer prices are appropriated by government as an implicit tax. Thus tax reform enters the sequencing problem.

Concern about high levels of unemployment influences both the speed and the sequencing decision. The simple model of transition determines the process of the reallocation of resources, but there are two stages to the explanation as to why this should inevitably lead to a situation of concurrent high unemployment and very low wages. The first is the acceptance that before resources can be transferred to high productivity employment, they must be identified as slack,[2] and then released from that position, with the intervening period being a time of unemployment. The second, which accounts for the low wage level, is that to bring about the redistribution of productive factors in the economy, the non-productive are forced out, which in the case of labour, is achieved through low wages in firms facing a newly imposed hard budget constraint. Managers reduce labour levels by either firing, which they are reluctant to do, or providing an incentive to find a higher wage elsewhere, preferably with time for job searching in an incomplete and unfamiliar market.

However, some qualifications are required here. The first concerns the interaction between capital and labour. In many CEE countries, the structure of capital was wrong, but nevertheless the pattern of employment

---

[2] See Chapter 5 where programming models are used to determine slack variables.

was designed to match the capital in place. Reducing labour while retaining the current stock of capital, where the latter is probably fixed in the medium-term, is not likely to increase productivity, and simply makes the assessment of the value of the enterprise more difficult. Thus changes in the levels of capital and labour, both in proportional and quality terms, will only result in productivity increases in the long run.

Another factor is the responsiveness of labour to wage levels. As the labour market develops, and differential wage structures are observed, workers begin to consider their own employment contracts. A reduction in wage rates and subsequently incentives, results in lower productivity, and contributes to the overall decline in output, rather than provide an instrument of macroeconomic adjustment. In fact it is clear that lay-offs did not keep pace with the decline in production and hence labour productivity, which was low at the beginning of the reform period, declined still further, due to a number of factors including strong trade unions and inadequate industrial policy (see Balcerowicz, 1995).

The final difficulty in the sequencing of reforms concerned with unemployment is the effective provision of a social safety net to support those displaced during the transfer of resources from one use to another. For many transition economies unemployment is a new phenomenon, although Hungary had already begun to establish a social security model in the early 1980's. The social expenditures, once the responsibility of the state owned enterprises, now are financed by the government. Unfortunately, this conflicts with the requests for a balanced budget urged by the IMF. The private provision of health insurance and pensions requires a financial sector that incorporates a system of intermediary institutions for household savings and deposits, and a fully developed capital market. So the sequencing debate goes on.

Enterprise Reform

Many authors argue that a substantial part of restructuring will take the form of newly emerging enterprises with a manufacturing technology and product mix that reflects a longer-term comparative advantage. Innovations in the approach to operations and marketing will influence the product mix chosen as well as the size and organisational structure of the firms (see Halpern (1995) for Hungary and Bucktikova and Flek (1993) and Charup and Zemplinerova (1993) for the Czech Republic).

The present study is concerned with the assessment of the progress of the reform within enterprises, but such an exercise is only possible within the context of changing institutions. Therefore the reform of the organisation of enterprises and the introduction of revisions in institutions is considered next.

Organisational models

The analysis of economic behaviour in a society with diffuse ownership and control structures is inevitably more complex than in one dominated by either a command or a market system. Coase (1937) defined a firm to be a collection of assets that are managed together, and since then the debate has continued on the effect of different ownership structures on productive efficiency. However, whatever the form of ownership and control, in market economies certainly, and now those in transition, a clearly defined concept of property rights is normally required.

Much of the modern economics literature assumes the separation of principal and agent and considers the nature of contracts between them, frequently in a situation of asymmetric information. Examples include Grossman and Hart (1986) who define ownership as the purchase of the residual control rights over physical assets not initially contracted for, and Milgrom and Roberts (1989) who prefer the definition to include the collection of residual returns rather than residual control. Another approach is that of Jensen and Meckling (1976) who consider the importance of the efficient management of assets, particularly the impact on productivity in a situation where the utility functions of the various claimants on those assets may differ. This behavioural view is relevant here, since there is no reason to assume the objective function is same in all firms.

However, while there are differences in the precise definition of ownership, there is a overall assumption that firms function well in a competitive environment. Equally common to all are the incentive problems of the principal-agent type, and the primary task of the reforming economies is to set out a structure for managers and other employees which can be implemented while firms are still in the public sector but preparing for privatisation in some form of other.

The joint objective of competition and corporate governance provides an appealing model, and allows a number of organisational forms to co-exist, although this has only recently become an acceptable view (see Brada, 1996). For many early observers in the transition debate, the privatisation of all enterprises was the only route to reform. A number of

22

studies have now shown that, after an initial hesitation, many state owned enterprises in the former Czechoslovakia (Estrin, Gelb and Singh, 1995), Hungary (Brada, Singh and Torok, 1994) and Poland (Pinto and van Wijnbergen, 1994) have responded quite successfully, and certainly no worse than those which have been fully privatised. Furthermore, a number of enterprises disguise a good deal of privatisation in the form of the transfer of assets to the private sector and in the contracting out of some parts of the operation.

As well as there being a range of firm structures, the means of achieving this also varied. The most common methods have been restitution to previous owners, if they can be found, and they can demonstrate their past ownership; privatisation through the sale of state property; redistribution through a system of vouchers; and the growth of newly emerging small firms directly into the private sector. Details of the operational aspects of the various privatisation schemes is given in Balcerowicz (1995), while a discussion of the nature of private versus public ownership of firms, within a framework of the fundamental theorems of welfare economics and Coasian property rights is in Stiglitz (1994, ch 10).

Institutional framework

The formulation and implementation of appropriate institutions are major components of the transition of enterprises and the economy as a whole, and many new institutions have been put in place. Institutions and professions long taken for granted in market economies have been re-created and reformed to support the functioning of markets. In particular, reform of the legal system is necessary for the completion of the privatisation programme as is a method of reporting to assist the valuation of enterprises. Activities such as accounting and auditing are a fundamental part of the monitoring and regulation of financial and other organisations.

Svejnar (1991, p.132) commented on the concern about the slow progress in institutional reform, and the inactivity of governments in eliminating major obstacles to a market economy, noting a number of areas where change could be implemented more efficiently. These include the creation of a complete and consistent legal framework to guide economic activity; an adequate emphasis on the creation of competitive market institutions, infrastructure and supporting practices in the areas of financial services, real estate, domestic trade, transport and telecommunications; the creation of accounting, auditing and other information systems; and strong market-oriented managerial and worker incentives in state enterprises.

In any discussion about a framework for establishing the rules, a balance between the market and the state is essential. For example, the financial system, while established as a system of banks and other institutions are clearly part of the private sector, regulation and supervision is a state level responsibility initially. Further comments on the disclosure of accounting information and the need for the provision of valid and useful information about the financial state of firms are in Chapter 4.

Performance Measurement: A Selective Survey

The importance of measuring performance, both in terms of overall national statistics and the production levels and efficiency of firms requires a consistent approach, and is only meaningful for policy if a reasonable amount of faith can be placed in the performance indicators. Kravis (1976) noted that since economics is concerned with the organisation of inputs (scarce means) to produce outputs (satisfy wants), comparisons of productivity is the focus of any assessment of economic performance. But this has proved to be problematic in a number of industry and country studies, and for transition economics is particularly elusive. This section considers some of the work in this area, and concludes there is little evidence of agreement.

Aggregate level

Balcerowicz (1995) notes that even in the established market economies statistical indicators do not provide a fully adequate description of economic reality. Problems with the statistical representation of changes in product quality, or the levels of unemployment are well known, with data open to misinterpretation or inappropriate aggregation.

It is clear that aggregate analysis in the transition economies fails to provide consistent national performance measures, to an even greater extent than those in the West. In one study by Roy (1995),[3] as part of the International Comparisons Programme, the productive efficiency of 26

---

[3] Seminar paper by Donald Roy (Home Office), London Business School, 1995.

OECD countries plus six transition economies was measured following methodology used in Kravis, Heston and Summers (1978). These results for 1990 reported productivity per capita in the former USSR higher than that of Australia, Denmark, Finland, Greece, Iceland, Ireland, New Zealand, Portugal, Sweden, Turkey and the United Kingdom as well as the other five transition economies. The same measurement procedure applied to the manufacturing sector only, reported productivity in Romania higher than in Greece, New Zealand and Norway. Common sense leads to questions about the accuracy of these measures.

But a range of clearly ambiguous statistics exist. Portes and Spaventa (1990) introduce a paper showing the extent of the diversity of aggregate measures, giving various estimates of GDP per capital for six CEE countries reported by a number of private organisations. In addition, estimates from the World Bank as well as national accounting data are included, which differ significantly and further illustrate the lack of a consistent measure. These data are shown in Table 2.1.

It has always been difficult to compare data from Western and Eastern Europe on the basis of GNP per capita. There are three basic problems. Firstly, real differences exist in the method of compiling national accounting data between the countries of Eastern and Central Europe and those in the West. For example, in the Net Material product (NMP) figure used in Table 3.1 (the row labelled National Accounting Data), services are excluded, and it was necessary to estimate the value of these. Since many collective services were provided free, the data was inflated by 30% (arbitrarily) to make a number comparable to GDP.

The second dilemma is the choice of a suitable exchange rate. The currencies of Eastern Europe were non-convertible and a number of black market rates was used, where multiple rates reflected product groups or the purpose for which they were used (ie commercial and non-commercial rates), all of which were grossly overvalued according to the official rate. In order to construct comparable series (as in Table 2.1), the dollar exchange rate was adjusted to a rate three-quarters of that on the black market.

Finally there are barriers which are a natural consequence of the autarky and subsequent isolation of the socialist countries from the West. This allowed seriously distorted prices and exchange rates to add to the inherent political accounting biases, such as the ambiguous incentives of those reporting from the firm level, all of which contributed to the difficulties in constructing consistent values at an aggregate level.

Table 2.1   Selected Estimates of GDP per Capita for Transition Economies

1988 US dollars	Bulgaria	Czecho-slovakia	GDR	Hungary	Poland	Romania
CIA[a]	7510	10140	12480	8660	7270	5490
ECE[b]	4244	7591	12608	2621	1818	3072
PlanEcon[c]	5633	7603	9361	6491	5453	4117
Paribas[d]	na	6500	8500	3000	na	na
CSFB[e]	1500	3500	4000	3000	2000	1000
National Accounting Data[f]	na	2610	2610	2830	640	470
World Bank[g]	na	na	na	2460	1860	na
Coefficient of Variation	0.46	0.41	0.46	0.53	0.74	0.67
1992 US Dollars						
EBRD[h]	5130	7160[Czech Rep] 5620[Slovakia]		5740	4880	2750

Table from Keating and Hoffman (1990), supplemented by the author.
Sources: a)   Central Intelligence Agency, *Handbook of Economic Statistics*, 1989, US Government Printing Office, Washington DC. Table: Preferred Estimates of GDP per capita
b)   UNECE Secretariat, Common Data Base
c)   *Western Investor's Guide to Eastern Europe and Soviet Union*, PlanEcon Reports, **5:42-43**, November 1989
d)   Paribas Conjuncture, **1**, January 1990
e)   Credit Suisse First Boston. These are based on national accounting data.
f)   Adjusted Net Material Product from national accounting data
g)   *World Development Report*, Oxford University Press for the World Bank, New York, 1990
h)   Financial Times (11 Nov 1994)

The major distortions in national statistics are noted by Bratkowski (1993). The main effect is a large systematic bias in the official statistical indicators, with this likely to be larger in those countries opting for a radical, wide ranging transition and so are more pronounced the faster the speed of economic change. Bratkowski suggests the following explanation. A radical change of economic system means there is a shift from a situation where there are strong incentives to inflate output and value added data to one where under-reporting is more attractive because of tax liability. Further, an increased market orientation reduces the scope of the public sector and increases that of the private sector. But historically, accounting practice has focused on the former and is unable to move very quickly to a private sector structure and growth in the latter is not recognised in terms of total output and GDP. Finally, reform involves positive changes in the quality and range of goods and in the composition of output, which are under-represented in aggregate statistics.

Enterprise level

Enterprise reform is still sufficiently recent for there to be little firm level empirical research undertaken on their performance, although a comparison of various organisational firm structures has been done using representative sample groups. Then, these results have been extended to the transitional economies with varying degrees of success. For those countries where the transition is fairly advanced, for example Hungary and the former Yugoslavia, privatisation is progressing and managers/owners are able to exert some choice about the productive and managerial structure of their firms. However, the analytical framework still has to reflect the historical control mechanisms that were imposed and the legacy of past restrictions. In particular, an efficient capital market will impose high costs on private investors who have no credit history and so the cost of capital to privatised firms remains high.

A number of papers comment on the efficiency levels of firms operating under different organisational structures. Zou (1992) directly addresses the efficiency of co-operatives, and concludes that where ownership is established at inception and if clear and efficient rules for control are set up, including the design of incentive mechanisms concerning the sharing of future cash flows, co-operative ownership can lead to economic efficiency. However, this does not allow for the opportunity to change the ownership structure, which is an important aspect of the analysis of a transitional economy.

Berman and Berman (1989) compare the behaviour of two groups of US firms, one labour-managed, similar to the Yugoslav model, and the other investor-owned operations. Although product and input markets are competitive, and the two groups face the same technological opportunities, their estimated production functions show significant differences. However, papers of this sort have generally concentrated on western firms, and therefore most analysis relating efficiency to ownership type has assumed

27

competitive markets and flows of information between agents, even though these flows may be imperfect. Estrin (1991) examines the parallel firm structure in Yugoslavia, but uses data from the Italian producer co-operative sector for empirical testing. These enterprises are able to compete successfully with profit maximising firms. As in Berman and Berman (1990), both groups face the same input prices, so management decisions which favour labour derive from a philosophical, rather than an economic bias.

Two papers analyze enterprise level data from Central and Eastern Europe. Piesse, Thirtle and Turk (1996) compare co-operatives and private farms in the dairy sector in Slovenia, and find that the important factor in overall productivity is size and not ownership structure, even though there were considerable advantages accorded the state owned farms compared with the purely private ones. Prasnikar, Svejnar and Klinedinst (1992) use an enterprise level sample of industrial firms in Yugoslavia, not to measure efficiency, but to test the impact of several structural and policy variables that enjoy popular support in the literature as the determinants of efficiency. Joint ventures, and the restructuring of the market and the enterprise are not found to be conducive to higher productive efficiency. Export orientation really is a reflection of resource use, and therefore accounts for improved allocative efficiency, but the lack of price information precludes a test of this.

Several papers with a comparative performance theme are reviewed in Murrell (1991), who also questions the use of neoclassical economics in the evaluation of the reform process at all. Perhaps contrary to the general perception, economies of scale may not be sufficient to outweigh the disincentives of collective organisation.

Some controversy can be found in the literature relating to the interpretation of efficiency measures. Pasour (1981) suggests that a level of performance which is achievable only under ideal conditions of perfect knowledge is not an appropriate standard against which to measure observed performance. He also argues that performance standards derived by assuming profit maximization should not be used to measure the performance of economic agents whose objective functions involve elements other than profit. A third question relates to the accuracy of empirical measures. In particular, it is argued that observed inefficiency is due solely to our inability to accurately measure input values, both the true nature of the inputs and the differential quality across firms. Finally, the notion of efficiency is relevant only within the narrow confines of the perfectly competitive equilibrium and thus not relevant to other organisational forms. All of these problems are relevant in what follows.

Another aspect of efficiency measurement which causes some disquiet when extended to the determination of policy decisions is the uncertain objectives of any single firm within the economy. Kirzen (1979) claimed that efficiency only has any meaning when goals are set, and are known. Then a technically efficient firm is more desirable than a technically inefficient one, as long as resources are scarce. When efficiency is measured relative to a peer group, which in all cases in the current study it is, informational considerations are not relevant since it may be assumed that all information is equally available to all members of the group. The lack of a purely profit motive does not affect the undesirability of inefficiency, although in this case it may be due to factors other than poor management or irrational decision-making by individual producers. From this perspective, the difference between management expertise and efficiency is indistinguishable, since either may be completely explained by the ability to utilise available information.

A direct concern of this study is the individual performance of firms, rather than the promotion of particular firms, or indeed industries, as winners. At present the diversity of performance within the same industry is huge. Kolanda and Kubista (1991) report a spread of productivity performance across firms within an industry to be as high as 1:60, compared with an equivalent range in Western Europe of 1:6, a difference that can be explained by the pressures of competition and an active market in firms themselves. Also those that continue to perform poorly exit the market altogether, due to the existence of well established bankruptcy legislation. Differences across industries are also substantial, for example, in Germany the value added per worker in engineering is close to that in metallurgy, whereas in Czechoslovakia a similar measure is twice as high in metallurgy than in engineering.

Industrial Policy and Structural Transformation

The final section in this chapter provides a rationale for efficiency measurement. A central feature of policy in the transition economies is the establishment of an industrial structure that will allow output growth and a rise in per capita income. But this cannot be seen as the imposition of an economic plan reminiscent of the past. In the West the case for industrial policies is made on the basis of what the market cannot achieve, due to externalities, economies of scale, information problems or capital market imperfections (see Grossman, 1990). But for reforming CEE countries, industrial policy is required to redistribute resources which in the past have been allocated to the principles of a command economy, and may not be appropriate for a market one. Hence the case for state intervention is not based on market failure, but the non-existence of markets.

The direction and detail of industrial policy is discussed by Landesmann and Szekely (1995). They emphasize strategies that will achieve an increase in the responsiveness of firms, households and employees to the newly emerging market environment, and to equip them with the ability to react to market signals. The state should also address any remaining barriers to entry and exit, that is, the institutional reform discussed earlier.

Geroski and Jacquemin (1985) distinguish between two kinds of industrial policy. One is the picking winners approach, when governments try to anticipate and make decisions about the allocation of resources to be invested for future growth. The alternative is to provide an institutional framework in which private sector adjustment is facilitated, and, rather than promoting national champions, lifting the general level of performance. In this way, winners will emerge of their own accord. Cowling (1990) argues that the role of the state should be limited to strategically overseeing development, rather than determining the organisational detail, and even then this is only necessary in a small number of key industries. Therefore it is important to find the best way to identify efficient firms and industries, in order that policy can reflect the aim of increasing performance in the inefficient firms and pushing forward the frontier of the best practice ones. Thus, we spend considerable efforts on measuring efficiency change and technical progress in later chapters.

Given the past orientation of industrial development patterns in Eastern Europe, certain skills have been neglected and serious under-investment has led some industries to be very much behind their counterparts in the West. Recognising this may help to explain the rather curious relative performance of particular sectors now, justify the decline of what are expected to be leading sectors, and determine the pattern of decline and recovery apparent in the results of the current study. This is the rationale for the comparison of the changing relative productivity of agriculture, industry and services as the transition from plan to market takes place.

30

Conclusion

This chapter has both provided some general background on the transition, outlining the policy decisions associated with change of this kind, and also identified the areas of central interest for the remainder of the study. Emerging from the considerable debate surrounding the effects of the political and economic changes which have occurred in the countries of Central and Eastern Europe, is a degree of consensus about the factors affect the success of those undergoing transition to a market economy. These are identified as: systematic transformation, including the establishment of institutions and enterprise reform, structural adjustment, macroeconomic stability and economic growth. Of these, only enterprise reform and structural transformation are addressed here.

But for any analysis undertaken at enterprise level, the institutional context cannot be completely neglected. Therefore, following an introductory section on the process of reform in general, some organisational models are discussed as well as the rules which define the framework for enterprise development. Now it is possible to consider the performance of firms within this new framework. In order to judge the success of a new system, it is necessary to find a method of evaluation.

The third part of this chapter presents the problems associated with this evaluation, pointing out the huge discrepancies in performance measurement at the national aggregate level. Any inherent problem in the basic interpretation of data at this level is further exacerbated when the firm is the unit of analysis. But despite the limitations of any method of evaluation, a technical relationship can be constructed and measured. Against the background of non-competitive enterprises, limited access to economic information, and a variety of objectives on the part of decision makers, a systematic method of measuring efficiency in production can be addressed. In turn, this can be used to inform industrial policy and provide a direction for structural transformation. This is the theme of the remaining chapters.

3 Parametric and Nonparametric Measures of Efficiency and Total Factor Productivity: Theoretical Relationships

Introduction

Two major advances dominate the production economics literature in the last quarter of a century. These are the dual forms of the production relation such as the cost and profit functions, and the discovery of flexible functional forms which can be viewed as second order approximations of any unknown production function. Thus in an ideal world, the appropriate procedure to follow in applications such as a firm or sector level measure of efficiency would be to fit a profit function version of one of the latest flexible functional forms. This chapter outlines the models available. But perhaps more importantly it explains why neither of these developments have proved more than marginally useful when analysing transition economies, and using accounting data.

Much research in economics has focused on measuring the productive efficiency of firms, with applications extending to a number of countries, and encompassing a variety of organisational forms. This is based on the concept of a transformation function which provides a direct, or primal, description of production technology. A common characteristic, regardless of the approach used, is that of optimality, a maximum or a minimum value that can be achieved within the constraints imposed by the available technology and price structure. Having constructed a boundary or frontier, and assuming a common set of constraints, efficiency is measured by the distance of individual firms relative to that frontier.

The techniques used to construct the boundary arise from two broadly different approaches: econometric estimation of the production (or equivalent dual) function, and programming techniques which determine the shape and position of the frontier. A different interpretation of the deviation of firms from the frontier follow from these two approaches. The methods commonly employed to measure efficiency again can be split into two broad categories: parametric and nonparametric. Parametric models are used to construct a production, cost or profit relationship based on a specified functional form and provide a consistent framework for investigating technical, allocative and scale efficiency of profit-maximising firms. These can be deterministic or stochastic. Deterministic models most frequently define a productivity frontier. There is no disturbance term, and thus no allowance for measurement error or noise to enter as a residual, and any firm level deviations are attributed to technical inefficiency associated with that individual unit compared with those firms which define the frontier. In contrast, stochastic models are estimated using econometric techniques based on the underlying behavioural and economic relationships. They include a disturbance term to allow for random variation around the average relationship, and capture the effects of noise and/or measurement error as well as shocks exogenous to the firm.

One disadvantage of parametric estimation is that the primal form of the production function admits to only one output, a situation which must be overcome by aggregation to a single output, or by recourse to a dual form, such as the profit function. This difficulty does not occur at all in nonparametric analysis, which has the additional advantage of imposing no *a priori* functional form on the underlying technology, and allows disaggregated inputs and multiple output technologies. Results are obtained through programming models rather than estimation and do not embody any economic or behavioural assumptions. The approach is deterministic (non-stochastic), and no accommodation is made for environmental heterogeneity, omitted variables and exogenous effects. These models define frontier functions only, stating the technical efficiency of firms relative to the best practice frontier, rather than fitting an average relationship to all data in the sample as in standard econometric estimation. Then, once a time dimension is incorporated, it is possible to measure growth in efficiency or the shift to new technologies over a number of periods, that is, to incorporate technological change. Finally, it is a fairly straightforward procedure to construct productivity indices from both the parametric and nonparametric representations of efficiency in production.

In summary, this chapter provides a review of some of the approaches to modelling efficiency in production, with special reference to technical efficiency, which is the predominant measure of interest here. It includes parametric and nonparametric methods and the measurement of the distance between individual firms and the best practice ones. After incorporating technical change, this leads to the construction of performance indices derived from the underlying production theory, which are used later to measure growth rates within and between Hungarian industrial sectors. The chapter provides a rational for the techniques used in this study and concludes with a critical comparison of the available alternatives.

The Measurement of Productive Efficiency

In standard microeconomic theory a transformation function provides a direct, or primal, description of the production technology. It describes either the maximum amount of output that can be produced by a given level of inputs, or alternatively, it describes the minimum amount of inputs required to produce a given level of output. Corresponding to the primal transformation function are three dual functions. The cost function describes the minimum cost of producing certain outputs with given input prices and technology. The revenue function describes the maximum revenue obtainable from certain inputs with given output prices and technology. The profit function describes the maximum profit that can be obtained with given output prices, input prices, and technology. Under certain conditions the primal transformation function and the three dual functions provide equivalent descriptions of the structure of the production technology (see Diewert (1982)).

Production possibility sets and the transformation function

In order to formalise primal and dual theories of production, the underlying Production Possibility Set (PPS) must be defined. This is determined by the underlying technology available to the producer. Then the PPS in turn determines the properties of the Transformation Function (TF), as demonstrated below. The Production Possibility Set (PPS), T, summarises the technical opportunities that a firm faces by giving all feasible input/output combinations. This is a purely technical relationship and does not rely on any economic or behavioural assumptions. Indeed, the aims of the firm are not known, nor whether these aims were met. This is very much in contrast with dual approaches which assume profit maximisation or cost minimisation, both of which may be reasonable in the context of established and recognised competitive markets but make little sense in the transition economies. The most general representation of T would be in terms of θ, an $(m+n)$ dimensional vector of outputs (positive elements) and inputs (negative elements). This representation is purposely general as it allows for the fact that the distinction between outputs and inputs can become vague, for example, if an output is also used as an input (or vice-versa), is an intermediate good, or adds to the stock of capital.

The vector of M non-negative outputs can be denoted as $y = (y_1,...,y_M)$ and the vector of N non-negative inputs as $x = (x_1,...,x_N)$. The PPS is then the various combinations of y producible in a given production period using the various combinations of x. There are a family of such PPS's over time, each representing the technological opportunities available in that period.[1] Having described the PPS, and hence the underlying technology, the Transformation Function (TF) can be defined as the set of efficient input-output combinations. This is the boundary of the PPS and can be written symmetrically as $F(x,y) = 0$.

Several conditions or properties are required to characterise the structure of the underlying technology, which have important implications that hold in both parametric and nonparametric analyses of production systems. Some are to ensure theoretical consistency, but other restrictions are imposed to simplify (or make possible) empirical estimation. These are necessary to compensate for a frequent lack of quantity or quality of data, and result in the adjustment of a theoretically desirable model to a usable restricted form. The two most important of these properties are homogeneity and output separability. The first is where a change in the inputs implies a change in output, and the proportional changes leads to the analysis of scale effects while the second is a trivial issue in this case, as aggregation is implied by the value nature of the data.

The simplest primal approach that can be derived by restricting the PPS to a production relationship between outputs, Y_i and inputs X_j. Following the growth accounting framework of Solow (1957), the simple form of the production function is defined as

$$Y = F(X_1, X_2 : t) \qquad (1)$$

where a single output (Y) is determined solely by the quantity of the two inputs, most commonly capital and labour, and an index of technology (t)

---

[1] This definition can be with respect to time over a particular time period, or across firms or industries for single period, cross section data. It can also be extended to intertemporal as well as interspatial panel datasets, such as that in this study.

assumed to be collinear with time. This is a purely technical relationship, characterised only by the assumption of output maximisation subject to the constraint of the available technology.

Duality

The TF is the primal representation of the technology. The dual offers an alternative but equivalent definition of the technology available to the firm, where assumptions of competitive, rational economic behaviour are valid. To characterise the dual function, the input price vector is defined as $w = (w_1,..,w_N)$ which corresponds to the input vector x (where w_i is the price of input x_i). Similarly, the output price vector is defined as $p = (p_1,..,p_M)$. The input requirement set, V(y), represents all the input combinations capable of producing the output bundle y. The producible output set Y(x) represents all output bundles that can be produced given the input bundle x. These can be expressed as

$$V(y) \equiv [x: (x,y) \in T) \tag{2}$$

and

$$Y(x) \equiv [y: (x,y) \in T) \tag{3}$$

respectively.

These are alternative representations of producer behaviour, which are reciprocal or dual forms of the same problem given neo-classical market conditions, and is described in detail in McFadden (1966) and more recently extended by Chambers (1988).

There are similar formulations for the other functions outlined earlier in this section. The cost function assumes that the firm, when facing competitive input markets with strictly positive input prices, attempts to minimise the cost of producing a given output bundle. That is

$$C(w,y) = Min[w.x: x \in V(y)] \tag{4}$$

and the Revenue Function is defined as

$$R(p,x) = Max(p.y: y \in Y(x)]$$ (5)

where the firm is attempting to maximise its revenue, given a certain input endowment. Finally, profit maximisation, the basic behavioural assumption of the neo-classical theory of the firm, is represented by the profit function. This can be stated in three alternative and equivalent forms, illustrating the interrelationships between the indirect objective functions presented above

$$\pi(p,w) = Max[p.y - w.x: (x,y) \in T: w,p>0]$$
$$= Max[p.y - C(w,y): w,p>0]$$ (6)
$$= Max[R(p,x) - w.x: w,p>0]$$

The equivalence of the above relationships is clear. The first equality is simply the profit function defined as the maximum of revenue from output (p.y) minus the cost of inputs (w.x), and subject to the PPS constraint. The second equality illustrates the simultaneous optimisation process of maximising profit for a given level of output (short-run optimisation) and choosing output levels and combinations to maximise long-run profits. The Cost Function determines the minimum cost of producing the optimal output scale and combination. In equilibrium, the profit maximising output combination is exactly the same as the cost minimising input combination.

Therefore for duality based empirical investigation, the technology is defined in terms of a PPS with the appropriate properties to ensure a well behaved function but also which allows the progression to production, cost, revenue and profit functions. These conditions apply to both parametric and nonparametric analysis although they may not always be useful in non-standard environments. Relatively little use is made of dual forms in the empirical analysis in this book. A profit function approach based on a very simple functional form failed to produce consistent results, so this approach was abandoned. The cost function is of some interest since the within transformation for the Cobb-Douglas when applied to panel data gives estimating equations that are exactly equivalent to the equations for cost minimisation.

The nature of efficiency

To move from a production relationship to a measurement of performance or efficiency is evaluated by the distance of an individual firm from the feasible boundary defined by the technology. The efficient transformation of inputs into output is characterised by the production function, such as the two input function in equation (1), which shows the maximum output obtainable from capital and labour inputs. A firm attaining this maximum is technically efficient. If costs are minimised by this choice of input proportions, the firm is also allocatively efficient.[2] In a situation of competitive markets, a firm that is both technically and allocatively efficient earns the maximum possible profit and is also known as profit efficient. It produces its chosen outputs with the minimum possible inputs and produces the maximum possible outputs with its chosen inputs. That is, it is technically efficient. It also produces the correct mix of outputs, given output prices, uses the correct mix of inputs, given input prices, and adopts the correct scale of operation, given input and output prices. That is, it is allocatively efficient and scale efficient. Similarly, where a firm is technically and allocatively efficient with respect to outputs and output prices, the revenue obtainable from its inputs is maximised, and is known as revenue efficient.

Farrell measures of efficiency

The model used for measuring firm-level efficiency follows the basic framework introduced by Farrell (1957). This is defined in terms of Shepard's (1953) distance function where $D^t(y^t,x^t)$ is the contraction of x^t that would take any inefficient observation, for any firm i, to a position on the frontier. The Farrell efficiency measure, $F^t(y^t,x^t)$, is just the inverse of the distance function. It is based on radial measures and its simplicity makes it especially appealing in empirical work.

Farrell's measure of overall (technical and allocative) efficiency is shown in Figure 3.1. The underlying production relationship again uses equation (1), but this is the input minimisation approach, with inputs x_1 and x_2. Assuming that there are constant returns to scale, this can be written

---

[2] Thus, following from the previous section, a fixed effects panel data estimation of the Cobb Douglas can be viewed as incorporating allocative efficiency, even though the lack of price information prevents this in all other cases. This is included in Chapter 8.

$$1 = F\left(\frac{X_1}{Y}, \frac{X_2}{Y}\right) \qquad (7)$$

and the boundary of the set $L^+(Y)$, in Figure 3.1, is the best practice unit isoquant. The unit isoquant defines the minimum combinations of inputs required to produce some unit output level Y^*. Observations B and C are efficient and define the isoquant, in this simple example, whereas observation A uses more of both inputs X_1 and X_2 to produce the same unit of output, Y^*, and is thus inefficient.

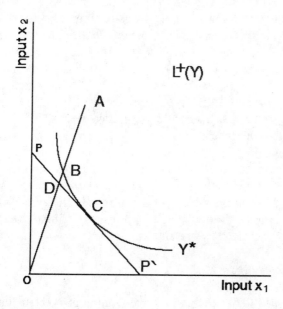

Figure 3.1   Farrell Measures of Efficiency

The vector OB shows the minimum combination of inputs x_1 and x_2 that firm A could use to produce Y^* efficiently, using its individually chosen factor ratio. OA is the actual combination of inputs used, and Farrell's radial measure of the technical efficiency level of firm A is OB/OA, a value between zero and unity. The ratio of prices is PP'. The ratio OD/OB measures allocative inefficiency, since the cost of D is the same as that of the allocatively efficient C, and is less than that of the technically efficient but allocatively inefficient B. Thus OD/OA measures total efficiency. This simple figure is the basis of efficiency measurement. The alternative output maximisation formulation of the problem uses equation (1), with firms on the production function defining the frontier and the efficiency of other firms being measured relative to this boundary of the PPS (see Figure 3.2 later in the chapter). Where this approach is used to incorporate scale efficiency, it is excluded from the input measure and relies on the unit isoquant.

Deterministic and stochastic parametric frontiers

The preceding section makes clear that efficiency measures are based on distances from the efficiency frontier. Thus, whereas parametric estimation typically relies on determining functions by estimating a line of best fit, in which all the observations are assumed to be efficient (in the sense of being on the production frontier or the isoquant), it is the boundary of the set that must be found for the analysis of relative efficiency. The simplest approach is known as corrected ordinary least squares (COLS), in which the OLS regression line is shifted until none of the residuals are positive, so that it then defines the frontier. Instead of assuming that all the firms are efficient, this approach typically assumes that a single firm defines the frontier and all deviations from this solution are due to inefficiency. This is equally unrealistic, so the preferred model is the stochastic frontier approach, which decomposes the error term into background, environmental factors, which are beyond the control of the firm and efficiency differences which are not exogenous. These frontier approaches are discussed in more detail in Chapter 6, where they are applied.

Efficiency vs technical change

Solow (1957) defined the distinction between output growth attributable to movements along the production surface (input growth) and output growth caused by shifts in the production surface (technical change). However, this assumes that production remains technically efficient. If this assumption is relaxed, the rate of total factor productivity growth can be decomposed into the rate of technical change and changes in the level of efficiency. Then, it is possible to attribute observed output growth to: 1) movements along a path on or beneath the production surface (input growth); 2) movement toward or away from the production surface (efficiency growth or decline) and 3) shifts in the production frontier (technical progress or regress).

Identifying the difference between efficiency growth and technical change is important since they are determined by fundamentally different phenomena, and require different policies to address them.[3] Later chapters separate these entities and illustrate the implications of each for the firms in the current sample. The transition may perhaps be viewed mostly as an efficiency problem, with technical change being a more long term issue, that is, establishing the preconditions for growth, rather than explaining long-term growth. This distinction was emphasised originally by Myint (1971) who argued strongly that for the less developed countries, even sustained growth is much more a matter of continually moving closer to the efficiency frontier, rather than shifting it outwards. If the same is true of the transitional economies, then institutional and organisational change are needed rather than R&D expenditures.[4] This issues are pursued in Chapter 7 and in Chapter 9, where TFP growth is decomposed into efficiency and technical change.

Productivity Indices Derived from Parametric Functions

The previous sections outline the way in which econometric estimation can be used to investigate efficiency at the firm level. An alternative, which is particularly useful for considering changes over time, is the index number approach to total factor productivity measurement. This is pursued in Chapter 9 and in this application the fact that the input data available is in value terms is actually an advantage rather than an impediment because it makes the calculation of the share weights for constructing the index accurate and straightforward. By contrast, if the inputs were expressed as physical quantities the lack of price information would preclude the calculation of shares in total costs. In such circumstances, previous studies have used the estimated elasticities from the Cobb-Douglas function as the

---

[3] There may be a complementary relationship between these two effects when moving from a single to a multiple period analysis. Thus, a shift in the frontier in $t+1$ may cause a single firm to move to that new frontier, with no real change in the level of efficiency between t and $t+1$. This is explained more formally later in this Chapter.

[4] This is perhaps too simplistic. The empirical results show that in the transition it is often a matter of restricting technological regress due to the lack capital maintenance and obsolescence.

share weights. Thus, in this case, actual shares can be calculated rather than using estimated coefficients.[5]

Evenson, Landau and Ballou (1987) have shown that there are equivalent measures of technological change based on the dual relationships between the production, cost and profit functions and that these measures are equivalent to economic accounting measures that are based on index number theory. They also show that changes in total factor productivity (TFP) can be explained by means of determining variables, such as R&D, and levels of education. This approach to explaining technical change is referred to as the two-stage decomposition, as opposed to the integrated approach, in which the determining variables are incorporated directly in the estimation of the production, cost or profit function.

The TFP index is related to the production and profit functions and is measured by the Tornqvist-Theil approximation of the Divisia index. Beginning with the profit-function approach, which allows the analysis of production with more than one output, the model begins from the general specification

$$g(Y,X,F,E) = 0 \qquad (8)$$

where Y, X, F and E are vectors of outputs, variable inputs, fixed inputs and determining variables, respectively. Variable profits are defined

$$\pi = PY - RX \qquad (9)$$

where P and R are vectors of output and input prices. Maximising profits, subject to equation (1), gives the first-order conditions for the Y and X vectors as functions of P, R, F, and E. Substituting these expressions into (2) gives the dual form, that is, the maximised variable profit function

---

[5] The negative aspect of this situation is that although the cost shares are readily available, the index itself has to be calculated from physical quantities and thus the lack of good price indices for deflators is still a problem.

$$\pi^* = \pi^*(P,R,F,E) \tag{10}$$

which expresses profits as a function of prices of inputs and outputs, the quantities of fixed inputs and determining variable exogenous. This is the integrated approach, in which the determining variables are included.

The two stage methodology drops the determining variables E and imposes long-run equilibrium, in which no abnormal profits are made. This leads to the accounting derivation of the TFP index, written using summations and subscripts, instead of vector notation as an equilibrium condition

$$\sum_i P_i Y_i = \sum_j R_j X_j \tag{11}$$

The fixed factors are treated as having a rental price for the service flow they produce. In the second stage of this approach, TFP changes are explained by the determining variables in the E vector.

The total derivative with respect to time, allows the derivation of an equation of factor shares (S_i) and factor costs (C_j), written as

$$\sum_i S_i \hat{P}_i + \sum_i S_i \hat{Y}_i = \sum_j C_j \hat{R}_j + \sum_j C_j \hat{X}_j \qquad where \ \hat{P}_i = \frac{1}{P_i} \frac{\partial P_i}{\partial t} \, dt$$

$$\tag{12}$$

and similarly for the other variables, or more compactly

$$\hat{p} + \hat{y} = \hat{r} + \hat{x} \tag{13}$$

where the terms represent the rates of change of aggregate output prices, output quantities, factor prices and aggregate factor quantities, respectively, using the shares as weights for aggregation.

The accounting derivation leads to the proposition that if both inputs and outputs change, the rate of change of TFP is given by

$$\hat{T} = \hat{y} - \hat{x} \tag{14}$$

as shown by Evenson, Landau and Ballou (1987, p.2).

The equivalence of the accounting and the production function approaches can be established by showing that the production function derivation of a TFP index also leads to equation (14). For a single output Y and several inputs $X_1,....X_n$, the production function may be written as

$$Y = F(X_1,....X_n:E) \qquad (15)$$

which is assumed to be a linearly homogenous function and where the determining variables are held constant. Differentiating totally with respect to time t, gives

$$\frac{\partial Y}{\partial t}dt = \sum_j F_j \frac{\partial X_j}{\partial t}dt + F_t dt \qquad (16)$$

where $F_j = \partial Y/\partial X_j$ is the marginal product of the jth input. Then productivity change, $F_t dt$, is equal to the change in output, minus the sum of the changes in the inputs.

The first-order conditions for profit maximisation are

$$F_j = \frac{P_j}{P_y} \qquad (17)$$

where P_j and P_y are the input and output prices respectively. Assuming that the marginal value products of the inputs are equal to their prices allows the substitution of (17) for F_j in (16). Dividing by Y gives

$$\frac{\partial Y}{\partial t}\frac{1}{Y}dt = \sum_j \frac{P_j}{P_y Y}\frac{\partial X_j}{\partial t}dt + \frac{F_t}{Y}dt \qquad (18)$$

Multiplying each term by X_j/X_j, and using the zero-profit condition for equilibrium, gives $\Sigma_j P_j X_j = P_y Y$ (the production function equivalent of (18) in the accounting derivation) and results in

$$\frac{\partial Y}{\partial t}\frac{1}{Y}dt = \sum_j C_j \frac{\partial X_j}{\partial t}\frac{1}{X_j}dt + \frac{F_t}{Y}dt \qquad (19)$$

where C_j is again the cost share of the jth factor. Equation (20) relates output growth to input growth, and can be written as

$$\hat{T} = \frac{F_t}{Y}dt = \hat{y} - \sum_j C_j\hat{X}_j = \hat{y} - \hat{x} \qquad (20)$$

which is the expression for the rate of change of TFP obtained in (16) using the accounting derivation.

If the profit-function derivation, or the cost-function approach, were to be pursued further, equivalent expressions can be obtained. If all input and output prices and quantities are observed, the rate of change of TFP can be calculated without estimation, but this result applies exactly only to data that are generated continuously. Since economic data come in discrete observations, (14) and (20) are approximations. The expression following the summation sign in (19) defines the *Divisia input index* and the commonly-used Tornqvist-Theil discrete approximation of the Divisia input index (Chambers, 1988) is written as

$$\hat{x} = \frac{1}{2}\sum_j (C_jt + C_{j,t-1})\ln\left(\frac{X_{jt}}{X_{j,t-1}}\right) \qquad (21)$$

which is the logarithm of the ratio of two successive input quantities weighted by a moving average of the share of the input in total cost. If there are multiple outputs, as well as inputs, the same aggregation procedure to gives the Tornqvist-Theil output index

$$\hat{y} = \frac{1}{2}\sum_i (S_{it} + S_{it-1})\ln\left(\frac{Y_{it}}{Y_{it-1}}\right) \qquad (22)$$

which is the logarithm of the ratio of two successive output quantities weighted by a moving average of the share of the output in total revenue. This TFP index is calculated by taking the exponent of the difference between (22) and (21) and chaining it (see Chapter 9 for application of these indices).

This process applies the quadratic approximation lemma (Capalbo, Denny, Hoque and Overton, 1991). Chambers (1988) shows that if productivity change is Hicks-neutral and the underlying quadratic production technology is the translog, then (23) is an exact measure rather than an approximation. Diewert (1986) has called an index which is exact for a flexible functional form, such as the translog, a *superlative index*.

Any TFP index is restrictive (relative to the econometric estimation of flexible functional forms of the production, cost or profit function), because the TFP approach imposes equilibrium, Hicks-neutral technical change and constant returns to scale. However, because the translog is a flexible functional form, there are no further restrictions imposed by the specification of the underlying production relationship. In this respect, the index used here is superior to alternatives (such as the arithmetic index, discussed by Lingard and Rayner, 1975) that correspond to restrictive production functions. For example, if the production function was Cobb-Douglas, which is separable in outputs and inputs, the first order conditions for profit maximization require that the cost shares, C_j, remain constant over time. In this case, equation (21) becomes

$$\hat{x} = \ln\left(\frac{x_t}{x_{t-1}}\right) = \frac{1}{2}\sum_j (C_j + C_j)\ln\left(\frac{X_{jt}}{X_{jt-1}}\right) = \sum_j C_j\ln\left(\frac{X_{jt}}{X_{jt-1}}\right) \qquad (23)$$

Taking exponents of (23) gives

$$\left(\frac{x_t}{x_{t-1}}\right) = \prod_j \left(\frac{X_{jt}}{X_{jt-1}}\right)^{C_j} \qquad (24)$$

which is the *geometric input index*, which is a special case of (23) and is exact for the Cobb-Douglas.

It can similarly be shown that the commonly used Laspeyres and Paasche indices, and predominantly used in national income statistics, are exact for the restrictive linear production function (and others). The geometric index is appropriate only if the revenue shares stay constant over time. Using arithmetic indices such as the Laspeyres and Paasche implies that all inputs (or outputs) are perfect substitutes and an increase in the relative price of any one input should cause its use to be discontinued altogether (Christensen, 1975).

Nonparametric Production Models

This section outlines the general results of the nonparametric approach to productivity analysis. The models reviewed here and applied in later chapters are again based on Farrell's (1957) work on radial measures of

46

efficiency, which was introduced in section (a). Farrell's approach used a system of linear programmes to construct the transformation frontier and to compute primal and dual efficiency relative to that frontier, including a framework for both technical and allocative efficiency.

Formally, Farrell's measure of technical efficiency is

$$F_i(y,x) = Min \ [\lambda : \lambda x \in L^+(Y)] \qquad (25)$$

where the minimised parameter, λ, determines the amount by which the observed input combination can be reduced. The efficiency level is defined as the solution to the programming problem

$$F_i(y_i,x_i) = Min \ \lambda,$$
$$subject \ to \ z_iY_i \geq y_i$$
$$z_iX_i \leq \lambda x_i \qquad (26)$$
$$z_i \geq 0$$

where Y is the output matrix, X is the input matrix and z is the vector of firm-specific non-negative intensity parameters, which are used to construct convex combinations of observed inputs and outputs, and where i denotes the individual firm. The parameter λ allows for radial scaling of the original observations and their convex sets, to determine the minimum input usage needed to produce the given level of output.

Decomposition of technical and scale efficiency

The original programming problem implicitly imposes constant returns to scale (as in Figure 1), so relaxing this restriction allows the total efficiency measure to be decomposed into pure technical efficiency and scale efficiency. Following Fare et al (1985), the relationship between total efficiency, F(y,x), pure technical efficiency, T(y,x) and scale efficiency S(y,x) is

$$F_i(y,x) = T_i(y,x) \ S_i(y,x) \qquad (27)$$

The left hand term is the total efficiency level, explained above, and now $T_i(y_i,x_i)$ is calculated as a programming problem in which constant returns to scale (CRTS) is not imposed, so that technical efficiency is measured independently of scale effects. To achieve this, the constraint that

47

the sum of z, across the inputs must equal unity, is added to the previous programming problem, that is

$$F_i(y,x) = Min \; \lambda,$$
$$subject \; to \; z_i Y_i \geq y_i$$
$$z_i X_i \leq \lambda x_i \qquad (28)$$
$$z_i \geq 0$$
$$\sum z_i = 1$$

The additional constraint on the z vector has the effect of enveloping the data more closely, allowing variable returns to scale to be exhibited. Figure 3.2 uses the production function representation, rather than the isoquant approach of Figure 3.1, to explain this result. With output Y and one input X, the constant returns to scale (CRTS) frontier is denoted by the straight line total product curve, OP, which passes through the observations for the efficient firms B and C.

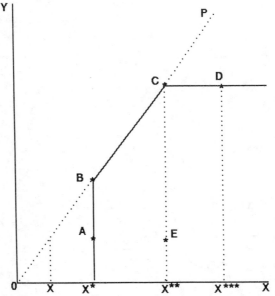

Figure 3.2 Decomposition of Technical and Scale Efficiency

Firms A and D are inefficient as they lie below the CRTS frontier. When non-constant returns to scale are allowed, the technical efficiency frontier, shown by the solid line segments, X^*,B,C,D, is concave and the

48

input-output combinations A and D are technically efficient, as well as B and C. Scale efficiency, $S_i(y,x)$, is calculated as $F_i(y,x)/T_i(y,x)$, since $F_i(y,x)$ includes both technical and scale efficiency and eliminating the pure technical efficiency leaves scale efficiency. Therefore in the Figure, firm A is scale inefficient by OX/OX^*, as it is too small, although is technically efficient. Firm D is similarly technically efficient, but is too large and is scale inefficient by OX^{**}/OX^{***}. Finally, firm E is technically inefficient by OX^*/OX^{**} and scale inefficient by OX/OX^*, giving a total level of inefficiency, relative to the CRTS frontier, of OX/OX^{**}.

Varian (1984) provides a very comprehensive summary of the main results of the previous work in nonparametric production analysis. This includes how to test for consistency of the observed data with cost minimisation and profit maximisation assumptions as well as how to test for some of the technology characteristics such as homotheticity and weak and additive separability, also testing for constant returns. Where it is appropriate to assume perfect competition, it is possible to reformulate the production theory in this way. Then the advantage is that it represents the optimization conditions as inequality constraints that can be easily used to verify, directly from observed data, the consistency of the optimization assumptions. Parametric tests for the consistency of the data with the optimization assumptions (and for tests of the underlying structural characteristics of the technology) are always subject to the maintained hypothesis that the model/functional specifications are correct.

A major advantage of the nonparametric approach is that the models are independent of any specific functional form. Furthermore, since the data used is unit neutral, it is not necessary for all firms to have positive values for all possible inputs or outputs. The disadvantages of this approach is the lack of straightforward hypothesis tests, and the extreme sensitivity of the model to an additional input or output vector, and to outliers.

Once a time dimension is added, the programming approach outlined above extends quite naturally to incorporate technical change. This forms the basis of an alternative approach to TFP measurement, as the next section shows.

Productivity Indices Derived from Nonparametric Functions

Parametric TFP indices were discussed in section b) above, and their usefulness noted. The alternative approach to TFP is the Malmquist index

(Malmquist, 1953), which is a natural extension of the nonparametric models in the last section. The attraction of the Malmquist index, and the reason for pursuing it here is that it allows the separation of efficiency change and technical progress. Following Fare et al. (1992, 1994), the Malmquist TFP index is defined, for firm i and year t+1, in terms of distance functions as

$$M_i^{t+1}(y_i^{t+1},x_i^{t+1},y_i^t,x_i^t)=\frac{D^{t+1}(y_i^{t+1},x_i^{t+1})}{D^t(y_i^t,x_i^t)}\left[\frac{D^t(y_i^t,x_i^t)}{D^{t+1}(y_i^t,x_i^t)}\frac{D^t(y_i^{t+1},x_i^{t+1})}{D^{t+1}(y_i^{t+1},x_i^{t+1})}\right]^{1/2} (29)$$

The first ratio on the right hand side is the efficiency measure for year t+1 relative to that for year t and continuing in the same manner in the next year gives the distance function for year t+1. The other four distance functions define the shift of the technical progress frontier. Two of these terms are identical to the efficiency measures just described. The value of the inter-temporal distance functions are explained by Figure 3, which shows the input requirement sets, factor ratios and isoquants for years t and t+1.

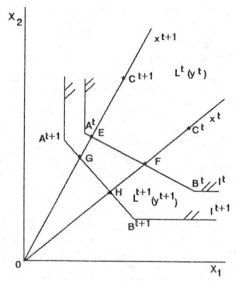

Figure 3.3: **The Rate and Bias of Technical Progress**

The base-year frontier, I^t, is defined by two hypothetical efficient firms, with observations A^t and B^t, and the efficiency of a third firm, at C^t, is calculated relative to this frontier. Thus, $D^t(y^t,x^t)$ is equal to OC^t/OF, on the initial vector x^t. In the next year, the frontier has moved to I^{t+1} and firm C now has an input ratio x^{t+1} and is at C^{t+1}. The efficiency measure is now OC^{t+1}/OG and the efficiency term in (4) is measured by these ratios show in equation (5). The first technical progress term is already defined above and is divided by $D^{t+1}(y^t,x^t)$, which is equal to OC^t/OH, giving the ratio OH/OF. The Figure shows that this is the shift of the frontier measured at the factor ratio x^t. Following the same reasoning, the last term in equation (30) is measured by OG/OE in the Figure and this is the shift of the frontier measured at the factor ratio of the second period, x^{t+1}.

$$M_i^{t+1}(y_i^{t+1},x_i^{t+1},y_i^t,x_i^t) = \frac{OC^{t+1}/OG}{OC^t/OF} \left[\frac{OH}{OF} \frac{OG}{OE} \right]^{1/2} \qquad (30)$$

The technical progress element of the Malmquist TFP index is the geometric mean of the two alternative measures. The product of the efficiency terms and the measure of technical progress is a Malmquist TFP index. This can be compared with geometric indices constructed using conventional accounting techniques, such as the Tornqvist-Theil approximation in the previous section.

Parametric vs Nonparametric Models of Efficiency and Productivity Measurement

The choice of parametric or nonparametric models to measure efficiency ultimately depends on the economic behavioural assumptions, and perhaps more crucially, on the constraints of the data. The parametric approach allows for the relaxation of the assumptions of neutral technical change and constant returns to scale. Therefore this may be preferable if the biases of technical change is of particular interest or there is the likelihood of considerable scale economies which would distort the nonparametric results. The parametric approach also has the advantage of providing statistical confidence intervals for the biases and technical change measures as well as tests for the significance of the inputs.

The disadvantages associated with the use of the parametric approach include the usual range of estimation problems such as robustness of estimators and the degrees of freedom problem associated with the use of flexible functional forms. A related problem is that a high degree of aggregation is often necessary to employ a flexible form which implicitly imposes separability between the input groups. Furthermore, as discussed above, the parametric approach usually estimates a system of the objective function together with the derived input demand equations. This requires the assumptions of efficient resource allocation and competitive markets.

The nonparametric approach offers an integrated test for consistency of the data with profit maximisation and includes the separation of efficiency change and technical progress. Furthermore it does so without any maintained hypothesis as to the form of the implicit objective function.

Conclusion

Where there is full information on prices of inputs and outputs, and in competitive markets with production decisions made on the basis of rational economic behaviour, the dual form of the profit function is generally the model of choice. Then the profit function is a favoured dual representation as both the optimal input levels and optimal output levels are easily derived as partial derivatives of the profit function. It requires only price information, unlike the revenue or cost functions which require both price and quantity information. It also has the advantage that p (vector of output prices) and w (vector of input prices) can be treated as exogenously determined, and so it is possible to solve for optimal input and output levels. Given the profit function uses input and output prices, the output includes output supply and input demand elasticities, with respect to prices. None of this information is available from the direct estimation of the production function.

The cost function, on the other hand, assumes some given target output level for cost minimisation and the revenue function maximises revenue for some given input endowment. Under perfectly competitive market conditions, prices will be exogenously determined as opposed to input or output levels. Therefore the profit function is less restrictive in the sense that input and output levels are allowed to adjust optimally to specified exogenously determined prices, that is, respond to the market.

However, it is clear that in certain circumstances, the firm's objectives may be better represented by cost minimisation, such as under policies of output quotas or production taxes, or where there is imperfect competition). Conversely, revenue maximisation may be the appropriate goal if inputs are restricted or rationed, or where managers behaviour is not necessarily profit maximising. In particular, these conditions may well be pertinent to a new market economy, where the transition is not yet complete and incentives may not be clearly defined. In these cases, the alternative dual forms may be favoured.

But practice may fall short of theoretical rigour. Cobb-Douglas is the chosen functional form if there is a trade off between parsimony of parameters and ease of interpretation, in which case it is excellent, and generality, where it fails abysmally. The Cobb-Douglas is very restrictive, basically because it treats each input as strongly separable from all others and, due to its construction, the elasticity of substitution is set equal to one rather than being estimated. Indeed there is only one parameter estimated for each exogenous variable, which must mean that the relationship between variables is imposed rather than estimated from the data. In comparison, the CES includes one more estimated parameter, the elasticity of substitution, although this is the same between all pairs of inputs, again because of the separability restriction.

Flexible functional forms overcome this difficulty because they are not separable and sufficient parameters are estimated to endogenously determine all elasticities of substitution. Thus functions like the translog are second order approximations of any unknown production function and may be regarded as very general representations of the production process. However, this is achieved by including cross product terms for all the variables, which in single equation estimation leads to multicollineary problems unless the data is extremely rich. Interpretation of the parameter estimates is also considerably more difficult and there may also be degrees of freedom problems.

Turning to the estimation using the Hungarian accounting data, a number of approaches were attempted. In empirical work, the choice of function is limited by the availability of price data for inputs and outputs and in the current study this choice is limited to a production relationship. The attempt to exploit duality maximises the chances of success by sticking to a simple functional form which is a CD/CES hybrid that is estimated as a simultaneous system of equations. It depends on relatively few parameters and puts the smallest possible dependence on prices, for which there is poor information. But even this fairly simple system, where solely own prices were required, still did not work.

One problem identified early in the Hungary study is that production inputs tend to be collinear in the first place and adding cross products exacerbates the problem to the extent that robust estimations are not obtainable. This difficulty can sometimes be overcome by adding structure to the model and estimating a system of share equations but in this instance, even this transformation gave poor results. The other attempt to exploit these recent developments dispensed with duality altogether, estimating the translog production function as a seemingly unrelated system of share equations. Predictably, this approach was also unsuccessful. Consequently, the functional form used throughout the econometric analysis is the Cobb-Douglas, directly estimating the production function.

Fortunately, there are two advantages to this choice of techniques. Firstly, in this analysis of Hungarian firms and sectors, it is very useful to have available a function that does not require an assumption of profit maximisation, although it does assume technical efficiency. Secondly, the Cobb-Douglas asks as little as possible of the data.[6] The other approaches widely used are nonparametric, where again there are no behavioural assumptions, and in addition, no imposed functional form. Finally the index number techniques used in the efficiency measurement over the whole period, also model the technical relationship rather than economic behaviour, again making this a useful method for transition economy applications.

The only instance in which it can be claimed there is a behavioural hypothesis is in the panel data estimation of the Cobb-Douglas function. Here Schmidt (1988) has shown that the within transformation for the fixed effects model when applied to the Cobb-Douglas function gives estimating equations that are equivalent to input demand equations derived from the cost minimisation problem. Thus, in this particular analysis which does use panel data to estimate a technical production relationship, the work can be viewed as either a technical relationship or as a cost minimisation problem.

---

[6] This complies with the general rule in practice that the poorer the data, the simpler the preferred functional form.

4 The Contribution of Accounting Information in Efficiency Measurement: Hungarian Firm Level Data[1]

Introduction

This chapter describes the data, the selection of firms and industry sectors, the way additional series were constructed and what proxies were used. It also puts the practice of compiling accounting information into a social and cultural context. From the discussion in earlier chapters it should be apparent that data availability has had a considerable influence on the techniques used in this study. Many more interesting aspects of economic efficiency measurement are excluded from this analysis because of the nature and limitation of the accounting information. But there is still a lot to be gained from constructing quantitative measures of productivity in order to access the speed and direction of changes during the early part of the transition that is the focus of this study.

The chapter begins with an overview of the function of accounting data at a general level in order to clarify its limitations. This is followed by a brief description of the transition of the Hungarian accounting system from one which simply reported production activity for purposes of aggregation at a national level to one which provides some information about the economic performance of the firm. Then the variables are

---

[1] This chapter is a shortened version of Piesse (1993), The Transition to a New Accounting System: The Case of Hungary, *Journal of European Business Education*.

explained in detail, in the form in which it was originally reported with descriptions of the series used in the empirical chapters that follow.[2]

The Characteristics of Accounting Information

Financial reporting and disclosure practices vary from country to country, with the differences reflected in presentation, the degree of flexibility in accounting practice and accounting practice itself. Presentation differences exist even between countries with similar financial systems, such as the US and the UK, where the position of items on the financial statement is one example. The degree of flexibility in accounting practice varies, with international reporting having greater levels of choice than, for example, the US, where there is none. Finally, accounting practice differs in a number of ways, but those areas where there is most diversity include consolidation, valuation of fixed assets, accounting for goodwill, inventory costing, contingency reserve policy, income tax allocation, pension accounting, accounting for research and development expenditure, foreign currency translation, and accounting for long-term leases and contracts.

The role of accounting data in the developed market economies is central to the informational aspects of market efficiency. However, while the transition literature seems to consider the introduction of new accounting systems inevitable, very little research has directly addressed the choice of system most appropriate to the reforming countries. Appealing to the relevant international accounting literature is useful, particularly that on developing countries, since this provides an adaptive framework for the transitional economies.

Accounting has a dual function in the transition process, having a different role at the micro and macro levels, although the former would appear to be more imperative. At the micro level, firm specific accounting information is required by the State and those involved in the privatisation programmes, for other enterprises and for potential foreign investors. Each firm is subject to valuation, although this may sometimes bear little relation to reality, and all are required to disclose information about their financial position and performance. It is required as part of the system of collecting

---

[2] Clearly, these difficulties in the construction of this dataset are peculiar to the transition economies. Data problems associated with production economics in the West also exist but are of essentially different character.

and transforming economic and social statistics and disseminating relevant data for decision making by the firm. At the macro level, accounting is used to construct national income accounts and various economic performance indicators as well as measuring social indicators to assess the adequacy of planning in the national areas of concern, such as health and education.

Historically, data collection at the national level in the transition economies has been rigorous, particularly with respect to detail and rigid categorization but at the enterprise level little value was associated with it as decisions were not informed by it. More recently, the skills, techniques and judgement required to prepare enterprise level accounting information have been recognised as essential to the development of industry and public administration. Government departments need data from the private sector to assess tax liability and to use in reindustrialization and the efficient allocation of capital. Accounting also monitors the progress of transition (Seider, 1967):

> Enterprise accounting is a supplier of information, a device for increasing the efficiency of resource allocation and a mechanism for controlling productive operations. It seems logical that these skills, normally considered to be tools of private enterprise management, should be equally useful to the management of the process of [transition].

Comparative Accounting Systems

Major differences embodied in the structure and compilation of national accounting systems have developed, largely to reflect the needs of the society in which they existed. Two factors are responsible for these differences, namely, the structure of ownership of economic and productive resources, and the mechanisms used in the conduct of economic activity. Both reflect the way in which data is reported.

In general terms it can be claimed that in a demand led, market economy, the ownership of the factors of production, and of the finished output can be private or public, although they are predominately private. Thus economic exchanges occur through a system of individual transactions, where valuation and thus pricing, is a function of the interaction of a large number of market participants, acting both as suppliers and consumers. Conversely in a supply led, or command economy, ownership is solely in

57

the hands of the State, and value is assigned according to the costs of production. There is no judgement required on the part of the producer about output levels, and no concept of productive efficiency in determining supply. The allocation of resources is the responsibility of the State, while achieving targets is the responsibility of the enterprise. This may be done regardless of the input mix used, the appropriateness of the technology chosen or the levels of wastage or externalities associated with that production. Information relating these two activities is simply passed from one group to the other.

These differences have resulted in national accounting systems which have a distinctive structure and scope, and Bailey (1988) describes the particular characteristics of supply-led economies. In socialist economies, data from the individual enterprises were aggregated into a total means of production for the whole country, and the accounting information received from each unit was compiled into a national set of accounts. This aggregate information was used in two ways. The first was to formulate production decisions at the central planning level, and the second used to control the activities of the State owned enterprises. These accounting systems related to all production in all industries and therefore needed to be standardised so that accurate aggregation could take place. This created a separation of reporting and planning, with the former essentially a book-keeping task, purely recording past performance, but with strict compliance with the rules. The latter, on the other hand, was a response to any shortfall in past targets and exclusively under the control of the administration at a national level.

Thus, it is no surprise that a new accounting system was one of the institutional reforms required as part of the transition to a market economy, although no single model was adopted by all the transition economies. Accounting systems develop to incorporate a number of cultural influences, including religion, the impact of political systems and civil liberties, the level of openness in society, attitude to risk, language and organisational rigidity, and many others (see Gray (1988) and Hofstede (1980)), and historically these have varied. The next section describes the motivation for a new structure of reporting and some of the characteristics of the present Hungarian accounting system.

Development of the Hungarian Accounting System

From the early 1980's, the socio-economic structure of Hungary experienced considerable change, and democratic socialism and the elements of a mixed market economy began to emerge (see Clarke (1989) and Hienonyri (1990)). The successive failure of several Five Year Plans, reinforced by the comparative performance of the Hungarian economy with that of those countries operating under a capitalist market structure coincided with a strengthening of social movements for political reform. In Hungary and other neighbouring socialist states, there was demand for a changing role for the State.

In the move from the post World War II socialist State to a socially aligned market economy, a system of reporting had been developed which was intended to straddle the parallel demands of the market and the State. This attempted to provide information for State planning, and also to encourage foreign investment. But it worked poorly, since the State demanded an extraordinary level of detail and conformity across enterprises, to ensure that aggregation was still possible at a national level. However, it was of little use to the outside world since it presented a view of the firm which made investment opportunities impossible to compare, and therefore had no value in the assessment of expected risk and return.

It became obvious that to achieve a successful transition to a functioning market economy, the financial structure had to be in place to support it. This began with the introduction of the first of several banking reforms in 1989.[3] In particular, because of the chosen method of privatisation, it became necessary to provide enterprise level information to various interested parties. The need for detailed book-keeping required to maintain national production records had diminished and been replaced with the demand for an information system to provide an asset valuation for individual firms.

A major issue was the confirmation of ownership. Changes in the form of ownership required that claims on the business by shareholders needed to be recognised and property rights acknowledged. Furthermore, this commitment to private ownership and the growth of a capital market led to demands for widespread disclosure, especially transparent valuations to ensure investor confidence and promote an active secondary market in

---

[3] Details of these can be found in a number of the Hungarian Ministry of Finance publications such as *The Economic Plan* and *The Accountancy Act*.

equity and debt. At the same time, the growth of a private banking sector required similar reassurances to make decisions relating to solvency, creditworthiness and the profitability of the new private enterprises.

Satisfying these demands required a level of disclosure new to Hungary, and legislation was introduced to ensure compliance. Specific areas covered by the new Accounting Act include the publication of annual accounts, the valuation of assets based on purchase or production cost, with former State-owned property to be independently valued at a fair market price, and the need for an independent audit. A National Accounting Board was set up to develop and establish suitable accounting principles and practice, most of which reflect current EU Directives. The accounting legislation embodied in the 1990/91 Accounting Act was approved by parliament and passed into law in March 1991, effective on 1 January 1992.

Reconciling Accounting Definitions

The previous section described how the new approach to reporting information differed from historical practice in Hungary. From a practical point of view the difficulties that persist in the interpretation of this data follow from the separation of compilers (Ministry of Finance) and users (researchers, potential new owners), although these are not unique to the current situation.[4]

The data is a balanced panel of 1000 enterprises for a seven year period from 1985 to 1991, although it was not acquired until 1993, more than one year after the Accounting Act took effect. Since the information was originally collected while preparers were following the previous accounting rules some translation was required and this was done by the Hungarian Ministry of Finance. No information about this translation procedure was made available and, not surprisingly, some difficulties remain. These became clear very quickly when obvious conflicts with western accounting concepts made many of the series hard to interpret. The remainder of this section describes this process, relying heavily on

---

[4]   Halpern (1995, p279), in one of the few studies to use financial accounting data admits the data are generally heavily biased, despite threats of punishment for intentional disinformation, as accounts are seldom subject to independent audit. Particularly prevalent is manipulation of costs, and the timing of profit statements to maximise tax advantage.

information given in Alexander and Archer (1992). Full details of the procedure to identify and construct the accounting relationships is in the Appendix to this chapter.

The *General Compulsory Scheme of Accounts* is the basis of the 1991/2 Accounting Act and applies to every aspect of the national economy. It is intended to ensure uniformity of the economic contents of the financial statements and determines the basic requirements of physical accounts. The Scheme defines nine classes of accounts. Classes 1 - 4 include the balance sheet accounts, where Classes 1 - 3 are the asset accounts and 4 is liabilities, equities and funds.[5]   Classes 5, 6 and 7 are used for recording costs by type, place within the firm (department or section), and cost-bearer (product) respectively.   Class 5 contains all the material costs: labour, charges on labour (ie social security tax and benefits to employees), depreciation allowance and other costs. Class 6 includes indirect costs (overheads, by department) and Class 7, direct costs by product. Firms can choose between two methods when preparing their accounting statements, first reporting costs by type in Class 5 and then by department and product in Classes 6 and 7, or the reverse. Small firms can report production costs only, ignoring Classes 6 and 7. Finally, Classes 8 and 9 record the results of the firms activities, presenting expenses and revenues which allow some measure of economic performance.   Class 8 specifies the accounts for reporting direct costs and various other costs not represented in the direct cost of products or services, and other expenses. Sales and revenues are Class 9.

As can be seen from the detail in the Appendix, the two main approaches are driven by production or by sales. Each uses a different combination of the nine accounts, neither of which is entirely satisfactory. On balance, the production approach was chosen over the sales approach for two reasons. Firstly, the production function is the theoretical basis of efficiency measurement, see chapter 3. And secondly, the total sales is an

---

[5] It should be noted the nature of funds remains quite different from that in western accounting systems, and is essentially a capital/liability/reserve concept, representing money contributed by the state, and has nothing to do with the idea of funds representing liquidity. This bears some similarity to the UK 1948 Companies Act, where the Capital Redemption Reserve Fund is a designated account within shareholder equity. Historically, these funds were kept separately for particular purposes, thus creating self-balancing aspects of the balance sheet. Thanks to Robin Jarvis for this.

aggregate of domestic, international and CMEA trading, with the associated inconsistencies of a heterogeneous structure for the terms of trade. This seemed to add an additional level of bias that was better avoided. The next section describes the data, both that provided directly by the Ministry of Finance and that taken from publicly available National Income Statistics (Magyar Statisztikia Evkonyv (1993)).

Data

Enterprises

No indication was given as to how enterprises were selected by the preparers of the data, or whether they were in any way representative of the enterprises in that industry, or what proportion of the industry they represented. Crude estimates indicate the sample enterprises account for between 10% and 14% of the total economy in terms of gross output in each year, with some variation across the time series. In this analysis, all enterprises were included unless data was missing or reported as zero, although there was no way to differentiate between these. Unfortunately many records were completely empty and the size of the potential dataset a long way short of that anticipated.[6] Some entries were illogical or unreliable, such as a negative number of employees, a positive number of employees but with zero wages.

Only those enterprises lacking valid data in the relevant series required for the production analysis were omitted. This was because a production model only really makes any sense if output follows from some transformation of inputs, but also as in the econometric analysis the data was used in logarithms, zero values are a problem. Those with zero values for other items, such as taxation, were included even though whole industries were reported as paying zero tax. This basis for exclusion reduced the number of firms in total by approximately 30%, with some industries reduced to a very small number of firms. This led to the decision to consider a selection of industries only.

---

[6] For methodological reasons, industries and enterprises with a small number of firms were excluded. If pooling were appropriate and used rather than panel data methods, more sample would have been larger. However, the superiority of panel models dictated the approach.

Table 4.1   Classification of Industrial Sectors

INDUSTRY	NO. OF FIRMS		INDUSTRY	NO. OF FIRMS	
	Total	Used		Total	Used
General Industry			**Transport & Communication**		
Mining	15	0	Transport	41	2
Electrical energy	15	0	Post & telecoms	-	-
Metallurgy	26	2	**Trade**		
Engineering	135	6	Internal trade	177	25
Building materials	20	2	External trade	21	3
Chemicals	76	2	**Water Works and Supply**		
Manufacturing	82	43	Water works	-	-
Miscellaneous	5	0	**Other Economic Activity (Services)**		29
Food processing	55	6	Data processing & software	8	6
Construction			Other services	6	0
Installation	58	2	Personal & household services	3	0
Planning	10	0	Business services	16	10
Agriculture & Forestry			Financial services	33	13
Agriculture	150	117	Town planning	22	0
Forestry	10	0	Environment	1	0

The initial dataset included enterprises from 25 industry sectors, classified at the three digit level. Initially all industries were included and Table 4.1 shows the distribution of enterprises across industries. However, many were subsequently excluded because of an insufficient number of surviving enterprises with complete and usable data.

It clear from the difference between the total and used columns that much of the data had to be discarded prior to any analysis, mostly due to incomplete records rather than inconsistencies. Geographical regions are also available, but these reflect the location of the registered headquarters and not the establishments themselves and so do not provide any useful information about the special advantages or constraints affecting production. This is not on the whole a problem, as most of the firms are not involved in region-specific production. The exception to this is agriculture where knowledge of the geographical location of farms would be very useful. Nt only would climatic conditions be seen to affect production, but the location would give some indication of the nature of the output expected from that farm. Indeed, farms from a wine growing region may behave differently from those operating in arable land or pasture.   Three   industries were chosen for this study and are the basis of the empirical analysis which follows: agriculture, light manufacturing and services, representing the primary, secondary and tertiary sectors respectively.

Agriculture Agriculture is one of the largest industries in the dataset and is representative of the primary sector. The majority of records are complete and usable. Furthermore, the production technology used in this industry is traditionally fairly straightforward, with the result that these enterprises would have more homogeneous characteristics than do, say, those in the engineering industry which was the second largest group. As discussed below in the section on prices and price indices, it is more appropriate to choose a suitable deflator series when the inputs are known or can be approximated, adding further support to the inclusion of agriculture. Finally, agriculture has been an important sector historically in Eastern and Central Europe, and national statistics have been kept more rigorously than in others.

Manufacturing The secondary sector is represented by the light manufacturing industry. This was sufficiently large to provide acceptable degrees of freedom in the estimation, although presented difficulties in a choice of price deflators for raw materials and capital, since there was no information about the nature of the inputs or the outputs, or whether and which intermediate goods are used in the production process.

Services To construct a sample of firms in the tertiary sector, a number of small service industries have been merged. It is not clear how the business activity in these various service related industries differed, but as in any developing and or transitional economy they have proliferated to support the primary and secondary sectors. There does appear to be some overlap in these enterprises, particularly in the areas of data processing, business and financial service provision. Enterprises in the Personal and Household Services sectors were not included, so the firms that made up the service sector are essentially representative of a business services industry group.

Variables[7]

The records of each firm represent 64 items taken from the nine Classes of Account described in section c) above. The measurement of production relationships using econometric modelling or programming, requires data on those inputs that are expected to be transformed into outputs, using the available technology. Both inputs and outputs would ideally be in physical units with prices at the firm level.

      With no further information about the construction of the individual items of accounting information, the following series were used. All are denominated in Hungarian Forints and are in current prices. The series are then adjusted to constant values with a suitable price deflator (details of which are given later in this chapter). The exception are the labour variables which are measured in numbers of employees, separated into blue and white collar workers. Total labour is a simple addition of the two.

Output Referring to *The General Compulsory Scheme of Accounts* in c), there were four possibilities for obtaining a measure of output:

i   *Value of Gross output (5)* - using the cost of production model

ii   *Net Revenue on sales (7)* - using the cost of sales model

---

[7] The number in brackets is the item identifier in the original dataset, matching those in the Appendix.

iii   *Value added (6)*. Intuition says that this is the value of output, adjusted for intermediate goods, much as UK GDP is constructed. However this series was rejected since for many firms it is negative (and the logarithm undefined).

iv   *Gross operating profit (25)*. This reassuringly is the difference between *Total receipts (23) and Total expenses (24)*. But neither of these series matched anything else in the accounts, and therefore this was excluded.

The series used was (i) Value of Gross Output. This is because it was the simplest series and presents no risk of mis-interpretation and gave better results than other series that were tried. The value of gross outputs is defined in the notes to the accounts, The Statistical Yearbook of Hungary (1992) as the value of goods and services produced. Data on *output inventories (64)* was reported, but there was no information about whether output values represented that for the current year after adjustment for inventories. Since historical practice suggests that unusable or obsolete output existed from previous years, this item was not included.

Capital Of all the inputs, this is the least adequate, partly due to lack of information, but compounded by the number of approaches that can be taken. Normally in a production function, the capital variable would be the service flow from the capital stock, made up of interest, depreciation and running costs. This flow then enters the production function along with the other flow variables which are labour, energy and materials, all expressed as annual values. In this case the running costs component is contained in the energy and raw materials series, so it cannot be separated out, but is adequately dealt with. An attempt was made to construct a service flow series by combining the interest rate variable (see under the prices section in this chapter) and depreciation, since there is a *depreciation (58)* item, although no information on the method used to calculate it. The nominal bank rate reported by the National Bank of Hungary is the only interest rate available and could be deflated, although a resulting negative real rate can cause still more problems. There clearly are missing data and none of the items available combined to make a well-behaved variable.

      The other information available was the *Value of Gross fixed assets (54)*. Net fixed assets was also available, but whereas the expectation is that the difference between gross and net in this context is depreciation, this was not the case here. There is also investment in new, used and other assets and *Investment expenditure (60)*. These series were used to investigate alternatives for the capital input. A common approach to calculating the capital stock is the perpetual inventory method. The equation is $K_t = (1 - \delta)K_{t-1} + I_t$, where K is the real value of fixed capital, δ is the single-period depreciation rate of fixed assets, and I is the amount of real investment undertaken. Had it been possible to assemble the interest, depreciation and investment data in this manner, some confidence in the capital stocks would be in order, but this could not be achieved.

Given the data available, the *Value of Gross fixed assets (54)* was accepted as the capital stock variable, although the way in which it was constructed is not known. Nor are the depreciation and interest variables usable to construct a service flow. Thus, the capital stock series is used although it is a poor substitute for the service flow. A fixed depreciation rate can be applied to this series, in order to make it more like a service flow, but in a multiplicative function like the Cobb-Douglas, this can be factored into the constant term and in the programming approaches the scaling is arbitrary, so it makes little difference. There is at least some precedent in cases with poor data. Using the capital stock in this way is common practice in international agricultural studies, where the FAO data has capital items like animal herds and the quantity of machinery, with no further information available to convert these to flows.

Labour There is a choice of labour data that can be used as an input in production. Number of employees may be useful, although there may be severe underemployment, and the data does state the number of employees registered with the firm, rather than the hours worked. This is divided into blue collar *manual workers (66)* and *white collar (67)* managers, although there is no division into skilled and unskilled labour, even though the national income statistics make this distinction. These are the only series expressed in units other than values.

Another route is to use the information on *wages (16), other costs of wages (17)* (benefits paid to labour) and *social security tax (38)* payments contributed on behalf of labour. *Personal income tax (45)* is available and amounts to about 21-23% of wages in all industries, and for all years. However as this is the equivalent to UK PAYE, it is deducted from wages, and does not represent an additional cost of production. All of the wage data in value terms is for labour in total, providing no information about the cost shares assigned to manual and to management employees. Social security payments are equal to approximately 40% of the value of the wage and this seemed to be consistent across industries and throughout the time series. The amount allocated to employee benefits (noted as *other costs of labour*) showed no such pattern, and this series was not used in the analysis.

One last comment on the labour data is that no quality adjustment is made. No data on the educational level of employees by firm has been included, and while National Statistics do give aggregates, this is not available at the industry level. But since nothing is known about the production technology the issue of skilled vs non-skilled labour can be ignored. However, on the somewhat heroic assumption that wages do tend to reflect marginal productivity, the wages data can be viewed as including a crude form of quality adjustment.

Thus, in the analysis that follows the cost of labour is used as the labour input. This makes the units in all the series consistent, ie forints, although working in logged values makes this unnecessary. More importantly it does make the optimization procedures in the programming problem simpler if all the inputs are of a similar dimension. Only in the index number approach, where units are completely irrelevant, is labour represented by the number of employees in one series. Comparing the index where labour is the number of employees and that where it is the costs of labour show they differ very little (not significantly different at the 95% level).

Energy The only data available is *energy costs (15)*, with no detail of type of fuel given. Fortunately, this variable does appear to be reasonably consistent and it performs fairly well.

Materials Again this is completely non-specific, reported only as *net material costs (14)*. The limited information on the type of inputs, to a large extent, determined the industries chosen in this analysis. Missing data about intermediate inputs, or whether they use domestic or imported raw materials is a serious concern.

Other identifiers Apart from the accounting items, the data also includes a number of other details.

The enterprises are identified by scrambled codes, and the geographical location and ownership type are listed. The geographical location is ignored, since it adds no further information (see earlier comment). The distribution of ownership (as defined by the Ministry) is shown in Table 4.2.

68

Table 4.2   Classification of Ownership and Control

FIRM FORM	NUMBER OF FIRMS	FIRM FORM	NUMBER OF FIRMS
State Enterprise		**Co-operatives**	
State administered	156	Agricultural	114
Self-managed	282	Fishing	4
State affiliated	12	Specialised agricultural	5
Non-profit organisation	2	Other	199
Supervised by co-operative	1	Small	149
Other	6		
Corporation with Legal Status		**Corporation without Legal Status**	
Union	7	Partnership	1
Joint venture	17		
Limited liability company	13	**Other**	
Company limited by shares	6	Organisation financed by State	26

Missing from this list is the year the firm was established, and the year of privatisation. The lack of variability of ownership meant it was impossible to test for a change in performance after restructuring. Also, since the data began in 1985, and only for those firms that were of the same ownership status throughout the period, there are few firms properly in the private sector included in the sample.

Price indices

No price information for the variables was included in the dataset, with the exception of labour, for which it is possible to compute the price of labour by dividing the wage bill by the number of employees. Obviously this gives an average wage per worker, without differentiating between manual and managerial employees. For output and the non-labour inputs price series were constructed from price indices reported in the Hungarian

69

national statistics (Statistical Yearbook of Hungary, 1992), although these are at the industry level only.

In order to exploit the time series as well as the cross section characteristics of the data, that is to use panel estimation techniques, the series require some transformation to take account of price changes. The lack of variability in the prices across firms is a shortcoming, and limits the number of ways it is possible to model such a large group of diverse firms from different industries. As it is, the assumption is that all firms in the industry face the same input prices in the cross section and the only movement in the price ratios is in the time series, which is just seven years.

All the data were initially in current values. But changes in these values over the period of the sample can result from changes in price or quantity, an ambiguity not very useful in production economics. A number of techniques can be used to address this problem, leading to a greater degree of choice in estimation procedures and measurement approaches than in the construction of proxy prices. In practice, the following price indices were used to adjust the value data for the effects of inflation, creating a constant series and in some instances, served as surrogate prices.

Price of output Definitions in the Statistical Yearbook state the basic output price is that used for the valuation of production, ie costs of production, realised profit or loss, plus subsidies and minus production taxes, where this last item is a tax to the firm on imported materials. Basic producer price indices are reported. These are in aggregate and by broad industry category only. Sales price indices are available separately for domestic and export sales at the industry branch level and reported in The Statistical Yearbook of Hungary, (1992) pages 123-5. All of these are constructed as Laspeyres price indices. These indices were used as deflators, and to construct the price ratios used in some of the time series econometrics.

If it is assumed that an output price deflator from one industry can be used for the inputs to other industries, there is potentially a lot of information in these indices. In the cost of sales model, the sales price indices by industry branch is used. Similarly the cost of production approach uses the producer price indices. In both cases it is necessary to ignore any special pricing arrangements negotiated by the firm for the purchase of raw materials or any bulk purchase agreement concerning outputs. This information is simply not available.

Price of capital The usual practice of using the price of capital facing the individual firm cannot be followed here. The bank rate reported by the

National Bank of Hungary is the only interest rate available and, after adjusting for inflation, this is the one that was used. The real interest rates were deflated by the consumer price index, in the absence of anything preferable, and the resulting series used as a price index for capital. Depreciation was not included here as adjusting an already weak variable by another arbitrary value did not appear to add anything useful.

The reform of the financial sector remains a major priority for Hungary. The nominal interest spread is reported to be below the market interest spread due to nonpayment of interest by borrowers.[8] Inflation has been maintained at the lowest possible rate, reported by The National Bank to be 22% in 1993. The National Bank refinancing rate is important in the structure of interest, as banks use it as their base lending rate (for prime customers) and is their marginal costs of funds. In June 1994, the Central Bank base rate rose from 22 to 25%. However Banks are still not very responsive to risk, and spreads are only slightly wider on high risks than on low.

Price of labour The series for wage costs was used as a price of labour. The wage differentials for the breakdown of manual and white collar labour is taken from the Statistical Yearbook of Hungary (1992). Nine industries are reported individually. Gross and net earnings are given, and the difference is assumed to be personal income tax. However, the levels of tax paid differ from those reported at the firm level, that is, tax paid by manual workers is between 25% and 30% and by white collar labour is between 33% and 38%. What is clear from the government statistics is that the wage differential between manual labour and management is substantial, with management earning between 60% and 100% more than manual workers. There are only two years of data available, 1991 and 1992, but the spread appears to be widening, since the year to year increase for this period is up to 10% greater for management. Using these data, the price of manual and management labour at the individual firm level was computed, although for some industries averages were used.

Price of energy Price indices for energy consumption are not available. The best approximation was taken to be the output (sales) price of the industry, where the relevant sectors are electrical energy and crude oil

---

[8] As an illustration, many firms in this sample report positive levels of debt, but no interest payments.

processing. The average of these was used as a single energy price index, and since the correlation between them was 0.89, this has some justification. No information about the specific energy type used is available so a more accurate deflator would not have improved the analysis.

Price of materials The price of materials is probably the most controversial, and ultimately determined the estimation procedures throughout. It certainly influences the choice of industries included, since it is only where the nature of the material inputs is fairly unambiguous that a suitable price deflator can be used. For example, in agriculture, price indices exist for inputs such as fertilizers and plant protectives or pesticides. For the construction industry, price deflators exist for building materials; for the chemical industry, chemicals; and for the food industry, food disaggregated into meat, dairy, canning and milling. For other industries, decisions made are essentially best guesses. A simpler view of all this is that if the input and output price changes are the same they will cancel out in the production function and programming approaches.

Some Comments on Decision-Useful Accounting Information

The difficulties encountered in constructing economic series which can usefully be applied to model production or measure performance and economic efficiency do not arise solely from the nature of the current data. In the absence of a method to separate prices and quantities, value data is not ideal. Equally, in the case of time series, current prices rather than constant are not very useful. But as will be seen in the current analysis, good quality value data from financial statements is valid in a number of practical and research applications. The following comments raise some general questions on the information content of financial statements arising from the present Hungarian accounting system.

The success of institutional reform relating to systems of reporting and the structure of corporate governance, including the role of audit and the nature of the bank-enterprise relationship, depends on its ability to provide confidence and thus promote future partnerships. Established accounting theory indicates that the demand for an accounting system arises from two distinct requirements; the need to control, that is, to ensure stewardship or accountability and the need to inform, or to provide information as an input into decision making and planning (Bromwich, 1992). Accounting systems (including prices) are recognised as an essential part of the market economy's control mechanism, as are inventories, an example of a frequently used standard accounting item suggested by Stiglitz (1992). Inventories are a control mechanism and also an indicator of failure. This information is increasing in use in Just-in-Time production systems, which show up weaknesses in supplier relationships or the communication system between the firm and its suppliers. A good system allows the detection of inefficient operations and the opportunity to correct them. Thus inventories are a signalling device: input inventories signal that production is held up, while output inventories signal poor judgement about consumer tastes and preferences, poor marketing or poor distribution.[9]

The planning and decision-useful role of accounting requires that the financial statements contribute additional knowledge, providing decision-relevant information, an important issue for the transition economies. An example is information on enterprises that is made available to domestic and international investors (or banks) in a way that allows comparisons with other opportunities (or credit requests). The new market economies are highly informationally inefficient, and will remain so until capital market reforms are sufficiently established. But while the rapid adjustment of prices to new information will not occur until the transmission technology is in place, the practice of reporting firm level data is an essential preliminary step.

Regardless of the system of accounting selected, ex ante decision makers require the ability to calculate the future value of cash flows, have an understanding of outstanding debt obligations and make an assessment of future income and wealth. Although considerable differences occur across national accounting systems, if these are known, and the basis of asset valuation defined, all participants will converge on a similar outcome.

Conclusion

A major objective of this study is the wish to develop a series of productivity indices that are robust and consistent, in a situation where information is not transparent and where the established forms of economic analysis which rely on the assumption of competitive markets are not

---

[9] Sadly, input and output inventories in the present data provided no useful signal at all!

appropriate. Where this is successfully completed, appropriate policy can be designed and implemented to correct shortcomings.

But one basic cause of the inefficiency that this study wishes to measure is the lack of useful information. Most damaging is the lack of price data, which is a difficulty for enterprise managers, for investors, domestic and international, and for researchers who wish to understand how resource allocations are made. Therefore almost from the beginning this project was bound to be full of imperfections.

This chapter has explained the importance of *good* data and described the process of checking the validity of the present data, including the experimentation that was carried out prior to the technical efficiency measurement and construction of the productivity indices which form the basis of the study. It has also clarified the limitations imposed by these data omissions, which simply compound the constraints on the theoretical models available because of the lack of competitive market conditions.

From the viewpoint of western accounting methods, the data presented is often tautological. Many series can only be deconstructed in such a naive way that no information appears to be contained in them. Others overlap such that it is not possible properly to balance items that a system based on accrual accounting can achieve. The only approach is to impose as much methodological and theoretical rigour as possible, with proxy data and estimates to fill in the gaps. Both the proxies and the fudges have been openly admitted and the procedures made clear, even if they may border on the unorthodox. For instance, one of the more successful techniques for making the time series consistent in Chapter 8 was to avoid using the inaccurate deflators entirely and resort to the time effects from the error components models.

Appendix: Reconciliation of Accounting Data[10]

The following definitions are taken from the balance sheets and income statements in the Hungarian accounts.

To consider a production approach:

Operating costs *by type* are in Class 5 account. Include material costs, labour, benefits, social security tax, depreciation and other.
Class 5 is used for National Statistics.

Operating costs *by department* are in Class 6 account. Include overhead (indirect) costs.

Operating costs *by product* are in Class 7 account. Include direct costs.

Enterprise chooses between primarily 5 and secondarily 6 and 7 or primarily by 6 and 7 and secondarily 5.

Classes 8 and 9 are *result* accounts. These include expenses and revenues. Class 8 records direct costs and others not represented in the direct costs of products or services and other expenses.

Class 9 includes *sales and revenues*.

Balance sheet

Intangibles now separate, but none in this data. Have to assume part of *Gross Fixed Assets (54)*. This may still include bad debts not written off.

Profit before tax (Gross profit (25)) also called *Operating Profit* may be for the previous year.

---

[10] The figures in brackets are the codes given in the data.

Income statement - Profit and Loss

Total revenue from sales and other income and total costs (costs of sales, overhead costs - not distributed to products - so assumed primary, period costs - could this be investment expenditures new and used? and other expenses.

To consider a cost of sales approach:

Cost of sales (as used in US) - income statement based on functions. Profit against net sales, compare manufacturing costs of products and services sold, marketing costs and general administration.

This could mean:
Gross Profit (25) = Total receipts (23) - Total expenses (24)

which works in totals, but where the expenses do not break down very cleanly.

Cost of sales method used in Hungary, but not the functional approach. Following direct costing, separate fixed and variable costs. Rather than net sales, try to find direct cost of goods sold.

Direct cost of goods sold include: direct marketing costs of products and services and manufacturing costs. Revenues, cost of goods sold and contribution margin are separated by activity (like Figure 4 European Accounting Guide).

Direct cost of goods sold - production and selling (#5 in Figure 8 European Accounting Guide)

Net sales revenue (7)

Profit or loss is based on the cost of sales model (based in turn on direct costing). Looks like this:

Profit or loss = operating profit (*gross profit (25)*) + *subsidies (28)* - other expenses - interest payments where *gross profit (25)* = *net revenue (7)* - direct costs of production - costs not charged to products, where

direct costs of production =
materials (14) + *labour (16)* + *labour benefits (17)* + *SST (38)* + *energy (15)* + *costs of selling* (which could be *fixed costs of domestic sales (19)*) + direct costs related to machinery (which could be *depreciation (58)*), and where

costs not charged to products = *factory overheads (22)* where this could include: wastage, general overheads, R&D and maintenance

Gross Income Statement

The sales revenues are adjusted for changes in inventories, and revenues are compared with total costs and expenses.

Income statement also includes breakdown of activity of the firm, according to distribution of sales, ie domestic, foreign, rouble or non-rouble.

Statement of costs by type

This reflects the production activity, and excludes selling (see Figure 6 in European Accounting Guide). This reflects central planning when production and selling separate. Therefore while this is probably what we want, the construction may reflect previous philosophy and be distorted and was prepared for national aggregation. Should reflect value added in production (fear it does not).

Simplistically, see Figure 4 which says:

Costs of production + costs of selling = costs of goods sold.

By type, this looks like this:

Total production costs = *materials (14)* + *labour (wages (16)* + *benefits (17)* + *social security (38))* + *depreciation (58)* + *other costs (energy (15)*

+ *tax (?profit tax (46)) + investment (perhaps - new and used and other (60, 61, 62 or 63))*

If full unit cost is used for evaluation of production, the connection between costs of good sold and produced would be:

Total production cost = Total costs of goods sold +/- change in inventory

Total production cost (as above) = *Gross output (5) +/- Output-input inventory*

This relationship is generally used in calculation of profit and added value of production, using total cost model.

This is rather speculative, but it looks as though the costs may not be strictly fixed and variable, but that *(14-17)* are the cost of production approach and *(18-22)* are the cost of sales approach.

The following relationships should exist. Where these definitions were violated, firms were removed from the sample.

Output

1   Output inventory (64) = Gross output (5) - Net revenue (7)

         Value of output inventory = Value of good produced - value of good sold

Sales

2   Net revenue on sales (7) > = Domestic sales (8) + Rouble exports (9) + Convertible exports (10)

         Total sales revenue > = Sales, domestic + CMEA + outside world

3   Convertible exports:convertible exports in $US = $/HUF   (10:12)

Costs

There are two representations of costs.
One based on units produced:

4   Total costs (13) > = Net material costs (14) + Energy costs (15) + Wages (16) + Other costs of wages (17)

and one based on units sold:

5   Total costs (13) > = Primary costs of: (domestic sales (19) + rouble exports (20) + convertible exports (21)) + overhead costs (22)

6   Total costs (13) > = Primary costs (18) + Overheads (22)
        (Total)   (Variable)   (Fixed)

Profit

7   Gross profit (25) = Total receipts (23) - Total expenses (24)

8   Gross profit (25) > = Profit after taxes (26)

Taxes

9   Indirect tax (37) = Social Security (38) + Tax on Production (39)

10   Tax on Production (39) = Tax on production for: foreign trade (40) + rouble exports (43) + convertible exports (44) + domestic use (42) + use of imports (41)

Subsidies

11   Indirect subsidies (28) = Subs for: domestic sales (29) + exports (30)

12   Subsidies for exports (30) = Subs for: rouble exports (31) + convertible exports (34) + rouble trade (32) + rouble intervention fund (33) + convertible trade (35) + convertible intervention fund (36)

Founders Equity

This is founders property fund - privatisation process

13   Net worth of owners equity (49) $>=$ Founders equity (50) + Retained earnings + Reserves

14   Net worth of owners equity (49) = State owned net worth (51) + Share capital (52) + Foreign investments (53)

Financial structure

Gearing: (Short term liabilities (47) + Long term debt (48)) / Founders equity (50)

Investment

15   Consumption of fixed capital (start of year) (59) = Invested assets (end of year) (56) + Residual

16   Stock of depreciated assets (59) = Net fixed assets (56) + Residual

PART II:
MODELS, ESTIMATION AND RESULTS

Introduction

The four chapters in this section contain the results from the econometric estimations and the programming approach. The chapters each address a different problem in the transition. Chapter 5 begins by attempting to incorporate relatively recent developments in production economics. Experimentation shows that even a simple version of the dual profit function approach produces poor results and offers explanations as to why this should be so with these data. Then, having established that dual forms are not appropriate, functional forms for the production function estimation are considered. Modern flexible functional forms, such as the translog were tried, both in single equation estimation and by fitting cost share equations as a simultaneous system. Not much is made of this, as these functions are too demanding of the limited data and give poor results. Thus, with some justification, the Cobb-Douglas form is chosen, despite its well-known limitations. The meaning of the Cobb-Douglas when fitted to cross section data is discussed in some detail, as these venerable old techniques prove to be more useful than the modern developments.

The annual cross section data results in Chapter 5 show the shift in emphasis of the various inputs from what can be described as the pre-transition period for Hungary. Those enterprises that have already begun to prepare for restructuring are compared with the ones solidly under state ownership, assuming that the most successful firms are likely to be selected for privatisation first.

Chapter 6 is less archaic and shifts from average OLS regressions to parametric and nonparametric stochastic and non-stochastic production frontiers. This gives alternative views of the spread of relative efficiency levels amongst the firms and changes in efficiency over time. This is worthwhile, as improving efficiency may prove to be more important than technical change in the transition (see the reference to Myint (1971) in Chapter 1).

The scale of production is the focus of Chapter 7, which follows on from the discussion of cross-sectional estimation of the Cobb-Douglas in Chapter 5. In the econometric analysis the firms are divided into groups, according to their size, to investigate the presence of increasing and decreasing returns to scale. The econometric analysis is supported by nonparametric programming techniques and this alternative approach proves to be complementary. The choice of firms selected for inclusion in the dataset does not allow a really adequate analysis of scale, because although differences do exist, all the firms are relatively large.

The last chapter in Part II exploits the panel data characteristics of the sample. Chapter 8 begins by attempting to improve the quality of the information gained from this data and struggles to correct for missing price information. Recent methods in panel data econometrics do provide firm and time effects which go some way to drawing out more worthwhile results than simply using poor price deflators and pooling. In fact, the outcomes show that the results are not very sensitive to the different deflators.

5 Primal and Dual Approaches and Functional Forms: Production Function Estimation and Explanation

Introduction

This chapter begins with an attempt at modelling profit maximisation, although not surprisingly, this is unsuccessful and dual specifications are pursued no further. Similarly, direct estimation of the share equations for the translog production function give very poor results and so flexible functional forms are also abandoned. Consequently the chapter concentrates on the Cobb-Douglas form of the capital, labour, energy and materials (KLEM) model (Berndt and Khaled, 1979), which is applied to cross sectional data at the industry level. Then annual changes over seven years of data for each of the three industries are compared.

This makes it possible to consider the choice of factor combinations and to investigate shifts in the use of these factors during the early years of the transition. Given constant returns to scale for the Cobb-Douglas, the coefficients can be interpreted as factor shares, which, in the absence of price information, allows some inference to be made about the relative importance of the individual factors. Note though, that the shares can be calculated directly from the data since, by its nature, it is expenditures. However, a big share does not guarantee that the factor is significant in the production process, but simply costs a lot, so the estimated elasticities are discussed along with the associated t statistics. Finally, the data is partitioned by form of ownership and the division between those firms that have been privatised and those still under State or co-operative control are compared.

Primal and Dual Functions and Choice of Functional Form

The production function is a purely technical relationship between outputs and inputs. It is also clear that single equation estimation of the production function is bound to result in simultaneous equation bias, as all the inputs which are actually decision variables are treated as exogenous. This has been understood at least since Marschak and Andrews in 1944. The dual cost and profit functions are derived from the corresponding cost minimisation and profit maximisation problems and therefore incorporate these behavioural assumptions in the estimation. Either assumption would be true under an organisational arrangement such as perfect competition, but neither are likely to be correct for Hungarian industries in this period. Indeed, this observation mitigates against dual forms and makes a programming approach a good alternative because it neither imposes a behavioural hypothesis nor does it care if the economic agents succeed in their attempts to maximise or minimise.

Both the dual approaches use input and output prices as exogenous variables. Again, under perfect competition this is preferable to having exogenous input quantities. At the firm level these prices can be expected to be exogenous to the enterprise, but in this case firms may be sufficiently large to influence prices, and hence the estimating equations may not be reasonable. However, in this particular application, although price data is available it is thoroughly untrustworthy and does not match up with the firm specific input data. Thus it is unlikely that a cost or profit function will give good results. This was confirmed by using a system of linear input demand functions with cross equation constraints derived from maximising profits subject to a nested Cobb-Douglas/constant elasticity of substitution production function.

The constrained profit maximisation problem is

$$Max\ \pi = P_y Y - P_m M - P_e E - P_w W - P_k K$$
$$- \Lambda (Y - \nu (\theta (M^\alpha E^\beta)^{-\rho} + \eta (W^\lambda K^\gamma)^{-\rho})^{-\frac{1}{\rho}}) \tag{1}$$

where Λ is the Lagrange multiplier. Y, M, E, W and K represents output, materials, energy, wages (labour) and capital respectively, ν is the efficiency parameter, ρ the substitution parameter and θ and η distribution parameters. Solving the first order conditions for the inputs gives the input demand functions

$$LnM = -\left(\frac{\rho\beta}{\rho\alpha+1}\right)LnE - \left(\frac{\rho}{\rho\alpha+1}\right)Ln\nu + \left(\frac{1}{\rho\alpha+1}\right)Ln\alpha +$$
$$\left(\frac{1}{\rho\alpha+1}\right)Ln\theta + \left(\frac{\rho+1}{\rho\alpha+1}\right)LnY - \left(\frac{1}{\rho\alpha+1}\right)Ln\frac{P_m}{P_y} \qquad (2)$$

$$LnE = -\left(\frac{\rho\alpha}{\rho\beta+1}\right)LnM - \left(\frac{\rho}{\rho\beta+1}\right)Ln\nu + \left(\frac{1}{\rho\beta+1}\right)Ln\beta$$
$$+ \left(\frac{1}{\rho\beta+1}\right)Ln\theta + \left(\frac{\rho+1}{\rho\beta+1}\right)LnY - \left(\frac{1}{\rho\beta+1}\right)Ln\frac{P_e}{P_y} \qquad (3)$$

$$LnW = -\left(\frac{\rho\lambda}{\rho\lambda+1}\right)LnK - \left(\frac{\rho}{\rho\lambda+1}\right)Ln\nu + \left(\frac{1}{\rho\lambda+1}\right)Ln\lambda$$
$$+ \left(\frac{1}{\rho\lambda+1}\right)Ln\eta + \left(\frac{\rho+1}{\rho\lambda+1}\right)LnY - \left(\frac{1}{\rho\lambda+1}\right)Ln\frac{P_w}{P_y}$$
$$(4)$$

$$LnK = -\left(\frac{\rho\lambda}{\rho\gamma+1}\right)LnW - \left(\frac{\rho}{\rho\gamma+1}\right)Ln\nu + \left(\frac{1}{\rho\gamma+1}\right)Ln\gamma \qquad (5)$$
$$+ \left(\frac{1}{\rho\gamma+1}\right)Ln\eta + \left(\frac{\rho+1}{\rho\gamma+1}\right)LnY - \left(\frac{1}{\rho\gamma+1}\right)Ln\frac{P_k}{P_y}$$

This is an example of the general linear structural equation model (see Dhrymes 1978, Ch 6), and is estimated as a simultaneous system using full information maximum likelihood (FIML), taking account of the cross-equation restrictions. Fitting this model to the Hungarian data showed that although only one relative price occurs in each equation, even this was enough to give totally unacceptable results (wrong signs and insignificant coefficients) and frequently the model failed to converge. Attempting to estimate such a system was not entirely without foundation, since all the prices used are indices (see chapter 4) and the correlations between them very high. Furthermore, given inflation rates differed little between industries, the ratio of prices, for example, P_m/P_y in equation (2), is close to unity. But perhaps this was the problem, and the price indices are meaningless. Added to the probable mis-specification, such an approach was doomed, as was any attempt to utilise other flexible functional forms of cost and profit functions, in which all the prices appear as exogenous variables in each equation.

So this route was abandoned in favour of production functions. Estimating a system of cost shares for the translog again gave poor results, mostly because the inputs tend to be collinear (see Table 5.1.) and this is exacerbated by including squared terms and cross products. In such situations the Cobb-Douglas demands less of the data and gives better results. However, it is not entirely acceptable, in that joint variable deletion tests showed that not all the squared and cross product terms could always be deleted.

Fortunately, there is a real gain to using the Cobb-Douglas system consisting of the production function in conjunction with panel data models. Schmidt (1988) has shown that the within transformation for the fixed effects model gives estimating equations that are exactly the same as those derived from the cost minimisation problem with the Cobb-Douglas functional form as the constraint.[1] Therefore, at least these panel results may be interpreted as having a behavioural assumption incorporated in them, in the only way possible for this data.

While the Schmidt insight adds support for the use of the Cobb-Douglas despite its well known limitations, the restrictions associated with the function are substantial, including the imposition of elasticities of substitution of unity between all input pairs and constancy of the elasticities across all the data points. These restrictions result from the form of the function, which does not incorporate sufficient parameters to take account of the interaction between variables, or to allow for non-linearity in parameters. Furthermore, each input is treated as its own separable group which itself means that all pair-wise elasticities of substitution have to be the same. Because of these constraints, the Cobb-Douglas has been largely replaced by flexible functional forms, such as the translog which incorporates cross products and squared terms. Whilst this can be an obvious improvement if the dataset is sufficiently large, production inputs are generally collinear and this is certainly true for the Hungarian

---

[1] Note too that if the errors in the production function are independent of those in the first-order conditions, this result does not require cross-sectional price variation.

88

agricultural sector data, although less so for the other two sectors, as Table 5.1 shows.

Table 5.1   Correlations Coefficients between Inputs

Inputs	Agriculture			Manufacturing			Services		
	Materials	Energy	Labour	Materials	Energy	Labour	Materials	Energy	Labour
Energy	0.906			0.723			0.294		
Labour	0.905	0.926		0.837	0.673		0.580	0.913	
Capital	0.909	0.916	0.911	0.773	0.785	0.668	0.267	0.718	0.767

Adding squared and cross product terms to the already collinear variables resulted in wrong signs and insignificant coefficients, although variable deletion tests showed that there are very few subsets of the data for which all the cross effects and squared terms can be jointly deleted. This suggests that the Cobb-Douglas functional form is inappropriate in this case, but a single equation flexible function form is not a viable alternative. The preferred method of estimation for a flexible function form is as a system consisting of the production function itself, and the cost share equations (Berndt and Christensen, 1973). While this approach was investigated and may prove to be useful it has the limitation that estimating the cost share equations requires the imposition of constant returns to scale. Wald tests for the validity of the constant returns to scale restriction showed that it frequently did not hold. Indeed, this is confirmed by the Cobb-Douglas estimates that follow, and it is intended that returns to scale should be a major area of investigation.

For these reasons the Cobb-Douglas is chosen as the preferred functional form, despite its limitations, a choice further justified by the messy nature of the data. Tybout (1992) has argued recently that for noisy data there is little to be gained from using sophisticated functions, and the Cobb-Douglas technology is chosen as it affords maximum flexibility in dealing with data imperfections.

Single Industry Level Elasticities and Factor Shares

Following from the review of production theory in Chapter 3, the relationship between the amounts of the inputs used and the quantity of output resulting from this activity can be described by a general production function

$$Y = F(K, L, E, M)$$ 	(6)

where Y is output, M is raw materials, E is energy, L is labour and K is capital equipment (as described in Chapter 4). This input set has been commonly used in the production economics at least since Berndt and Khaled (1979) and has become generally known as the KLEM model.

The econometric estimation adopted a Cobb-Douglas specification for reasons stated above, and in general this fitted the data well. In logarithms, the value of the coefficients represent the percentage change in output for a given percentage change in the input. In this way, the coefficients are output elasticities and constant across the sample. The form of the production function is

$$Y = A K^{\beta_1} L^{\beta_2} E^{\beta_3} M^{\beta_4}$$ 	(7)

There is a substantial literature on fitting the Cobb-Douglas to cross-sectional data and the rather dated work of Walters (1963, 1969) proved to be especially useful. Walters points out that the usual assumptions of the theory of the firm under perfect competition (U-shaped cost curves, same technology and same input and output prices) means that if the theory was complied with all the firms would produce the same amount equally efficiently. The data would all occupy the same point in input/output space and no econometric estimates of elasticities would be possible.

Two assumptions on the nature of producer differences reconcile the model with useable data, one associated with the level of output and the other with managerial ability, or entrepreneurship. So, it is assumed that mistakes are made in the level of output, in both directions, ie some firms are too big and some too small. But, on average the sample will exhibit constant returns to scale and estimation is consistent with the model and this is the most common approach in practice.

The other possible scenario is that managerial competence varies from one firm to another. This represents a more or less constant relative efficiency level for the individual manager. This entrepreneurial variation is captured in the disturbance term and can accompany the mistakes in the level of output. Then, the results will depend on the relative importance of the two effects. The entrepreneurial variation will result in a downward bias in the measurement of the scale effect. Therefore, simply summing the coefficients and finding unity cannot be interpreted as evidence of constant returns over all the firms in the sample. The suggested solution is to divide the sample into groups according to size and this old-fashioned technique is used in Chapter 7.

One realistic assumption in the present analysis is multiple prices for inputs. There is no reason to presume that all firms face the same price for any of the four inputs included here. The only variable for which there is price information is labour, and the average wage per employee is not constant across the sample. This means the rationale for the substitution between factors is different for each firm, even though the direction and magnitude of any reallocation is hidden, given the limitation of value data.

In the absence of accurate input prices, the Cobb-Douglas factor shares can be used as weights for aggregation in constructing a TFP index (see Kawagoe and Hayami (1985)). However, this again requires that the coefficients are constrained to sum to unity. For the Hungarian data used here, this constraint was rejected in many cases, but this was not a problem since the input shares were constructed directly from the input cost data and the option of using the coefficients as weights was not necessary. These variable shares are what is needed for the construction of the Tornqvist-Theil approximation of the Divisia index in Chapter 9. Since the geometric index is a special case of the Tornqvist-Theil (with constant weights), these indices are suitable for in comparative studies, although this is not necessary here.

Yearly Cross Section Results: Industry Comparisons

This series of annual cross-section results relate to the individual industrial sectors, each estimated separately and reported in Tables 5.2, 5.3, (with an alternative model for manufacturing in 5.4) and 5.5. These show evidence of a difference in emphasis in the use of the inputs in the three industries, although commonality was identified in other areas and these are summarised and then discussed in more detail by industrial sector.

Raw materials and labour were the only variables significantly different from zero in the three models and for all years. Raw materials also had the highest elasticities throughout, although no information about the nature of the materials used is available. Neither is it clear where the materials came from, that is, are they domestically produced, imports or intermediate goods intrinsic to the enterprise? Labour also is a significant factor throughout, with the second highest elasticities, when measured as wages.

Table 5.2 **Agricultural Sector - Annual Unconstrained Cobb-Douglas**

Year	Constant	Materials	Energy	Labour	Capital	δ_i's	Adj R^2
1985	1.257	0.542	0.122	0.312	0.030	1.005	0.974
	(6.64)	(14.32)	(2.76)	(7.00)	(0.92)		
1986	1.165	0.522	0.106	0.382	0.010	1.020	0.976
	(6.58)	(14.04)	(2.41)	(8.86)	(0.32)		
1987	1.036	0.532	0.065	0.408	0.020	1.025	0.974
	(5.42)	(13.21)	(1.39)	(8.99)	(0.55)		
1988	1.208	0.467	0.112	0.399	0.038	1.016	0.977
	(6.98)	(12.09)	(2.15)	(9.21)	(1.10)		
1989	1.103	0.435	0.110	0.509	-0.016	1.038	0.968
	(5.22)	(9.76)	(2.10)	(9.33)	(-0.45)		
1990	1.321	0.513	0.008	0.364	0.109	0.984	0.967
	(6.35)	(13.47)	(0.21)	(6.455)	(3.17)		
1991	0.722	0.421	0.052	0.361	0.212	1.045	0.958
	(2.88)	(10.07)	(1.27)	(5.42)	(6.50)		

Firms = 117. The t statistics are in brackets: The 95% confidence level critical value for a two tailed test is 1.98. It the appropriate test is considered to be one-tailed, since elasticities must be positive, then the value is 1.66. The 90% critical value is 1.66 for the two-tailed test and 1.29 for the one-tailed version.

The series of annual cross section regression estimates gives some indication of a trend shown by the changing shares of individual inputs. But the data in these cross section equations are all current values, retaining, at this stage, the original values given. Therefore, comparing the annual results does not allow any inference to be made about reallocation as a response to price movements or other forms of rationing from one year to the next. Changes may be largely the result of relative differences in inflation between the inputs.

Agriculture Table 5.2 reports the annual cross-section estimates of the elasticities for agriculture, from equation (7). The coefficients sum to close to one in the unconstrained equation. To test for robustness of this result, the equation was re-estimated with constant returns imposed and the Wald test indicated that the constant returns to scale (CRS) restriction could not be rejected. Therefore in all the years where the coefficients sum to very nearly one, these can be safely interpreted as factor shares.

As shown in the table, the independent variables explain more than 95% of the variance throughout the time period. Established practice has denoted the constant term to account for otherwise unmeasured level of technology. This is a significant factor in all years although it probably accounts for errors in the other variables rather more than technological change. As can be seen in the table, this value fluctuates considerably over this time period, ending at almost half the first year value, which can be interpreted as an indication that the average level of technology in agriculture available to the firms in this sample has fallen. This implies that even if there has been technological progress in the industry, not all firms have been able to incorporate the new innovation into their production technology.

Table 5.3   Agricultural Sector - Annual Constrained Cobb-Douglas

Year	Constant	Materials	Energy	Labour	Capital	Adj R^2	$F(1,112)^*$
1985	1.313	0.545	0.121	0.304	0.030	0.974	0.107
	(16.91)	(15.24)	(2.75)	(8.45)	(0.93)		
1986	1.338	0.535	0.097	0.355	0.013	0.976	1.199
	(16.89)	(15.19)	(2.24)	(9.97)	(0.41)		
1987	1.263	0.549	0.056	0.375	0.020	0.973	1.748
	(15.09)	(14.34)	(1.21)	(9.96)	(0.57)		
1988	1.344	0.480	0.099	0.379	0.041	0.977	0.786
	(16.75)	(13.46)	(1.99)	(10.33)	(1.20)		
1989	1.455	0.467	0.093	0.455	-0.014	0.968	3.317
	(16.88)	(11.22)	(1.78)	(9.83)	(-0.39)		
1990	1.253	0.508	0.009	0.375	0.109	0.968	0.115
	(20.40)	(14.16)	(0.25)	(8.17)	(3.17)		
1991	1.167	0.448	0.050	0.293	0.209	0.957	3.341
	(18.8)	(11.37)	(1.21)	(5.26)	(6.35)		

* Test results for $F(1,112)$ of restricted vs unrestricted regression. Critical value = 3.84 at 95% significance level.

Raw materials has the highest output elasticity in all seven years, and this variable is always a significant input to the production process.

Energy is significant in the early years, but becomes smaller and then not significantly different from zero in later years. During the last two years the energy coefficient is falling and insignificant, suggesting that the value marginal product (shadow price) is not significantly different from zero. This suggests that energy is being used up to the point that its VMP is zero, or in terms of the linear programming, energy is not a constraint on production. As with raw materials, there is a high output elasticity on the labour input.

The poorest performing input is capital, which is not surprising given its unsatisfactory construction, and the inability to derive flows from the stock series. Only in the last two years is this significant, and in earlier years the elasticity is small, with a maximum of 3.8%, and in one case is negative. The accounting statements for the firms in this sample show high expenditures on capital equipment, compared with other inputs, and one possible conclusion is that machinery is old, poorly serviced or incorrectly used. Alternatively, it is quite possible that capital only became a scarce factor with the reforms towards the end of the period. Quality adjustments are not possible for materials, energy or capital. However, the division between blue and while collar workers may indicate some quality difference. This is pursued further in the case of manufacturing, where the results were more interesting.

The constrained (CRS) model results are in Table 5.3. These are very similar to those from the unconstrained equation, and results for the $F(1,112)$ test of the restricted versus the unrestricted regression shows that the constraint cannot be rejected. However, since Walters (1968) shows that the CRS outcome tends to occur when in fact there are increasing and decreasing returns in the sample, the returns to scale issue is deferred to Chapter 7.

Manufacturing Table 5.4 reports similar regressions for manufacturing. As in the agricultural sector, the constant term falls over the period and is insignificant and negative for two of the seven years. This can be interpreted as a fall in the average technology level or an indication of the recession in the Hungarian manufacturing industry during these early years of the transition and the associated high levels of underemployment existing in the factories. Commonly too, raw materials and labour are significant at the 95% level throughout the period. The elasticities vary considerably for both.

Table 5.4   Manufacturing Industry (Version 1) - Annual Unconstrained Cobb-Douglas

Year	Constant	Materials	Energy	Labour	Capital	Adj R^2
1985	0.071	0.961	-0.166	0.224	0.009	0.940
	(0.09)	(15.35)	(-3.38)	(2.45)	(0.16)	
1986	1.338	0.301	-0.117	0.557	0.237	0.960
	(1.41)	(5.23)	(-1.73)	(5.47)	(4.49)	
1987	3.213	0.384	0.156	0.256	0.070	0.962
	(4.71)	(9.39)	(2.08)	(4.34)	(1.00)	
1988	1.277	0.585	0.021	0.313	0.069	0.991
	(4.25)	(21.11)	(0.41)	(3.77)	(3.35)	
1989	-0.455	0.481	-0.307	0.947	0.003	0.893
	(-0.61)	(5.22)	(-1.94)	(4.17)	(0.05)	
1990	1.172	0.331	0.095	0.628	-0.034	0.946
	(2.99)	(10.38)	(1.41)	(14.74)	(0.97)	
1991	-0.700	0.623	-0.327	0.698	0.142	0.983
	(-0.80)	(8.04)	(-2.49)	(6.55)	(3.29)	

Firms = 43. t statistics in brackets. The 95% critical value is 2.02 for a two tailed test. The alternatives are very close to what was reported below Table 5.2, so they are not repeated.

In the case of labour, the contribution increases over the period, such that the last three years are on average three times as high as the first year. Because of the unstable behaviour of the labour variable, other series for labour were used (Table 5.5). In this formulation, blue collar labour has a higher elasticity than white collar, although it did not perform any better when white collar was omitted.

One useful piece of information is provided by these two specifications. In the first, where the cost of labour variable is used, constant returns to scale is approximated, if not fully present. In the second, where the number of employees are used, labour is not always significant. This lends support to the underemployment view, repeating the argument earlier: there was too much labour in place in manufacturing prior to the transition which has still been retained, contributing to the transition recession. Unlike agriculture, the energy variable has a negative, although significant, effect for four of the seven years. Here too, capital is not especially well-behaved, with only three years significantly different from zero.

**Table 5.5   Manufacturing   Industry   (Version   2)   -   Annual
Unconstrained Cobb-Douglas**

Year	Constant	Materials	Labour - blue collar	Labour - white collar	Capital	Adj R^2
1985	0.071	1.028	-0.0001	-0.00008	-0.029	0.920
	(0.81)	(18.04)	(-0.65)	(-1.43)	(-0.46)	
1986	5.282	0.428	0.0005	0.0002	0.178	0.958
	(10.89)	(17.15)	(4.15)	(4.89)	(4.61)	
1987	3.982	0.542	0.0006	0.0001	0.184	0.949
	(7.31)	(15.38)	(4.86)	(2.89)	(3.18)	
1988	3.454	0.584	0.0003	0.0003	0.171	0.985
	(9.51)	(14.68)	(2.62)	(4.32)	(8.86)	
1989	3.696	0.632	0.003	0.002	0.043	0.865
	(3.53)	(7.19)	(2.20)	(2.68)	(0.66)	
1990	6.610	0.291	0.0015	0.0013	0.131	0.842
	(12.08)	(5.74)	(2.22)	(6.98)	(3.03)	
1991	4.318	0.560	0.0005	0.00008	0.142	0.953
	(8.69)	(7.07)	(1.79)	(0.91)	(2.80)	

t statistics in brackets.   The critical values are as for Table 5.4.

Thus, the wage series is retained for the manufacturing equations, partly because in this second series of equations energy was included initially, however it was not significant and variable deletion tests showed energy not to be an important input.   A translog equation, which is potentially a more appropriate functional form for production relationships with simple inputs such as labour and capital, failed to improve on the simple Cobb-Douglas.   Neither the cross-product, nor the squared terms in the translog function were significant.

Service industries   A similar series of cross section regressions was estimated for services, which is made up of the financial, business and computer services industry groups. Exogenous variables included were raw materials, labour (cost of labour) and capital. Energy was not included in the final model, since it was not significant in any of the cross section equations and unlike the other two industries, the assertion could be made that this is a less crucial variable here. Capital was included, although as in the other two industries, very little information was available about the

96

nature of capital used. However, intuition supports the case for a more homogeneous capital requirement (computing and other office technology) in the service sector than in the manufacturing industry.

Table 5.6   **Service Industry (Aggregate) - Annual Unconstrained Cobb-Douglas**

Year	Constant	Materials	Labour	Capital	Adj R^2
1985	1.133	0.264	0.705	0.067	0.986
	(3.15)	(5.05)	(7.59)	(1.62)	
1986	1.631	0.282	0.671	0.014	0.965
	(2.99)	(3.90)	(4.68)	(0.22)	
1987	1.027	0.236	0.755	0.050	0.988
	(2.179)	(4.29)	(6.48)	(1.35)	
1988	1.091	0.300	0.645	0.107	0.992
	(3.69)	(8.00)	(7.93)	(2.92)	
1989	1.230	0.288	0.651	0.838	0.994
	(4.54)	(7.39)	(8.86)	(3.17)	
1990	1.286	0.330	0.674	0.018	0.994
	(4.75)	(10.03)	(9.68)	(0.71)	
1991	1.091	0.299	0.712	0.026	0.987
	(2.92)	(6.32)	(7.05)	(0.65)	

t statistics in brackets. The 95% critical value is 2.06 for a two tailed test. The alternatives are very close to what was reported below Table 5.3, so they are not repeated.

In this group of industries, the positive and significant constant is assumed to be a measure of technology, and perhaps the wage variable can be viewed as a quality adjusted (skilled) labour variable, to reflect professional qualifications or other competencies. Table 5.6 reports these results. Not surprisingly, the labour input has the highest elasticity in the service sector, traditionally a labour intensive industry. This variable is significant in each of the cross section regressions, and has a mean coefficient of 0.687. Raw materials are also a significant input, and have a largely constant weighting of 0.3. Typically, capital does not perform consistently well, perhaps a continuation of the stock flow problem.

Cross-ownership Comparisons

The discussion in Chapter 2 included aspects of the transition which provided the initial interest and motivation for this study. One of the major tasks of systematic transformation identified by Sachs (1996) was the transfer from State to private ownership, and the subsequent reform of the enterprises. Already the privatisation programmes have played an important role in reversing the legacy of central planning, breaking up large, multi-product and multi-activity productive units. Much of the debate about the value of these privatisation programmes has focused on the order and process of the dismantling of State enterprises. However, any evaluation of their subsequent performance following privatisation must be considered with care. Any increase in the level of performance can either be an indication of the success or failure of the restructuring or a signal that the right choice was made in the selection of enterprises for privatisation. The analysis of data separated by ownership must reflect these possible outcomes.

Many studies of comparative efficiency are linked directly to the style of management or ownership. For example, Estrin (1989) used data from firms operating in a market economy but with alternative organisational structures, and Brada and King (1993) compared firms in the same industry but in different national environments. In this section it is acknowledged that the definitions of the ownership groups are not comparable to those of either Estrin or Brada and King, although some interesting results can be obtained.

The data in this study covers the period immediately prior to the established beginning of transition, and so any direct comparison between those enterprises designated as private and those still defined as co-operatives of various kinds, along with those still under state ownership, remains rather artificial. All of the enterprises labelled as private, were already so at the beginning of the period, that is, 1985. This was the result of the slow move towards the early liberalisation of markets, a situation that makes Hungary a special case in the group of transition states. The implication is that these were some of the earliest to be privatised, and they may be a non-representative group. Clearly, this analysis does little to shed light on enterprises whose reform is initiated during the transition itself. Rather, it is restricted to observations about the behaviour of the particular firms in this sample to the introduction of market structures and the increased competition they face following the privatisation of other firms in their industry.

The control and ownership categories outlined in Chapter 4 are used to divide the firms into two main groups, those enterprises remaining under the control of the state and corporations with legal status, including co-operatives. Unfortunately, the subtleties of different types of co-operative have been lost in aggregation, since no group was sufficiently large to consider in isolation. The service industries are not included in this section as only one firm was listed as being in the State owned group. Still, this division was in some sense arbitrary. A subset of the state owned firms are worker-managed, although overall control is with the State. Issues relating to the size of the enterprise, often a crucial element in the efficiency debate and certainly relevant here, are addressed in Chapter 7.

The analysis in this section first divides the data into two groups and then applies an ownership and control dummy variable (State-owned are 0, incorporated firms and co-operatives are 1) to test for differences in output elasticities. These results are reported in Tables 5.7 and 5.8. The results show a significant difference in performance in the agricultural and manufacturing sectors, when ownership is taken into account. To examine agriculture first, the dummy variable is not significant in any of the regressions, and the coefficients change very little from those in Table 5.2. More interesting is the split sample. In Table 5.7, the intercept is positive for the privatised enterprises but not significantly different from zero for those in the State-owned group, indicating a higher initial level of technology for the former. But the difference in the slope coefficients, in particular, those on materials and energy, shows that the sample should not be pooled in the first place. The table shows raw materials to be an important input, and is positive and significant throughout the period. However, comparisons between the state and private sector shows a higher coefficient on raw materials in the state owned enterprises, with the gap widening throughout the time period, except in 1990.[2]

Energy also is another input that behaves differently between the groups, being a significant input for the incorporated firms and co-operatives but not for the State managed firms. Following the discussion earlier in this chapter, the State owned firms are using energy up to the point that its VMP is zero, so energy is not a constraint on production. The price of energy will almost certainly have been different for the two groups, with the state owned firms probably having no incentive to

---

[2] The very different sample sizes for the two groups means these estimates are not strictly comparable.

conserve energy or maybe not the physical means to do so if they had wished. This is not the case for privatised enterprises. It is hardly new information that multiple prices existed before the beginning of market reforms, but these results are confirmation of this view.

Table 5.7   Agricultural Sector - Ownership Structure

Year	Ownership Group	Constant	DV	Materials	Energy	Labour	Capital	Adj R²
1985	State (n=14)	1.999		0.593	-0.010	0.286	0.055	0.934
		(1.36)		(6.49)	(-0.10)	(1.61)	(0.26)	
	Non-state (n=103)	1.296		0.535	0.131	0.314	0.024	0.969
		(6.03)		(12.85)	(2.75)	(6.59)	(0.69)	
	Total (n=117)	1.339	-0.032	0.540	0.122	0.312	0.027	0.974
		(5.95)	(-0.68)	(14.23)	(2.74)	(6.98)	(0.83)	
1986	State	2.071		0.650	-0.002	0.216	0.049	0.958
		(1.93)		(8.20)	(-0.20)	(1.60)	(0.33)	
	Non-state	1.209		0.508	0.114	0.392	0.005	0.971
		(6.02)		(12.52)	(2.35)	(8.52)	(0.14)	
	Total	1.279	-0.45	0.520	0.103	0.382	0.008	0.976
		(6.07)	(-1.00)	(13.94)	(2.35)	(8.87)	(0.24)	
1987	State	0.958		0.638	-0.078	-0.039	0.445	0.950
		(0.72)		(8.26)	(-0.75)	(-0.25)	(1.98)	
	Non-state	1.104		0.515	0.073	0.423	0.010	0.968
		(5.12)		(11.84)	(1.46)	(8.81)	(0.27)	
	Total	1.201	-0.22	0.527	0.064	0.407	0.016	0.974
		(13.08)	(-1.31)	(13.08)	(1.38)	(8.99)	(0.45)	
1988	State	2.004		0.636	0.003	-0.046	0.301	0.942
		(1.52)		(6.74)	(0.03)	(-0.31)	(1.81)	
	Non-state	1.263		0.450	0.138	0.412	0.016	0.973
		(6.51)		(11.04)	(2.45)	(9.13)	(0.43)	
	Total	1.355	-0.054	0.463	0.117	0.396	0.032	0.977
		(6.45)	(-1.23)	(11.96)	(2.24)	(9.16)	(0.91)	
1989	State	0.019		0.598	0.152	0.103	0.243	0.941
		(0.01)		(3.97)	(1.08)	(0.52)	(1.612)	
	Non-state	1.061		0.430	0.100	0.527	-0.015	0.963
		(4.38)		(9.05)	(1.73)	(9.02)	(-0.37)	

100

Table 5.7 continued

Year	Ownership group	Constant	DV	Materials	Energy	Labour	Capital	Adj R²
	Total	1.071 (4.17)	0.011 (0.22)	0.436 (9.72)	0.109 (2.06)	0.510 (9.26)	-0.015 (-0.41)	0.968
1990	State	2.761 (2.03)		0.882 (6.56)	-0.073 (-0.54)	-0.050 (-0.19)	0.070 (0.40)	0.952
	Non-state	1.286 (5.54)		0.490 (12.26)	-0.001 (-0.03)	0.384 (6.56)	0.123 (3.30)	0.964
Year	Ownership group	Constant	DV	Materials	Energy	Labour	Capital	Adj R²
	Total	1.304 (5.20)	0.006 (0.12)	0.512 (13.35)	0.008 (0.20)	0.365 (6.40)	0.110 (3.13)	0.967
1991	State	-3.255 (-1.20)		1.112 (3.53)	0.316 (1.66)	-1.524 (-2.17)	1.340 (3.20)	0.905
	Non-state	0.732 (2.81)		0.461 (11.27)	0.062 (1.57)	0.369 (5.73)	0.154 (4.66)	0.963
	Total	0.878 (2.80)	-0.53 (-0.83)	0.426 (10.08)	0.058 (1.39)	0.345 (4.98)	0.206 (6.22)	0.958

t statistics in brackets: The 95% critical values for State owned firms is 2.26 and for non-State is 1.98.

Capital remains a resource which according to the accounting data is costly, but is not shown by the econometrics to be contributing to any extent in productivity. The biggest difference between the groups is in the use of labour. Production in the non-state sector receives a major contribution from labour. In the state sector labour is not a significant input and, in some years, is even negative. As described in Chapter 4, the labour data is fairly extensive, with elements of the total costs of labour separated. These include the wage bill, social security tax, and *other costs of labour* which are assumed to be the additional services provided by firms to their employees in terms of benefits like health care, education and training and child care, many of which, historically, were an integral part of welfare services in the former command economies.

Since here, only the direct wage bill is used as the labour variable, the results in Table 5.8 can be interpreted quite straightforwardly, that is, either there is a large degree of underemployment in the state-owned firms in this sector, or labour is simply inefficient, or both. While these two outcomes will have the same effect on the enterprise in the cross section

101

estimation and are therefore not separable, extending the analysis to take account of changes in employment practice are more informative. The identified decrease in number of workers employed over the period, with no fall in productivity would lead to support of the underemployment hypothesis, whereas if the smaller number of workers led to a fall in productivity, the inefficiency of labour hypothesis would hold.

Table 5.8   Manufacturing Sector - Ownership Structure

Year Ownership Group	Constant	DV	Materials	Energy	Labour	Capital	Adj R^2
1985 State (n=27)	0.375 (0.66)		1.015 (12.20)	-0.111 (-1.56)	0.118 (1.11)	-0.021 (-0.35)	0.969
Non-state (n=16)	1.472 (3.22)		0.454 (6.84)	0.063 (0.62)	0.439 (6.08)	0.041 (0.95)	0.987
Total (n=43)	0.087 (0.15)	0.148 (1.09)	0.783 (11.65)	-0.092 (-1.29)	0.384 (4.95)	-0.0199 (-0.44)	0.972
1986 State	2.133 (6.54)		0.406 (6.89)	-0.083 (-1.30)	0.329 (4.74)	0.262 (5.92)	0.984
Non-state	1.026 (1.37)		0.422 (7.19)	-0.235 (-1.22)	0.625 (4.67)	0.180 (2.19)	0.974
Total	1.802 (4.61)	0.115 (1.13)	0.391 (10.20)	-0.103 (-1.66)	0.409 (7.69)	0.246 (6.07)	0.984
1987 State	1.516 (7.21)		0.643 (17.33)	0.0001 (0.02)	0.221 (5.43)	0.086 (3.13)	0.994
Non-state	0.353 (0.28)		0.544 (5.08)	-0.184 (-1.02)	0.660 (2.71)	0.033 (0.37)	0.962
Total	1.035 (1.80)	0.162 (1.26)	0.580 (11.76)	-0.041 (-0.66)	0.376 (5.23)	0.083 (1.84)	0.978
1988 State	1.699 (4.71)		0.560 (14.68)	-0.069 (-1.23)	0.321 (5.22)	0.130 (4.46)	0.987
Non-state	1.651 (1.59)		0.256 (2.04)	-0.163 (-1.36)	0.643 (3.00)	0.224 (5.95)	0.975
Total	1.921 (2.58)	-0.007 (-0.04)	0.411 (7.96)	-0.149 (-1.90)	0.457 (5.04)	0.206 (4.43)	0.964
1989 State	1.793 (4.29)		0.515 (9.89)	0.069 (0.96)	0.365 (4.99)	0.013 (0.29)	0.983

Table 5.8 continued							
Non-state	1.902 (3.31)		0.664 (11.47)	-0.128 (-2.08)	0.265 (2.88)	0.102 (2.58)	0.999
Total	1.388 (3.42)	0.080 (0.85)	0.553 (13.77)	-0.006 (-0.11)	0.363 (6.91)	0.069 (2.00)	0.988
1990 State	1.319 (4.73)		0.599 (9.69)	0.031 (0.53)	0.303 (4.40)	0.050 (1.17)	0.999
Non-state	0.580 (0.42)		0.530 (4.20)	-0.085 (-0.54)	0.581 (3.26)	0.015 (0.14)	0.965
Total	1.055 (2.13)	0.033 (0.30)	0.537 (9.13)	-0.003 (-0.05)	0.443 (7.28)	0.033 (0.72)	0.981
1991 State	0.924 (1.87)		0.488 (9.24)	-0.048 (-0.69)	0.529 (7.30)	0.057 (1.18)	0.980
Non-state			Regressors are collinear				
Total	0.993 (3.45)	-0.019 (-0.77)	0.479 (11.93)	-0.055 (-1.00)	0.539 (10.62)	0.057 (1.50)	0.999

t statistics in brackets: The 95% critical values for State owned firms is 2.07 and for non-State is 2.20.

This was investigated, although the State-owned enterprises did not report fewer workers, and the fall in labour was solely in the private sector. Further regressions included the disaggregated labour variables, but these were not significant. Furthermore, shifts in the distribution between blue and white collar workers, and the lack of any quality adjustment in labour made any real conclusions dubious. Therefore, while it is conventional wisdom that managers in State owned enterprises have higher levels of inefficiency, due to lack of motivation or straightforward incompetence, or both, or that there are especially high levels of blue collar underemployment because of lack of alternative opportunities, these hypotheses are not testable within this dataset.

Table 5.8 reports the results for the manufacturing sector. In this industry, the proportion of firms in the State sector is higher, a reversal of the situation in agriculture. The intercept is positive in all the regressions, although in five of the years not significantly different from zero for the privatised firms. The constant term can be an indication of the level of technology, consistent with earlier interpretation, or is perhaps a proxy for quality and a means of adjustment with respect to one of the exogenous

103

variables. As with the agricultural sector, the dummy variable does not differentiate between the groups with any degree of confidence. Apart from 1985, which looks generally unreliable, raw materials are significant and have similar elasticities for both groups.

Labour is an important input in both groups, although for most of the sample has a considerably higher elasticity, or equivalently, higher share in the non-state firms than the state managed ones, with the value often twice as much. Energy is negative and insignificant in both groups throughout, while capital is significant for four years, and has a predominately higher elasticity for the state managed firms, although this input makes a lower contribution than either raw materials or labour. Concerns about the nature of capital and therefore the appropriateness of the capital variable is particularly acute in this industry. In Hungary, some aspects of manufacturing have become highly technical during the last decade, and further information about the nature of these manufacturing enterprises, and their associated capital usage would be extremely valuable.

Conclusion

This chapter first tried fitting a dual profit function and then considered functional forms conventionally used to model production relationships. The profit function was rejected, which may be due to the non-competitive nature of the economic system in which the firms were operating, or to the lack of good information on prices of inputs or outputs. Flexible functional forms were tried and rejected because of poor results due to collinearity. These limitations led to the use of a Cobb-Douglas production function which enables the estimation of a purely technical relationship between the variables.

Two main questions were addressed. Since the use of the Cobb-Douglas allows the interpretation of the coefficients as shares in total expenditure on factors of production, it is useful to examine whether these relative shares had changed during the period leading up to the transition. The main result of this chapter is that all the regressions showed that raw materials and labour were the most important inputs, while capital was marginal (significant in agriculture and manufacturing by the end of the period). Energy was not a constraint on production, which is hardly surprising, since this was one of the most heavily subsidised markets. At the industry level, the regressions showed that the relative importance changed, with raw materials being replaced by capital in agriculture and by labour in manufacturing. In the service sector, labour was the predominant factor throughout. In all cases, energy was treated as a free input, while capital had a small elasticity, which tended to become significant at the end of the period. While it is not appropriate to make assertions about the reallocation of resources, since this usually implies price information, the shift in emphasis as measured by the coefficients or shares does indicate substitution effects.

The second part of the chapter investigated a specific aspect of the transition as a whole; the performance of firms that had been privatised, within the limits of the descriptions in the data. A number of results follow from this, but few conclusions. Again, using the share characteristics of the Cobb-Douglas, it is clear that decisions on the mix of inputs are price driven. Energy was not significant for the state enterprises in agriculture, while it was for the private farms. Thus, the implications are that energy has a positive shadow price to private farm managers, but not to State enterprise managers. Labour is underemployed, or inefficient, or both, in the State owned enterprises in agriculture, with little obvious attempt to reverse this. Indeed, the elasticities become increasingly insignificant. Conversely, for the private sector farms, the labour elasticities are large and highly significant. Employment levels have fallen and there has been some movement from the blue to the white collar groups. For industry, the results are less dramatic, since energy is insignificant for both groups and the labour variable is only insignificant in the first year for the state enterprises. For services, the exercise is not presented as there were too few state firms.

6 Firm and Industry Level Efficiency Measurement using Parametric and Nonparametric, Deterministic and Stochastic Frontiers

Introduction

The previous chapter showed how the functional form for the production relationship was determined and then used the appropriate specification to determine the contribution of the inputs to the resulting output. Ordinary least squares regression provided estimates for the enterprises as a whole, with subsets of the sample investigated as special cases.

This chapter extends that analysis from estimating an average relationship to determining the technical efficiency of each enterprise individually. There are a number of reasons why firm specific information is valuable. Those enterprises operating at or near the frontier have a clear advantage over those with low measures of technical efficiency. Once identified, their characteristics such as working practices, mix of inputs, etc can be analyzed and emulated by those operating at some distance from the frontier. At the same time, the nature of those operating some distance from the frontier can be examined in more detail and restructured with the aim of improving their performance. Finally, policy decisions concerning enterprise reform may be best targeted at those enterprises most likely to succeed in a privatisation programme. At the industry level, the average technical efficiency of the enterprises provides useful information, identifying leading and declining sectors, again to inform policy and economic regeneration. For both the enterprise and industry level technical efficiency measurement, changes in the relative ordering illustrates improvement or regression with respect to best practice.

The measurement of technical efficiency follows the method of Farrell (described in Chapter 3), and is simply the distance of each firm from a frontier of best practice firms. The difference in the various approaches to efficiency measurement lies in the construction of the frontier and three methods are presented here. Two frontier models are estimated, a correction to the OLS estimator in the previous chapter and a stochastic frontier model. The third frontier is constructed by nonparametric programming.

First the models are described and firm and industry specific measures of technical efficiencies for each year are generated and interpreted.[1] This is extended to consider the inter-temporal effects and the chapter concludes with comparisons of the frontier models used here.

Frontier Production Functions and Efficiency Measurement

The estimation in the earlier chapter has taken the form of a log-linear regression, where the line of best fit through the data is determined, resulting in an average relationship across all the firms with a random error term. From this, a frontier production function can be derived and is especially useful for individual firm level effects (see the survey by Greene (1991)). Frontier functions have been the subject of some debate, with some critics doubting the existence of technical inefficiency in firms at all. For example, Muller (1974) claims that little is known about the role of non-physical inputs, especially knowledge of the task at hand or other information which influence the ability of any single firm to use its available technology fully. When these omissions are corrected and all inputs are properly taken into account, efficiency differences might disappear, leaving only random disturbances. Then the frontier and the average functions would be identical, and all firms operate on the unit isoquant. Regrettably, empirical evidence indicates a wide divergence in outcomes which can hardly be described as random.

Another complication is that all frontier models, whether estimated or programmed, are extremely sensitive to outliers in the data. Therefore a single rogue firm, or more likely an error in the data, can define the frontier making the whole analysis invalid. But in many cases the difficulties are outweighed by the advantages of being able to obtain a value

---

[1] These methods are very output intensive. Therefore average efficiencies are reported in the tables in this chapter with details at the level of the enterprise in the Appendix. Many individual enterprises are discussed specifically, and these are identified by firm number in the Appendix.

which can be used as a measure of the technical efficiency of the individual firm.

Parametric frontiers

First, econometric estimation of fixed parameter models is considered. Two models are specified, one deterministic and one stochastic.

Deterministic frontier model   The simplest deterministic frontier model can be estimated using a straightforward adjustment to the OLS regression described in Chapter 5.   The procedure begins with the OLS estimator which is an average, or response, function. Then an adjustment transforms the average relationship to create a frontier. Formally, this takes the form of a fixed parameter frontier from the familiar form of the production function

$$Y_i = f(x_i: \; \beta) \; \exp(-u_i) \qquad i = 1,...,N \qquad \textbf{(1)}$$

where Y_i represents the possible production level for the ith firm; $f(x_i; \beta)$ is a Cobb-Douglas, translog, or other suitable function of the inputs. Then u_i is a non-negative random variable associated with the technical inefficiency of the *i*th firm.   The technical efficiency of the ${}_i$th firm is defined by $\exp(-u_i)$, which has values between zero and one.   Thus the technical inefficiency effect is now incorporated into the function to create a deterministic frontier production function. Most commonly, standard OLS regression using a Cobb-Douglas is used to estimate the coefficients, and then the intercept estimate is corrected by shifting the function until no residual is positive, and one is zero.

In the analysis below, cross-sectional data is applied to the following OLS regression to estimate the coefficients, following Timmer (1971)

$$\log y = \alpha + \Sigma \beta_j \log x_j - u \qquad u \geq 0 \qquad \textbf{(2)}$$

The validity for this approach is provided by Greene (1980) who has shown that a consistent but biased estimate of α, which imposes a sign uniformity on the residuals, will be generated by this procedure. The technical inefficiency of a given firm is defined to be the factor by which the level of output for the firm is less than its potential, that is, the level of output produced from the same amount of inputs by those firms on the frontier. Given the deterministic frontier model equation (1), the frontier output of the ith firm is $Y_i^* = f(x_i; \beta)$ and so the technical efficiency for the ith firm is the Timmer definition of technical efficiency is

$$\textit{Timmer Technical Efficiency}_i = \frac{Y_i}{Y_i^*} = \exp(-u_i) \qquad (3)$$

Technical efficiencies for individual firms in the context of the deterministic frontier production function equation (1) are predicted by obtaining the ratio of the observed production values to the corresponding estimated frontier values

$$TE_i = \frac{Y_i}{f(x_i: \beta)} \qquad (4)$$

where β is either the maximum-likelihood estimator or the corrected ordinary least-squares (COLS) estimator for β.

Stochastic frontier model In the last section the frontier is deterministic. All firms share a common production frontier and all variation in firm performance is attributed to differences in levels of technical efficiency relative to the common frontier. But this concept ignores the possibility that a firm's performance may be affected by factors outside its control such as the weather, industrial disputes, interruptions in the supply of raw materials, etc, as well as by factors under its control, such as managerial incompetence, poor resource allocation, the use of outdated and poorly maintained capital equipment etc, resulting in inefficiency. To combine the effects of exogenous shocks, both positive and negative, together with the effects of measurement error and inefficiency into a single error term may be inappropriate. In addition, there is statistical noise which is contained in every empirical relationship.

The concept of a stochastic, or composed error, frontier is that the error can be divided into two parts. A symmetric component permits random variation of the frontier across firms, and captures the effect of measurement error, other statistical noise and random shocks outside the firm's control. A one-sided component captures the effects of inefficiency relative to the stochastic frontier. Thus, this approach again uses parametric estimation to create a frontier from which firm efficiency levels are computed directly.

109

The stochastic frontier regression model is the classical linear regression model with a non-normal, asymmetric disturbance term but then the disturbance term is decomposed into the two individual parts, which are assumed to be independent of each other. The first is defined to be symmetric and normally distributed and represents the usual statistical noise and other random variation of the frontier across firms. The second part, the stochastic element, is non-positive and can assume a number of distributions. This represents some aspect of the firm's behaviour which results in a failure to produce maximum output, given the inputs at its disposal, and is under the control of the firm.

The stochastic frontier model presented here was developed by Aigner, Lovell and Schmidt (1977). The general formulation is

$$Y_i = \alpha + \sum_j \beta_j X_{ij} + \varepsilon_i, \quad where \ \varepsilon_i = v_i - u_i \qquad (5)$$

and where $\quad u_i \sim |N(0, \sigma^2)| \ and \ v_i \sim N(0, \sigma_v^2)$

In this production function the u_is are positive (although would be negative for a cost function), and subtracted from the v_i's. Hence the u_i's are defined as the one-sided error term representing technical inefficiency. The value of u_i is interpreted as the technical inefficiency of each firm in the sense that it measures the shortfall of output y_i from its maximum possible value given by the stochastic frontier. These terms will be used in the subsequent analysis. The v_i's are the two-sided error terms representing the usual statistical noise, and are uncorrelated with the regressors.

Assumptions relating to the two elements of the error term are their mutual independence and the requirement that the v_i's are normally distributed. In practice, the u_i's are most frequently distributed as either half or truncated normal or exponential. The assumption that the μ_i are uncorrelated with the regressors is intuitively appealing in the year by year cross section estimations, since it is reasonable to suppose that if the nature of the inefficiency is known to firm i in year t, decisions taken within the firm will reflect this new information and effect the choice of inputs in year t+1. That is, managers learn from past experience. Later analysis using panel data allows the relaxation of this assumption, since more information is available about each firm ex post and managers learn from their own and the experience of their peers. Estimating the model in equation (6) results in the usual residuals, the estimated ϵ_i's. The decomposition of this error term into the two component error terms to allow the actual prediction of

110

the technical efficiencies of individual firms from the stochastic frontier model is from Jondrow, Lovell, Materov and Schmidt (1982).

There are some constraints on this procedure and estimates from stochastic frontier models are not obtainable under certain conditions. Waldman (1982) has shown that the maximum likelihood estimator for the stochastic frontier production function model is simply OLS, and σ_v^2 and σ_u^2 are both equal to zero if the OLS residuals are negatively skewed (or positively for a cost function). Therefore if the model is mis-specified or the data is such that there is not sufficient variability in the error terms for the decomposition, the stochastic frontier model cannot be differentiated from OLS.

One possible specification error resulting in skewness of the residuals is heteroscedasticity. Prais and Houthakker (1955) found expenditures were more volatile in households with higher incomes than lower ones. Simply, the rich had more choice. This can apply equally to firms. Therefore, if the assertion is that the non-random, one sided element of the residual embodies factors that are under the control of the firm, large firms may also have more choice. This size effect creates less problems for average estimation, but, as stated above, frontiers are very sensitive to outliers in the data. Caudill, Ford and Gropper (1995) adjust for heteroscedasticity in a stochastic frontier cost function using bank data, although they have the luxury of a robust dataset with individual product prices. In the current application, the Hungarian enterprise data does not allow this although the issue of scale effects in the production technology or the operational aspects of the firm are highly relevant and addressed to a limited extent in Chapter 7. What is evident is that due to skewness of the data or resulting from mis-specification, not all the cross section stochastic frontier models produced useful results, as will be seen in the results section later in this chapter.

As with the corrected ordinary least squares frontiers, the technical efficiency of an individual firm from the stochastic frontier models is defined in terms of the ratio of the observed output to the corresponding frontier output, conditional on the levels of inputs used by that firm. Thus the technical efficiency of firm i in the context of the stochastic frontier production function equation (6) is the same as for the deterministic frontier model, that is

$$TE_i = \frac{Y_i}{Y_i^*} = \frac{f(x_i; \beta) \exp(v_i - \mu_i)}{f(x_i; \beta) \exp(v_i)} = \exp(-\mu_i) \qquad (6)$$

although now the statistical error has been filtered out to result in a less biased efficiency measure.

Deterministic vs stochastic frontier estimation Although the deterministic and stochastic frontier models involve the same expression for the technical efficiency of an individual firm, the estimates for the technical efficiencies will differ for the two models. For the deterministic frontier model, the ratio of observed to the estimated frontier output will generally give smaller values for the estimated technical efficiencies because no account is taken of the presence of random errors in the output data or the effects of omitted variables in the estimated frontier models.

This is confirmed by the empirical results, since if a firm has a higher level of technical efficiency measured from the stochastic frontier compared with the deterministic one, that is

$$\frac{Y_i}{Y_i^*} > \frac{Y_i}{f(X_i: \beta)} \tag{7}$$

it means that firm i is technically more efficient relative to the unfavourable conditions associated with productive activity ($v_i < 0$) than if its production is judged relative to the maximum associated with the value of the deterministic function, $f(x_i: \beta)$.

Conversely, within the framework of the stochastic frontier model, firm i could be judged technically less efficient relative to its favourable conditions than when its production is judged relative to the maximum associated with the value of the deterministic function, $f(x_i: \beta)$. However, for a given set of data, the estimated technical efficiencies obtained by fitting a deterministic frontier will be lower than those obtained by fitting a stochastic frontier. This follows from the inherent nature of the deterministic frontier which is constructed such that no output values will exceed it. The implications of this are that if a firm is in an industry which is subject to random shocks, the stochastic frontier is more appropriate.

Finally a stochastic frontier can be seen as allowing for some types of specification error and for omitted variables uncorrelated with the included variables. However, obtaining individual firm estimates of efficiency is more involved with a stochastic frontier than a deterministic one, which yields estimates of individual firm efficiency as the residuals from the estimation directly.

112

The third frontier model is not estimated but constructed from a linear programming model. This procedure uses all data precisely and does not include any disturbance term or residual. It can therefore be described as nonparametric and deterministic. The efficient production frontier is derived from all the observations in the sample, both efficient and inefficient. The best practice frontier is derived from an input minimisation procedure in the production of a given level of output. The production process assumes the technology which satisfies strong disposability of inputs, and the efficiency of each observation is measured as a ratio of actual to potential performance, as in the earlier estimation.

There are a number of advantages to this measurement approach. Firstly, it allows the comparison of each firm with a given input-output combination with others in the sector offering a similar range of products and services in different proportions. That is, the model identifies which of the sample firms are similar in order to choose appropriate reference groups and constructs a linear combination of these frontier firms. This provides an unbiased measure of total factor productivity in a multiple inputs and outputs framework.

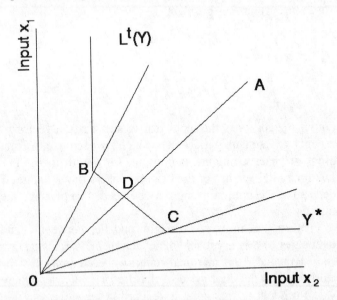

Figure 6.1   Nonparametric Efficiency Measurement

Following the Farrell efficiency measurement illustrated in Figure 3.1, the data is now used to determine the efficiency frontier (Y^*). Now repeated in Figure 6.1, it can be seen that one segment of the unit isoquant is determined by the linear combination of two efficient firms, B and C, both of which are using a similar mix of inputs in their choice of production technology. The efficiency of the non-frontier firm A is then OD/OA, where OD is the vector representing the lowest mix of inputs which firm A could use and still reach the isoquant, using its own factor combination.

Secondly, each input and output can be measured separately in its natural units without the need to apply a weighting system, such as individual prices, for aggregation. Thirdly, proportional input decreases translate into reduced costs and any input which is not used to its full potential is denoted by the measure of its slack. Therefore areas of possible cost reduction are identified.

Formally, the measure of overall efficiency of firm i is defined

$$F_i(y,x) = \min [\lambda : \lambda x \in L^+(Y)] \tag{8}$$

where the minimised parameter, λ, determines the amount by which the observed input combination can be reduced. The efficiency level is defined as the solution to the programming problem

$$F_i(y_i,x_i) = \min \lambda,$$

subject to
$$zY_i \geq y_i$$
$$zX_i \leq \lambda x_i \tag{9}$$
$$z \geq 0$$

where Y is the output matrix, X is the input matrix and z is the vector of firm-specific non-negative intensity parameters, which are used to construct convex combinations of observed inputs and outputs for the ith firm. The parameter λ allows for radial scaling of the original observations and their convex sets, to determine the minimum input usage needed to produce the given level of output.

Technical efficiency is measured directly, and lies between 0 and unity. The disadvantages of this approach is the lack of hypothesis testing or validation tests. However, the marginal values of each input can be retrieved, and interpreted as the dual price of that factor. In cases where the marginal physical product of that input is reduced to zero, the variable is slack, and contributes nothing further to output. Conversely, if there is a value not equal to zero, this is a constraint on production, and output

114

could be higher if there were not a scarcity of this input. Therefore while the level of significance in the estimated coefficients in the econometric models is subject to statistical tests and the programming is a technical construction and not testable in the same way, a correspondence between the insignificant variables in the regressions and the slack variables in the programming is reassuring.

Firm Level Efficiency Measurement

Seven series of annual efficiency levels for all firms within each industry were obtained from the three frontier models. In the case of the stochastic frontier model, a number of specifications were attempted, with normal-half normal, normal-exponential and normal-truncated normal underlying distributions for μ. The normal-half normal was the model of choice for all three sectors. In the agricultural sector, skewed residuals in 1989, 1990 and 1991, allowed the OLS estimates only and stochastic frontier results are available for the first four years. The model was only estimable for a subset of the period in the manufacturing sector too. Maintaining all four inputs in the analysis to date, the model converged in only one year. Dropping the energy variable resulted in a higher rate of success in this sector, with 1985, 1989 and 1991 converging. Similarly in the service sector, with raw materials, labour and capital, 1986, 1988 and 1989 provided results. All firms were included for the three sectors.

The real value of the stochastic frontier models in this application is in the efficiency measurements for the individual firms, since not surprisingly, the estimated slope coefficients from the stochastic frontier estimation were very similar to those of OLS, reported in Chapter 5, and it is the error term that is of particular interest.[2]

The intercept of the stochastic frontier model is higher than that obtained by OLS, which is to be expected. Olson, Schmidt and Waldman (1980) showed that in the case of a production (cost) function, OLS estimates of all parameters except the intercept are unbiased and frontier estimation has the effect of raising (lowering) the intercept in the estimation of a production (cost) function.

---

[2] The details of the individual regressions are given in the Appendix to this chapter in Tables A6.1, A6.2 and A6.3 respectively.

The number of firms on the frontier varies considerably between the three approaches, and is an obvious outcome of the procedural differences in the construction of the frontiers. By the nature of the corrected ordinary least squares procedure, the performance measure is derived as a deviation from the most efficient firm, and all others are adjusted with respect to that firm. Thus only a single firm is defined as being fully efficient. For the stochastic frontier, no firms are on the frontier as statistical noise and other random effects are not part of the efficiency measure and remain as the unexplained residual.

Table 6.1   Econometric Frontiers - Summary of the Firm Level Efficiency Measurement

Industry	Agriculture (n = 117)			Manufacturing (n = 43)			Services (n = 29)		
	Corrected Ordinary Least Squares								
Year	Mean	Std.Dev	Minimum	Mean	Std.Dev	Minimum	Mean	Std.Dev	Minimum
1985	0.669	0.094	0.437	0.626	0.119	0.232	0.657	0.132	0.442
1986	0.628	0.086	0.399	0.708	0.113	0.504	0.668	0.147	0.211
1987	0.637	0.093	0.408	0.570	0.115	0.396	0.618	0.115	0.399
1988	0.715	0.094	0.413	0.713	0.112	0.541	0.720	0.109	0.485
1989	0.499	0.084	0.281	0.622	0.138	0.340	0.755	0.095	0.532
1990	0.669	0.106	0.419	0.593	0.099	0.447	0.752	0.093	0.599
1991	0.478	0.097	0.278	0.677	0.133	0.245	0.623	0.119	0.390
	Stochastic Frontier								
1985	0.865	0.075	0.565	0.817	0.120	0.199	na	na	na
1986	0.898	0.046	0.547	na	na	na	0.767	0.150	0.184
1987	0.946	0.012	0.538	na	na	na	na	na	na
1988	0.896	0.049	0.451	na	na	na	0.953	0.008	0.616
1989	na	na	na	0.762	0.174	0.280	0.885	0.063	0.564
1990	na	na	na	na	na	na	na	na	na
1991	na	na	na	0.799	0.117	0.014	na	na	na

The nonparametric models allow any number of firms to form the frontier, and firms with very different combinations of inputs can be technically efficient. But which ever method is used, it is relative levels of efficiency and changes in the position of firms in the total ranking of firms that are important, as well as the nature of the inefficiency of any one firm.

The three frontier models described generated measures of technical efficiency, with each industry considered separately, so that all the enterprises in the agricultural sector are compared with others in that sector. Full details of the individual firm efficiency scores are available on request. If information on the firms were available, as they would be to local users, then it would be possible to use the firm level results fully, as was suggested in the introduction. However, in this case no such information has been made available and the discussion tends to be based on the aggregate results.

Thus, Table 6.1 provides a summary of the results from the corrected least squares and stochastic frontier models, with the range of efficiency measures between 0 and 1. Tables A6.1 to A6.3 report all the test statistics for the stochastic models, which are not especially interesting. Referring to the results in the table, the efficiencies constructed from estimating a stochastic frontier model are higher than those derived from the deterministic one, for all years and for all firms. The COLS results are interpreted first.

The industries cannot be compared in terms of technical efficiency scores directly, but the means, variance and changes over throughout the period are interesting. The lowest minimum values occur in each sector in different years, making the argument for a general slow-down in the overall economy too unreliable to be used as an explanation of poor performance. A more likely explanation is that the causes of inefficiency are not the same for each industry. Random poor years can be explained in agriculture, such as 1989 and 1991, as unfavourable weather conditions for some firms in some areas, but other factors must contribute to the equivalent poor result in 1987 for manufacturing. It could be that in some areas of manufacturing, agricultural goods were inputs to production in manufacturing, although this is speculative as food processing is a separate industrial classification altogether. The service industries achieved a consistently high level of productivity throughout the period, although in 1986 at least one firm performed particularly poorly.

The most obvious difference in the mean and minimum efficiency levels is that both the mean and minimum level of efficiency for agriculture fall by 30% and 36% respectively, with an exceptionally severe drop in

1991. Conversely, for manufacturing the efficiency measures are a little higher at the end of the period and for services there is considerable improvement, followed by a fall back to the starting levels, in the last year.

The variance in technical efficiency differs between the industries. For agriculture, the COLS efficiencies have a higher standard deviation throughout, while in manufacturing and services there is no clear pattern. Intuitively, this makes sense since an important component of the agricultural sector's production technology is the weather, which is common to all firms, at least at the regional level. The remaining individual firm level differences are therefore a smaller part of the total variation in performance in agriculture, compared with that in manufacturing and services.

The stochastic frontier results at this level are limited, as the skew of the frontiers led to the model being rejected in many cases. The few results available do not allow for agriculture's decline to be checked, since the model does not work for the later years. However, the results for manufacturing and services confirm the COLS presumptions of little change in the first and some improvement in the second.

The nonparametric frontier results are summarised in Table 6.2 below. A large number of firms are on the frontier for each industry which is encouraging, and indicates the frontier is not determined by a few outliers, but there are also many firms with very low efficiency scores. Apart from the first two years, when the means are almost equal for all industries, the service sector consistently has a higher mean level of efficiency. That is, services has a lower dispersion, as the next column shows, although the variance is high for all sectors with no obvious trend, apart from the fall in the case of services. Particularly in the case of nonparametric frontiers, the means are not very useful and are simply included in a summary table to give an overall picture. The more meaningful results are at the firm level. The nonparametric model does corroborate the decline in efficiency in agriculture and the slight growth in manufacturing efficiency, but it also suggests substantial growth for services, which is at odds with the econometric results.

Outliers clearly have an effect on nonparametric frontiers, and as a consequence, the programming approach can produce very unstable results. For example, in the manufacturing industry, 1985 has a minimum value of 0.20, which means that this firm is only 20% efficient (80% inefficient). This is firm 6, whereas the next least efficient firm has an efficiency level of 0.635 (firm 12). Following the progress of firm 6, it is clear this is not consistently inefficient. In fact by the next year this firm has moved from being the most inefficient to the seventh most efficient, although it's performance does fluctuate considerably with respect to others in the same industry throughout the period.

As noted above, the nonparametric frontier measures are constructed using all the firms in the sample. Therefore one particularly high performer in a single year will change the efficiency level of all the others, even though their own absolute efficiency score does not change. Thus the columns in Tables A6.2 and A6.3 which denote rank order are in many cases more informative than the actual efficiency values[3].

Table 6.2   Nonparametric Frontiers - Summary of the Firm Level Efficiency Measurement

Industry	Agriculture (n = 117)			Manufacturing (n = 43)			Services (n = 29)		
Year	Mean	Std.Dev	Minimum	Mean	Std.Dev	Minimum	Mean	Std.Dev	Minimum
1985	0.843	0.115	0.532	0.876	0.147	0.200	0.843	0.133	0.632
1986	0.803	0.120	0.469	0.843	0.116	0.621	0.838	0.161	0.239
1987	0.788	0.117	0.481	0.732	0.186	0.471	0.897	0.114	0.551
1988	0.787	0.109	0.459	0.832	0.125	0.554	0.924	0.082	0.703
1989	0.599	0.138	0.296	0.850	0.119	0.588	0.898	0.101	0.705
1990	0.759	0.123	0.483	0.882	0.091	0.720	0.927	0.078	0.776
1991	0.763	0.137	0.423	0.889	0.125	0.416	0.907	0.108	0.551

Number of Firms on the Frontier							
Industry	1985	1986	1987	1988	1989	1990	1991
Agriculture	16	10	8	7	5	9	12
Manufacturing	13	10	6	10	11	9	11
Services	10	8	13	12	11	11	9

Indeed, since the efficiencies are being measured relative to a frontier that is itself shifting, it is most odd that these efficiency measures are ever reported on their own, although this is common practice in the

---

[3] In Tables A6.2 and A6.3 the frontier firms are all ranked 1. Since there are a different number of frontier firms in each year, the ranked order value of the least efficient firm number varies.

literature. These are single year, cross section frontiers and the only information to retrieve from this exercise is to check that a single firm in isolation is not defining the frontier every year (probably a data error) or to compare the variance of technical efficiency scores across industries. It is not possible for efficiency to be measured independently of movements in the frontier, so common sense suggests that technical change should be reported as well, for the results to have any meaning. In this case, Chapter 9 will show that the efficiency results are thoroughly misleading, since when technical change is included, to give a TFP index, agriculture's decline in efficiency in the final year is explained by the frontier shift. Technical change shifted the frontier and led to some farms being less efficient, but the technology effect dominated and TFP rose substantially. Thus, the efficiency results alone should be treated as incomplete information. A second complication with the efficiency measures is tackled next.

Industry Level Efficiency Measurement

In the previous section, three separate frontiers were constructed for each year, so that all the enterprises were only considered with respect to others in their industry. On the other hand, generating measures of technical efficiency of the pooled sample provides different information, although this may be more of interest to industrial policy and the identification of sectoral trends than of enterprise management. In a pooled model, the efficiency scores are relative and not absolute, with the individual enterprises not necessarily compared with their industry peers at all.

However, the scope for pooling the sample is limited here. It has already been shown in the econometric estimation (Chapter 5) that the slope coefficients are different for the three industries, making aggregation of these industries invalid. Therefore only the nonparametric frontiers are constructed using the pooled sample since this method does not calculate parameter estimates but chooses a reference group for each firm and there is no reason why this need be drawn from the same industry. The measures of technical efficiency for the individual enterprises are then compared to a frontier comprised of the best practice ones from the three industries in total, so that cross industry comparisons are meaningful. The results are reported as industry averages, after the individual enterprises have been identified by sector. Full results are available from the author.

Table 6.3   **Nonparametric Frontiers - Summary of Efficiency Measurement - Industry Level (n = 189)**

Year	Agriculture Mean	Std.Dev	Minimum	Manufacturing Mean	Std.Dev	Minimum	Services Mean	Std.Dev	Minimum
1985	0.768	0.114	0.475	0.864	0.141	0.200	0.843	0.133	0.632
1986	0.721	0.119	0.424	0.832	0.114	0.621	0.823	0.155	0.239
1987	0.649	0.122	0.377	0.722	0.179	0.471	0.886	0.117	0.551
1988	0.774	0.110	0.395	0.812	0.123	0.511	0.922	0.081	0.703
1989	0.642	0.173	0.308	0.847	0.117	0.588	0.888	0.097	0.695
1990	0.745	0.118	0.479	0.868	0.085	0.720	0.916	0.076	0.776
1991	0.745	0.130	0.358	0.876	0.118	0.416	0.903	0.109	0.551

Number of Firms on the Frontier

Industry	1985	1986	1987	1988	1989	1990	1991
Agriculture	4	2	2	3	7	6	6
Manufacturing	8	8	5	6	10	5	4
Services	10	6	10	11	9	8	9

The nonparametric frontier results are summarised in Table 6.3. The mean levels of efficiency in the service sector is higher than that of agriculture and manufacturing for five of the seven years, while in 1985 and 1986 this sector is essentially parallel with the other two. The nonparametric results confirm that when the industries are considered together, and the relative efficiencies are generated, the service sector enterprises are on average more technically efficient, followed by manufacturing, with agriculture last.

The implications of this are discussed more fully in Chapters 9 and 10, which examine the importance of identifying growth and decline in particular industries and the relevance to this in policies of structural adjustment and economic growth. Finally, it is worth noting again that looking at efficiency changes over time without considering technical change is later found to be misleading. A discussion of measuring individual firm and industry effects follows in Chapter 8, and TFP indices are constructed in Chapter 9, where Figure 9 explains the joint determination of efficiency and technical change.

The Frontier and Factor Proportions

The number of firms on the frontier is substantially different for this pooled frontier reported in Table 6.3, as compared with the unpooled frontier of Table 6.2, especially in agriculture and manufacturing. In 1985, of the 22 total best practice firms, only 4 are from agriculture, as compared with 16 in Table 6.2. Equally in 1986, of 16 total frontier firms, those in agriculture is 2, rather than 10 from Table 6.2, and in 1991, of a possible 19, only 6.

Likewise in manufacturing, in 1985 only 8 out of 22 are on the frontier compared with 13 earlier, and in 1991, only 4 out of 19 are best practice, compared with 11 previously. Of the 19 firms on the frontier, 9 are in the service sector (out of only 29), which suggests that services dominate the frontier. This is not really true, as the frontier has four dimensions and firms will be on it if they have high output per unit of any of the inputs. Thus, service industry firms predominate because they are so labour intensive and conversely have high outputs per unit of the other three inputs. This high labour intensity can be seen most clearly in Figure 6.2, which plots the frontier firms for 1991, in the labour/materials plane.

The service firms, denoted by an S, are clustered around the tentative labour/materials ratio line that is shown, whereas the farms and manufacturing firms are far more materials-intensive.[4] Thus, the labour intensive segment of the frontier is determined by the service firms, while a manufacturing firm, M160 determines the material intensive segment of the unit isoquant.

---

[4] Note that there is one outlier: firm S164 is at the other end of the spectrum from the rest of the service firms and is highly materials intensive.

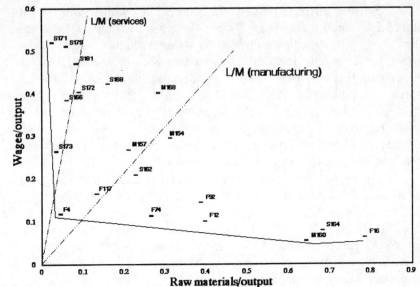

Figure 6.2   Inter-industry Frontier Firms, 1991 - Labour/materials
Factor Input Ratios

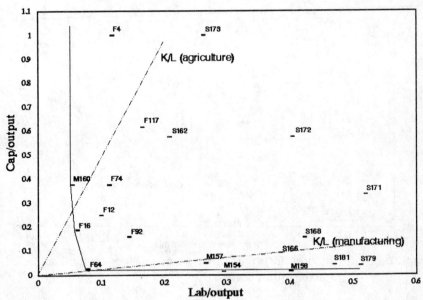

Figure 6.3   Inter-industry Frontier Firms, 1991 - Capital/labour
Factor Input Ratios

Between these extremes, the frontier is dominated by a farm, marked F4, which at almost any price ratio appears to be the most efficient single unit. The capital/labour plane is shown in Figure 6.3 where again the service firms have low capital/labour ratio shown, and this time it is a service firm that is in the pivotal position, closest to the origin. But, it is actually manufacturing firms M154 and M158 that define the labour intensive segment of the frontier, while farm F4 and manufacturing firm M160 determine the capital intensive region. Note too how inefficient some units are: S173 and S172 represent the firms at the bottom of the efficiency spectrum, at least with respect to these inputs.

Figure 6.4 repeats the exercise for the capital/materials plane, where the capital intensive end of the spectrum is determined by farm F4 (but almost the same position is occupied by S173) and by S171, with S179 the most efficient. Then, the materials intensive segment begins with S166, then M158 and M154 and finally at the extreme, S164. The procedure excludes the energy dimension because it was not important and would add three more diagrams but little else.

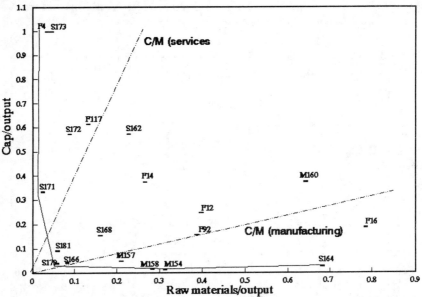

Figure 6.4   **Inter-industry Frontier Firms, 1991 - Capital/materials Factor Input Ratios**

Thus, over all the dimensions, it is not true that the service firms really dominate the frontiers. There is actually a very fair mixture of enterprises from each of the three sectors. Nor are the factor proportions consistently different between sectors, apart from the labour intensity of services. This can be seen in Figure 6.3, where the agriculture frontier spreads right across the full range of factor proportions. This is in some part due to the diversity of agricultural enterprises and the lack of information on this aspect of the dataset will cause problems in the next chapter, when scale is considered.

Comparative Methodologies

This chapter has derived efficiency measures using a number of approaches applied to the same data, with an acceptable degree of consistency given the quality of the information available. Some idea of the comparative results from the COLS, stochastic and nonparametric models can be gleaned from the Tables and it was suggested that COLS always has the lowest efficiency levels, followed by nonparametric and then the stochastic approach.

Figure 6.5 plots the efficiency measures for the 117 farms in 1988 (a year when the stochastic frontier worked), beginning on the horizontal axis with the most efficient and moving out to the least efficient. The nonparametric results lie between the stochastic frontier and COLS estimates, which is not a surprise since the COLS results are all relative to a single efficient farm, whereas the nonparametric has a dozen farms on the deterministic frontier and the stochastic approach does not attribute all the differences to variations in efficiency. Thus, for the stochastic model, no farm is fully efficient, but the least efficient has a far higher score than under the deterministic techniques.

The results can be compared more formally by following the *methodology cross-checking principle* recommended by Charnes, Cooper and Sueyoshi (1988, p.2)

> at least when large issues of policy are to be guided by the resulting inferences, it will generally be prudent not to rely on only one discipline ... but also to have recourse to other disciplines which employ different methodologies.

although this is not without necessary trade-offs in making such a comparison fair.

125

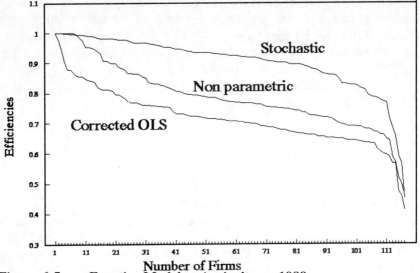

Figure 6.5   Frontier Models - Agriculture, 1988

There are obvious differences in the efficiency levels, particularly between the parametric and nonparametric production frontiers. Since the programming model is non-stochastic, noise is reported as inefficiency. Therefore it is expected that the extent of the inefficiency will be higher in a non-stochastic production frontier than a stochastic one. But the reverse seems to be true here. In a comparative study, Ferrier and Lovell (1990) suggest that such a lack of harmony between the efficiency results can be attributed to a number of factors, two of which may be appropriate to this Hungarian enterprise data. Firstly the programming approach is non-stochastic and so interprets noise as inefficiency. Second, the econometric estimation imposed a parametric structure on both the technology and the distribution of inefficiency, and so combines specification error with inefficiency. But there is the possibility that the specification was wrong in the econometric models, which provides a justification for any superior performance in the programming approach. Stated simply, if one method is wrong, it is invalid to claim the alternative is better, it simply is not wrong. The decomposed error in the stochastic frontier may be the model of choice, although the poor quality data in the current application does not do it justice.

126

Table 6.4   Comparison of Results - Sample Year

	Pearson Correlation Coefficients		Spearman Rank Correlation Coefficients	
Agriculture (1986)	**COLS**	**Stochastic frontier**	**COLS**	**Stochastic frontier**
Stochastic frontier	0.0194		-0.0017	
Nonparametric frontier	0.8635	0.1068	0.0678	0.0148
Manufacturing (1985)	**COLS**	**Stochastic frontier**	**COLS**	**Stochastic frontier**
Stochastic frontier	0.0656		0.1557	
Nonparametric frontier	0.5715	0.3897	-0.0776	0.0607
Services (1986)	**COLS**	**Stochastic frontier**	**COLS**	**Stochastic frontier**
Stochastic frontier	0.2387		-0.1621	
Nonparametric frontier	0.7598	0.4106	0.4951	-0.0778

The extent of the variation in the results from the three frontiers is illustrated in Table 6.4. The Pearson correlations are higher than the rank correlations in all sectors, although reasons for the differences in the comparative results are only speculative. It is noted that the extreme sensitivity to outliers in the nonparametric frontier and the crucial role played by the extreme value in the COLS provide a close relationship between these two models. Correlation coefficients of 0.8636, 0.5715 and 0.7598 for the three industries support this proposal. Conversely, the stochastic frontier model is further from the deterministic frontiers, more so in the case of COLS.

Predictably, the rank correlations are lower overall, since because the levels of technical efficiency are bunched closely together for all industries, a substantial shift of the position in the ranking of an individual enterprise can follow a very minor change in value. Also the large number of enterprises that are on the frontier in the nonparametric results compared with a single or zero frontier firm in the others, will distort the rank coefficient substantially.

More rigorous comparative tests present some difficulty as there is no equivalent of a significance test for individual inputs or a measure of overall goodness of fit in nonparametric programming. But even with data as suspect as these, there is some comfort in consistent results and the results from the programming models do support those of the econometrics. Information derived from the year by year production function estimates

127

provide an indication of the level of importance of the conventional inputs to the final output. Variables with a positive marginal value and zero slack are statistically significant, and the firm is production constrained by a shortage of that input. For those inputs with a marginal value of zero and a positive slack, the opportunity cost is zero and further units of this input remain idle, and hence inefficient. The variable most frequently slack is energy (for 54% of firms), followed by capital (35%), reflecting the insignificance of these coefficients in the estimation. The constraint on production for the majority of firms seems to be raw materials (no slacks), and to a lesser extent, labour. Labour was slack in 16% of cases, which is not surprising, since it was insignificant for the state farms in Chapter 5.

Obviously the choice of variables may be completely wrong, or too undefined and incomplete to be meaningful. Certainly any model that is mis-specified in the econometric sense will present similar difficulties when constructing a programming model. Unfortunately the tests are not nearly so specific in the latter. The result that materials and labour are the constraints on production are supported by a survey quoted by Kornai (1994), covering the period 1987 to 1993.[5] This study identifies the same variables and shows how the supply constraints, such as shortages of labour, materials, and intermediate goods eased steadily over this period. It appears as though even in this pre-transition period, Hungary has already progressed sufficiently for physical resource constraints to be rare and are not an obstacle to production. Labour as a constraint began to diminish by the 3rd quarter of 1989 and raw materials slightly earlier. The major shortage by the beginning of 1990 is access to funds, which Kornai claims is due to the immature nature of the banking system and similar institutional arrangements, and demand, which is slow, and exacerbated by increasing unemployment.

Conclusion

The extent of technical efficiency in an industry is important. But the source of any inefficiency is to be found at the enterprise level since it appears that the difference between best practice and average practice in an

---

[5] This is a survey applying a methodology developed by the German research institute IFO, where respondent are asked to mention impediments to production (see KOPINT-DATORG, 1993).

industry are explained by the decisions taken internal to the firm. These include the choice, mix and monitoring of the use of inputs, such as the level of investment in maintenance and new machinery and the quality of labour to employ, and the proportion of skilled to unskilled and managerial to blue collar workers. It also includes the introduction of personal and corporate incentives and a policy on research and development expenditures.

This chapter generates a number of measures of technical efficiency for the individual enterprises, following Farrell (1957), and extends this to the three industries. The basic methodology requires the construction of a efficient frontier and all enterprises are compared in relation to that frontier. Two econometric and one programming model are presented and the outcomes compared. The first set of results illustrate the range of technical efficiency levels of enterprises with respect to the others in their industry. There is a wide dispersion of efficiency scores, with the lowest firms at around one third efficiency, which suggests that large gains are possible if policies can correct these losses. This is the type of information that could well be used to ensure the reforms are achieving the desired objectives, but little can be said here, due to the lack of detailed information accompanying the data.

The second set of results compares the three industries and here some comments can be made, even without detailed local knowledge, although these are restricted to the nonparametric frontier only. The main finding is that the service sector is more efficient than manufacturing and that agriculture is the least efficient. Given all efficiency scores are between 0 and 1, the standard deviations are directly comparable. The industry with the simplest production technology could be expected to have the smallest variance, that is, there are less opportunities for inefficiency.

As was clear in Table 6.4 and Figure 6.5, the higher correlations for the individual industries are between corrected ordinary least squares estimation and nonparametric frontiers, both of which depend largely on outliers. However, the method used to determine the efficiency levels is almost immaterial relative to the real problem. This is that although the efficiency scores are all that can be observed in a single year, over time they depend on the movement of the frontier and should not be studied independently of technical change. Fortunately, later chapters using more data provide more useful performance measures, in the form of TFP's.

The variables that were most frequently slack in the nonparametric models were energy and capital, which corroborates the results of the last chapter. This result is also corroborated by a national survey which identified materials and labour as the supply constraints. Now labour is being reduced, with higher quality replacing quantity, and the supply of raw materials is not blocking output due to shortages. Indeed, the survey suggests that by 1989/90 it was demand that was constraining growth.

7 The Importance of Firm Size: Estimates of Returns to Scale and the Decomposition of Technical and Scale Efficiency

Introduction

This chapter considers firm level technical efficiency while taking account of the size of the organisation and the implications this has for productivity levels, particularly following the break up and distribution of state-owned enterprises. A large part of the reform programme has concentrated on privatisation programmes of various kinds and the move from state to private sector control and ownership of enterprises. A great deal of effort by transition governments has been directed towards finding the best method of achieving this transfer of control, along with the order of the reforms and the priorities with respect to industrial sectors and groups, all of which are discussed in Chapter 2. In addition to the general privatisation programmes there is the issue of restitution, or the returning of property and land to those holding a historic claim to it. This is primarily of concern in agriculture, while the other two sectors in this study are less open to such proprietorial rights.

While the form and progress of the privatisation is not included in this study, enterprise productivity and efficiency measures before and after the reform programme has serious implications for the structure of policy in the future. Certainly there is no reason to assume that the ideal size of enterprise is the same for all industries, if one exists at all. This chapter first considers the literature on firm size and determines whether there is an optimal scale of organisation for these industries. Then the measurement of technical efficient is decomposed into scale and purely technical efficiency effects and the overall performance of smaller and larger firms is compared. The sample is divided into groups determined by size of enterprise and these are considered separately and compared.

The optimal firm size is unknown. There is no evidence that large enterprises are significantly less technically efficient than smaller ones. While the transition is still incomplete, the market situation faced by smaller enterprises for any combination of factors of production, especially labour (as well as institutional factors such as credit and insurance, for which there is no data here) are still imperfect. Thus, any indication of apparent economies of scale may be temporary and the result of unresolved policy distortions. This is a problem for restructuring, as it is not clear how the large enterprises should be divided up, as when markets are better established, economies of scale may diminish or eventually disappear.

The Problem of an Optimal Firm Size

In theory, economies of scale are defined by a production function which exhibits a more than proportional increase in output for a given increase in all inputs (see Chapter 3). In practice, it is difficult to test for returns to scale because there is rarely an occasion when an increase in the magnitude of some inputs does not also imply other change in the factors of production. For instance, the introduction of the combine harvester increased the optimal farm size and it is hard to separate economies of scale and technological progress in such a situation.

Peterson and Kislev (1991) suggest that agriculture is different from industry in that increasing returns to scale are far less likely to be the case in agriculture. One possible explanation is the nature of the management problems associated with production which is very localised, compared with the physical locations of agricultural activity or, to extend this to services, with the individual nature of service activity. Clearly organisation and monitoring is different in an enclosed space than where production is spatially diffuse. Particularly, where incentives are not clearly defined, or do not enter the objective function of employees, maintaining high levels of productivity is difficult.[1]

The consensus of authors directing their work on firms in capitalist markets, whether developing or developed, tend to separate agriculture from other sectors. The general claim is that economies of scale in agriculture do not exist, except under very specific, and often temporary, circumstances, such as policies that favour larger farms over small ones.

---

[1] The classic work on why farming is different is Brewster (1950).

132

In cases where these distortions do exist, as firms increase in size they are able to take advantage of improved access to credit, storage facilities and marketing and distribution that small farms do not have. But this is assuming that markets for labour and other inputs function well, which is not clear for the transition economies, especially during the period of interest in this study.

Empirical studies typically report constant returns to scale, and it has been suggested that lack of scale economies is the primary reason why firms in agriculture are smaller than those in industry. Certainly, supervision is easier when labour and machinery are stationary in a plant or factory. In agriculture, both labour and machinery are mobile making supervision expensive and increasing management costs. Adams and Brock (1986) even suggest there is a tendency to exaggerate the extent of scale economies in the industrial sector, although many others would disagree, particularly with contemporary levels of global technology.

Of the three industries included here, agriculture is the one for which size has received most attention, and for which a special case may be made. In the development context, particularly south Asia, small farms have higher yields than the large ones. This makes perfect sense where the constraint is land rather than labour, and small family farms can maximise their yields. Binswanger et al (1995) suggests that these units are generally more efficient and preferred to other types of farming because of the way in which labour relations are organised, incentive structures are clear and family and hired labour work together, making it easy to monitor work effort. In terms of effective monitoring, Hill and Ingersent (1982) claim that for many European farms, a labour force greater than four workers will incur higher labour management costs. However, it is important to put this in context, since in the US, a small farm with just two to three units of labour will also have a very large amount of capital equipment, which allows farms of up to 800 acres to be successfully managed and therefore what is considered a small family farm in the US is a huge operation in Central and Eastern European.

In the transitional economies where primogeniture was not the rule, fragmentation of agricultural land holdings has resulted in very small family farms, and in many cases, these have frequently been collectivised as producer co-operatives. Rather than co-operative production, which raises incentives and labour management problems, Deininger (1993) proposes the collectivization of marketing arrangements and sharing of high cost capital investment such as equipment and machinery while avoiding collective ownership of land, which has never been popular with farmers in any country. For many peasant farmers, owning the land is a basic prerequisite for a satisfactory system because of the status associated with ownership. This attitude could cause problems for the implementation of the restitution programme and result in inefficient productive units unless the private ownership of plots can be combined with collective marketing and shared capital equipment arrangements.

Much of the research on farm size has focused on explaining the steady increase in the average size of farms in both developed and developing market economies, although agricultural enterprises remain far smaller than those in the industrial sector. It also appears that increased mechanization in agriculture has led to less expansion in the size of operational units compared with that in industry. Comparisons between profit maximising farms and the command economy agricultural enterprises have shown the two groups to be very similar, with both suffering from difficulties resulting from labour management of operations which are spread over a large area, rather than differences caused by their choice of alternative economic organisation (see Brooks, (1991), Johnson and Ruttan, (1994) and Piesse, Thirtle and Turk, 1996).

The debate in the literature on the merits of small versus large farms is not replicated with respect to other industrial sectors. In terms of market economies, Adams and Brock (1986) suggest that in industry generally, small firms were considered to be inferior in internal efficiency and especially weak in technological efficiency. Generating new technology was the economic challenge, the price of efficiency and progress. For Eastern and Central Europe there are no grounds for debate at all. Lavigne (1995) claims the large conglomerate firm that results from external expansion was unknown in the pre-transitional economies, and socialist enterprises were not allowed to expand in sectors different from their main scope of activities. Rather they became large as vertically integrated corporations, with complementary activities. Finally, in the service sector, the sample firms are generally small, when measured by number of employees. These are the firms most likely to be newly established, and comprise what is broadly the small and medium sized firm sector in a western economy, in many cases dominated by professional and other white collar workers.

The definition of small and medium sized firms is currently under review by the European Union, and will be incorporated into the Fourth and Seventh Directives, an issue of concern for Eastern and Central European states requesting membership. In the present analysis, there was a lack of small and medium sized enterprises altogether, although the issue is important when considered as an extension of any restructuring of the enterprises that are included. Reform of the larger enterprises on the basis of their inefficiency is not constructive if the result is the separation into a series of productive units that are too small.

A Review of Enterprise Statistics

Before beginning any analysis linked to the size of operation, some comments should be about the preferred variable for distinguishing between larger and smaller firms. A number of criteria are possible, even within the limits of the accounting information available in this dataset.

There is no generally accepted measure of firm size in the economics literature to guide the choice of decision variable. All the efficiency evaluations thus far are in the spirit of Farrell's ratios of outputs and inputs. Various measures of output (sales or turnover), of inputs, both flows or stocks, such as number of employees or value of fixed capital, and of income (in established market economies that accruing to equity holders) have been used in different contexts (see Lund (1983)).

In agriculture, empirical applications frequently use farm size in area terms, although clearly quality is important but ignored in such a delimiter, along with the various activities included in this sector. The value of output, or income, also says little about the size of operation, unless the type and quality of the final output is known.

Labour is one of the more reliable series in the current application. It is the only non-value series and consequently free from the effects of an uncertain inflation factor or of dubious valuation practices. The wage bill includes manual and white collar labour and the proportion of these may well change over time. This suggests that the real number of total workers is the preferred measure of firm size. The choice of this variable has been criticised by Sunderland (1980) who claims that a bias is introduced as more efficient organisations use less labour to produce the same level of output than an inefficient one. But here, in the absence of a better measure, the firms were ranked by number of employees and the value of output to denote size.

To give some substance to the concept of large and small firms in this discussion of scale, the range and mean of output, the number of employees and the output per unit of labour are shown in Table 7.1.

135

Table 7.1   Output and Labour Data - Descriptive Statistics

	Value of Output (Real Hun.Forint)			Number of Employees			Output per employee		
	Min	Max	Mean	Min	Max	Mean	Min	Max	Mean
Agriculture									
1985	14394	3376615	227951	89	3928	535	162	860	426
1986	14212	3747432	238046	80	4177	517	178	897	460
1987	14162	4030789	243326	77	4479	508	184	900	479
1988	12717	4237478	251897	77	4040	479	165	1049	526
1989	10849	4060956	239627	68	3922	441	160	1035	544
1990	7750	2594964	185794	61	3032	383	127	856	485
1991	7168	2025657	160844	27	2239	290	265	905	555
Manufacturing									
1985	26536	2126488	519025	77	4481	1008	345	475	515
1986	28391	1676458	536178	21	3829	1009	1352	438	532
1987	24266	1410075	416437	118	4120	991	206	342	420
1988	12486	1469878	400811	18	4369	985	694	336	407
1989	12304	1306177	354935	5	3150	1031	2461	415	344
1990	17119	971764	318321	101	4603	1022	169	211	311
1991	7088	709510	228401	51	3143	953	139	226	240
Services									
1985	1504	1250015	86451	20	1140	182	75	1097	475
1986	1556	1261142	70577	15	2197	193	104	574	366
1987	2004	120608	80436	22	3468	251	91	348	321
1988	1576	900127	70798	22	3677	273	72	245	260
1989	1110	822152	63273	14	3152	230	79	261	275
1990	708	845553	57963	19	3544	267	37	239	217
1991	813	537536	39080	11	2765	224	74	194	174

The integrity of the data has already been discussed in Chapter 4, and clearly there are many questions around the quality of the information, and so it may still be data error that accounts for some of the values in the table, particularly the minimum number of employees. The agriculture and manufacturing industries present some very unstable employee data. Thus, for the analysis in the next section, size is determined by the value of output.

The Identification of Scale Economies

Econometric estimation does not allow a straightforward separation of technical and scale efficiency. One approach is to test the sensitivity of the size of firm to the value of the summed coefficients of the estimated production equation, although Binswanger et al (1995) warns against this procedure as any mis-specification will result in incorrect results. But, this is common practice in empirical production econometrics. Generally if there are as many firms over-producing as there are under-producing, the regression of output on one of the inputs will show more or less constant returns to scale (see Chapter 5). But, if more firms are under-producing, then a general expansion of output by all firms in the industry would lead to constant and then decreasing returns to scale. These warnings add weight to the validity of the nonparametric models since the way in which RTS is measured is less vulnerable to the mis-specification problem.

Table 7.2   Small, Medium and Large Agricultural Firms - 1991

Regressors	Smallest firms (n=39)		Medium firms (n=39)		Largest firms (n=39)	
	Coefficient	t stat	Coefficient	t stat	Coefficient	t stat
Materials	0.52568	7.179	0.38828	5.262	0.36636	4.941
Energy	0.01121	0.183	0.11310	1.684	0.00016	0.002
Labour	0.54747	4.133	0.39573	3.628	0.43826	2.782
Capital	0.12519	1.905	0.21949	3.805	0.16661	2.604
$\Sigma\beta_i$'s	1.209		1.1165		0.97138	

Following Walters (1968), the approach is to estimate the Cobb-Douglas production function stated in Chapter 5, with the sample divided into three groups, on the basis of firm size, and this was done for agriculture.[2] Table 7.2 shows that with three samples of equal size, the smallest farms have substantial increasing returns to scale (IRS), with the output elasticities summing to 1.209. The IRS diminishes to 1.117 for the medium-sized group, but this is the only sub-set to have positive returns to all the inputs. For the largest farms, which should include some farms that are too small, some the right size and some too big (for their factor inputs), the elasticities sum to 0.97, and the CRS restriction cannot be rejected. Thus, by 1991 there is clear evidence of IRS, but none of decreasing returns to scale (DRS). This suggests that, on average, the group is not too large but there must be some individual units in this top group that are too big. This is confirmed by testing whether the three groups are statistically different from each other. The results showed that group 1 (smallest) is not the same as group 2 (medium) and group 3 (large) but there is no statistical difference between groups 2 and 3 at the 90% level.

The groupings are of course arbitrary, so to try to find further evidence, especially of DRS, the farms were divided into groups of ten. The left-hand side of Table 7.3 reports the results generated by estimating the function first for just the ten smallest farms, then the twenty smallest and continuing incrementally in this way. The right-hand side of the Table reverses the process, beginning with the largest firms and cumulatively adding increasingly smaller units. This is done to ensure that the results are not simply caused by the change in sample size. Table 7.3 shows that a clear pattern emerged in the agricultural sector.

Table 7.3   Scale Effects in Econometric Estimation - Agriculture 1991

Incremental from Smallest Firm				Incremental from Largest Firm			
Farms	$\Sigma\beta_i$s	Farms	$\Sigma\beta_i$s	Farms	$\Sigma\beta_i$s	Farms	$\Sigma\beta_i$s
1 - 10	1.67	1 - 50	1.22	108 - 117	0.96	68 - 117	1.01
1 - 20	1.37	1 - 60	1.11	98 - 117	0.96	58 - 117	1.09
1 - 30	1.40	Remainder 61 - 117	0.96	88 - 117	0.97	Remainder 1 - 57	1.11
1 - 40	1.29			78 - 117	1.00		

---

[2] This does necessitate an assumption of homogenous factor costs, which intuition says is false, but lack of prices has been a hurdle throughout.

The first cohort, of the ten smallest farms exhibited increasing returns to scale, but this diminished, and as can seen from the table, the summed coefficients became progressively smaller, reaching 1.11 for the smallest sixty farms. The remaining farms, which were at the top end of the size scale exhibited decreasing returns to scale, with the summed coefficients of the fifty-seven largest farms equal to 0.96, which is not significantly different from unity. Reversing the order, the largest ten farms showed evidence of decreasing returns to scale, ($\Sigma\beta_i$'s = 0.96) and the result was the same for the largest twenty farms, but again the CRS restriction could not be rejected. As the incremental farms became smaller, the coefficients summed to a greater than unity. Thus, although the technique is somewhat messy, there does seen to be reasonable evidence that the smaller farms are more efficient. But, even for the best case, reported in the table, the first group of the ten smallest farms did not have significant coefficients, because of lack of degrees of freedom. Nor did all seven years of cross sections work well, even for agriculture.

These results depend on the wider range of firm size in agriculture, whereas the light manufacturing enterprises were all larger than the median farm and the service sector firms were all smaller than the median farm. This resulted in a less clear outcome for the other two industries, where it has to be admitted that the lack of dispersion in the data means that nothing can be determined by this method.

The next approach is nonparametric, where scale efficiency is calculated for every firm in the sample, which is a considerable advantage.

The Programming Approach: Pure Technical and Scale Efficiencies

The nonparametric techniques of measuring Farrell technical efficiency has been extended by Fare, Grosskopf and Lovell (1985) to include the decomposition of total technical efficiency into pure technical and scale efficiency. It is noted that in measuring the scale effect, constant returns to scale is assumed to be a long-run equilibrium condition, ie firms operating at the lowest point of their total cost curve.

As explained in Chapter 3, the imposition of a constraint on the z vector has the effect of enveloping the data more closely, allowing variable returns to scale to be exhibited. The technical efficiency measure does not restrict the reference technology to satisfy strong disposability of inputs (as in the overall technical efficiency measure) allowing for backward bending isoquants. This is accomplished by changing the restrictions on the inputs, and is denoted as (a) in equation (1)

$$F_i(y, x) = \min \lambda,$$
$$\text{subject to } zY_i \geq y_i$$
$$zX_i \leq \lambda x_i$$
$$z \geq 0$$
$$\text{(scale constraint: a)} \quad \sum z_i = 1$$
$$\text{(scale constraint: b)} \quad \sum z_i \leq 1$$

(10)

The constant returns to scale restriction is relaxed by changing the restrictions on the z parameters. Finally, an further constraint, (b), is imposed in place of (a) to determine whether the non-constant returns are increasing or decreasing returns to scale. This is shown in Figure 7.1.

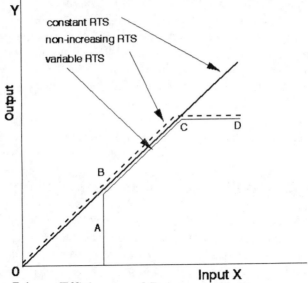

Figure 7.1   Efficiency and Returns to Scale

With output Y and one input X, the constant returns to scale frontier is denoted by the straight line total product curve, the ray from the origin, which passes through the observations for the efficient firms B and C. The efficiency measures, λ, for the producer at A are the same relative to the constant returns to scale and non-increasing returns, but higher relative to the variable returns to scale technology. If the efficiency measure under

140

constant returns and non-increasing returns are not the same, then the returns to scale are decreasing.

Comparison of Industry Scale Effects

The results in this section relate to the individual industry efficiencies. A summary is in Table 7.4. The table reports total technical efficiencies and the decomposition of this into a pure technical and a scale effect for the average of all the firms in each industry, with these results referred to in interpreting the Malmquist indices in later Chapters.

In Table 7.4, in 1985 the mean total efficiency for all firms in agriculture is 84.3%, but when adjusted for firm size, it is clear that many firms have a high level of technical efficiency, 93.67%, but are not the correct size of operation to ensure maximum total efficiency. The scale efficiency level of 90.25%, indicates that the mean agricultural enterprise is nearly 10% scale inefficient.

These results also show that if the scale of the enterprise is taken out, 16 firms are fully efficient rather than 10, implying that if they were size-adjusted, technical efficiency could increase. Over time, the total efficiency levels for the farms tends to fall, and this appears to be caused by scale inefficiency, rather than pure technical efficiency, which is actually higher by the last year. By 1991, agriculture is only 81% scale efficient. Finally, the dramatic fall in 1989, which is not common to the other industries, could be explained by poor weather.

Binswanger, Deiniger and Feder (1995) argue that in actual agricultural production, rather than marketing or related activities, there is no reason to expect anything other than constant returns to scale, and that to compare agricultural enterprises of different sizes requires total factor productivity measurement (see Chapter 9). This is particularly important in any system where subsidised factors of production, ie energy or capital equipment, have been made available to some enterprises and not others. For example, measuring labour productivity without taking account of machinery and equipment makes no sense if there are huge differences in the levels of capital investment.

Comparing the industries, excluding the first year, the service sector is the most scale efficient throughout the period, but even for these firms there are considerably more on the frontier when non-constant returns to scale are assumed. Manufacturing is second in terms of scale efficiency, and in four of the seven years has more than twice as many firms on the frontier after adjusting for size.

Table 7.4   **Nonparametric Frontiers: Industry Total, Technical and Scale Efficiency**

		Agriculture			Manufacturing			Services	
		Total	Technical	Scale	Total	Technical	Scale	Total	Technical	Scale
1985	**Mean**	84.30	93.67	90.24	87.59	91.081	95.59	84.25	91.26	92.32
	Std dev	11.46	12.79	6.33	14.66	12.635	8.33	13.34	9.92	9.98
	Minimum	53.16	60.17	68.83	19.98	39.300	50.84	63.24	70.71	68.95
	Fr firms	10	10	16	13	23	13	10	15	10
1986	**Mean**	80.28	94.10	85.8	84.32	92.770	91.05	83.84	90.41	92.33
	Std dev	11.98	13.92	9.09	11.64	9.597	9.19	16.08	14.637	9.27
	Minimum	46.90	54.38	52.33	62.11	66.750	67.06	23.85	36.800	64.81
	Fr firms	7	9	9	10	21	21	8	14	15
1987	**Mean**	78.82	91.70	86.48	73.19	91.907	79.81	89.74	92.746	96.88
	Std dev	11.73	14.89	7.87	18.60	12.052	17.01	11.35	11.057	5.64
	Minimum	48.10	55.62	58.39	47.10	52.860	49.23	55.05	55.080	80.32
	Fr firms	6	8	10	7	7	25	13	12	19
1988	**Mean**	78.71	91.87	86.43	83.21	93.883	88.57	92.36	96.081	96.15
	Std dev	10.86	14.59	9.13	12.53	8.899	9.57	8.19	6.131	6.19
	Minimum	45.86	51.49	55.05	55.35	70.400	66.65	70.33	81.010	80.99
	Fr firms	6	7	11	11	11	23	12	12	16
1989	**Mean**	59.85	80.21	75.76	85.01	91.970	92.47	89.75	93.801	95.69
	Std dev	13.80	18.45	12.94	11.92	10.035	8.22	10.07	8.250	6.42
	Minimum	29.57	51.46	48.94	58.76	68.300	68.62	70.51	75.750	70.51
	Fr firms	4	5	8	11	11	16	11	11	18
1990	**Mean**	75.85	91.17	84.34	88.22	92.707	95.24	92.67	96.529	95.99
	Std dev	12.31	17.33	10.62	9.12	8.020	6.22	7.75	5.830	5.16
	Minimum	48.29	61.48	44.84	72.00	76.620	74.70	77.55	79.370	81.88
	Fr firms	5	9	12	9	9	22	11	11	15

Table 7.4: continued									
1991 Mean	76.26	95.09	81.12	88.88	94.443	94.20	90.69	94.755	95.61
Std dev	13.70	18.38	11.49	12.53	8.981	9.94	10.27	8.132	7.004
Minimum	42.28	58.47	52.51	41.56	58.580	41.56	55.10	69.670	77.63
Fr firms	8	13	10	11	11	23	9	9	15

Testing for constant, decreasing and increasing returns to scale, in the manner of Fare, Grosskopf and Lovell (1985), completes the scale results. If the scale efficiency level is 100%, they are operating at constant returns, with the direction of the deviation from 100% calculated from equation (1), in the manner explained by Figure 7.1. Full results are available from the author, including an additional column to illustrate the scale effects. A summary of these results is in Table 7.5. Perhaps the oddest result is that a policy of breaking up the large enterprises in agriculture appears to have been followed without any gains.

Table 7.5   Firms Exhibiting Constant, Decreasing and Increasing Returns to Scale: Intra Industry

	Agriculture			Manufacturing			Services		
	Constant	DRS	IRS	Constant	DRS	IRS	Constant	DRS	IRS
1985	10	60	47	13	16	17	10	6	13
1986	7	73	37	10	25	11	8	12	9
1987	6	53	58	7	24	15	13	4	12
1988	6	63	48	11	23	12	12	11	6
1989	4	37	76	11	19	16	11	4	14
1990	5	69	43	9	19	18	11	10	8
1991	8	47	62	11	19	16	9	6	14

This table has some interesting inter-temporal implications. In agriculture, there is a relatively constant number of firms operating at constant scale economies, but the number of those producing at non-constant returns changes over the period. At the beginning, 60 firms have decreasing returns to scale, that is, they are too big, and only 47 increasing returns, that is, producing too little. By the end of the period this has

143

reversed, and 47 produce too much and 62 too little. Table 7.1 shows that both the output values at constant prices and the number of employees has fallen considerably, so these firms do appear to have reduced the overall size of their operations.

Thus, it appears to be true that the farms have become smaller, and Table 7.4 indicates the level of scale efficiency has fallen. This would indicate that farm size reduction is costly in efficiency terms, but are the smaller farms really less efficient? This question is answered in the affirmative by Table 7.6, which reports the average efficiencies for the small, medium and large farm groups of Table 7.2., for the first and last years of the sample. The 1985 results are quite useful, in that the small farm group are least efficient, but not because of size. Indeed, they are the most scale efficient, but they are technically inefficient. That the larger units are internally more efficient is the Adams and Brock (1986) point made earlier with respect to firms. It may apply to these agribusiness units too, but nothing further is available to allow more to be said.

By 1991, all the total efficiencies are lower, but the small group is still the most scale efficient and the least technically efficient. Thus, it does seem that the results are consistent. The agricultural enterprises have become smaller and less efficient, but because of lower pure technical efficiency rather than the scale efficiency itself.

Table 7.6   **The Impact of Farm Size on Efficiency in the Agriculture Industry**

	1985			1991		
	Technical	Total	Scale	Technical	Total	Scale
Smallest farms	85.4	79.2	93.7	85.2	71.6	84.1
Medium farms	94.6	86.6	91.7	94.1	79.3	84.1
Largest farms	100.00	87.5	86.3	100.00	79.5	76.2

Another aspect of the puzzle is that farm sizes have changed, but reducing the number of farms that were too large has not led to any increase in the number that are the right size and has decreased scale efficiency. It is not really possible to solve this problem with the available information, but a possible explanation may be that the wrong farms have been decreased in size. For instance, it could be that grain farms have been broken up and become less efficient, while the efficient small farms are horticultural enterprises. Breaking up a grain farm, or a large-scale animal farm does not make it a horticulture unit. Indeed, if there were scale economies, it could well make it a less scale efficient grain or animal unit. Thus, the fact that agriculture is made up of totally different enterprises, on which there is no information, makes it impossible to come to sound conclusions. This in itself, is a lesson in data collection, showing that this qualitative information is crucial for such an analysis.

For manufacturing, the proportion of firms which are too large or too small does not vary significantly, nor do those in services, although the tendency is towards enterprises which are too small, rather than too large for the majority of the years studied. These results are not pursued here to avoid repetition.

Conclusion

While it is tempting to return to the now familiar excuse of insufficient and spurious data, much can be gained from analysis of this kind. The importance of enterprise size is central to the privatisation programme, and the programming models allow the separation of pure technical and scale efficiency. The results show high levels of pure technical efficiency, particularly in the services sector where for several years, nearly 50% of firms are on the technical efficiency frontier, although only one third are fully efficient. The results for agriculture show that restructuring may not be of the optimal kind, and there is a strange reversal from more than half the enterprises being too large to the same proportion being too small, with no increase in the number that are totally efficient. The lack of information on the type of agricultural enterprises makes the data practically worthless for the purpose of determining farm size, when agriculture appeared to be by far the most interesting sample until now.

Despite this shortcoming in the data, it has still been possible to separate scale and technical efficiency. For all three industries the levels of technical efficiency are high at around 95%, so this gives little scope for improvement. However, while scale efficiency is also high in manufacturing and services, it is lower and falling to around 80% in agriculture, but the data deficiency prevents the reason being determined.

This analysis could be considerably improved without the constraint of confidentiality. Knowledge of the details of the enterprises, what they produce and the nature of their inputs is not available and so the characteristics of each firm cannot be observed. What is clear is that a change has taken place in the size distribution of firms, not just in these three industries, but across the board. The small and medium sized enterprises were almost totally eliminated under the socialist regime. But in Hungary, they have been reappearing, beginning during the period of reform socialism between 1968 and 1989, and only beginning to multiply rapidly since the changes in the political system. The proportion and absolute production volume of the large-firm segment are falling. But, it is wrong to say that the most significant organisational structures in the economy are the large and contracting industrial enterprises and the small, expanding, privately owned service firms. A more accurate way of describing the situation is to refer to contracting and expanding segments of the economy, without specifying their ownership, scale and production group. There is a fall in the proportion of state-owned industry and a rise in the purely privately owned and mixed-ownership sectors that cover various combinations of state and private ownership.

8 Inter-temporal Consistency, Panel Data Estimation, One and Two-Factor Error Component Models

Introduction

So far, no dynamic effects have been included in the estimation, largely due to the difficulty in converting current value data into a valid time series of input and output quantities. But, during the period of this sample, and subsequently, as discussed in the context of the transformational recession, the real value of output has fallen considerably (see Table 7.1 in the previous chapter). Inter-temporal efficiency has only been measured by comparing the annual results, which is of dubious value when the measures are relative to a frontier that is moving over time, due to technological progress or regress. Indeed, the conclusion to Chapter 6 pointed out that taking note of efficiency without considering technical change was likely to be misleading, as they frequently occur simultaneously and need unscrambling. Thus, it is essential to achieve inter-temporal comparability, to include technical change and move on to TFP measurement. The model is richer, as not only can inefficient firms improve such that they move closer to the frontier, but also the frontier can shift in response to new technologies. The product of these two effects is the Malmquist TFP index.

The chapter begins by trying to make the data inter-temporally comparable. It is clear there are changes over the seven years of nominal accounting data, but this is of limited value as these changes can be explained by changes in quantity, or in price, or in both. To fix one of these variables, and thus attribute variation in value to the other, some transformation is necessary.

Fairly naive methods are used to check on the deflators. The results from applying the inadequate price deflators are compared with those from using time dummies, adding a time trend and simply using the original

147

nominal values. Simply pooling the time series and cross-section and using plain OLS is sufficient to show that the problem is not insurmountable, since the results are not very sensitive to the choice of deflator. Then, to exploit the panel to the full extent, less restrictive specialised estimation techniques are used.

Panel data sets for this type of analysis are typically wide and short (117 by 7, for agriculture, for example) and heterogeneity across units is an integral part of the problem. One and two-factor error component models identify specific firm and time effects. Unfortunately, it was not possible to use the time effects as deflators, instead of the price indices, because they were too messy (including negative values), even though political and macroeconomic factors common to all firms would account for a large part of the time effect. Adding the time effects as an explanatory variable did not work well either because there was too little variation and they tended to behave like a constant term.

The firm effects from the two way error components model show that intra-firm differences are important, but are difficult to interpret in any further way. They can be interpreted as contributing to the measures of technical efficiency at the firm level, but too many other factors are at work. Finally, the power of the panel approach is fully exploited by pooling the time series and cross section, for all three industries at once. At this level, even energy can be shown to be significant, despite a very low elasticity.

The Value of Panel Data Models

Methods of estimation using panel data techniques have several advantages and can contribute to an application such as this in a number of ways. Basically, pooling cross section and time series lets both variances add explanatory power to the regressions, as well as ensuring ample degrees of freedom. The advantages are discussed in detail in Baltagi (1995), and include the following:

Gaining greater information

Panels give more informative data, more variability, less collinearity amongst the variables, more degrees of freedom and more efficiency. Time series data are frequently collinear when aggregate measures are used, but may exhibit sufficient differences at the firm-level to eliminate multicollinearity. Also the variation in the data can be decomposed into firms of different size or other characteristic. The wider choice of variables leads to more reliable parameter estimates.[3]

Separating cross section and time series effects

Panel data allow the cross-section and the time series aspects of the data both to contribute to the parameter estimates. Many variables can be more accurately measured at the micro level, and biases resulting from aggregation over firms are eliminated. Behavioural models using panel data incorporate model and measure technical efficiency across heterogeneous operational structures.

Controlling for individual heterogeneity

Panel data suggest that individuals, firms, states or countries are heterogenous. Time series and cross-section studies not controlling for this heterogeneity run the risk of obtaining biased results. Panel data are able to control for any firm- and time-invariant variables whereas a time-series study or a cross-section analysis cannot. Not accounting for firm-specific differences in economic or behavioural assumptions, such as firms operating under different management systems or more or less restrictive regulations, can cause serious mis-specification.

Adjusting for dynamic effects

Panel data are better able to study the dynamics of adjustment. Cross sectional distributions that look relatively stable can hide a multitude of changes. As was shown in Chapter 5, yearly cross-section results show some changes in the productivity of firms, but the rate of change is only identified in a panel estimation.

---

[3] A testable assumption is that the form of the estimating equation is the same for each firm: that is, the data must be poolable (see Baltagi (1995), Chapter 4, for a discussion of poolability tests).

Panel data models in the context of productivity measurement

A long-standing problem in productivity analysis has been the inability to distinguish economies of scale from technical change. The cross-sectional data provide information about the former, while time-series data confuse the two effects, making it impossible to separate them. Rather than assuming constant returns to scale in order to reveal a measure of technical change, it is preferable to capture the individual effects. Panel data methods of estimation allow this, making these techniques suitable for the present analysis. Finally, it is not implausible to assume that there is variation in the parameters across firms. However this raises a further question. If the coefficients are found to differ in the cross section, should these differences be attributed to random variation, and thus part of the disturbance term, or to fixed parameters that simply are different? The random coefficients model corrects some of the inefficiencies of the classical regression although tests of the constancy of the parameters are frequently not conclusive (see Greene, 1995, ch 16).

Short vs long run estimates

Finally, studies using panel data find the Between estimator (based on the cross sectional component of the data) tends to give long-run estimates while the Within estimator (based on the time series aspects of the data) gives short-run estimates. This supports the conventional wisdom that cross-section studies tend to yield long-run responses while time-series tend to yield short-run responses (see Kuh, 1959, and Houthakker, 1965). Baltagi and Griffin (1984) warn that in panel data models, the difference between the Within and Between estimators is due to dynamic mis-specification, and even with a rich data set, the shortness of the time elements allows dynamic under-specification of long-lived lag effects owing to measurement error.

Summary

Panel data estimation can be viewed as a way of averaging, but with the advantages that there are many more degrees of freedom and that both the cross sectional and time series variances will help to determine the parameter estimates. The cost is that this assumes that the slope coefficients are the same which may be inappropriate if they are not, as noted above.[4] In any event, panel data procedures are valid only if the firms are on the same production function, but using inputs in different proportions. Since there is no information about the activities of the firms in the sample, it has to be assumed they have access to the same technology, even if they choose a different combination of inputs. In any time series it is assumed that firms may change from one combination of inputs to another between periods as they adapt to new knowledge and as techniques are introduced, a dimension to the diffusion process that is typically ignored in cross-sectional production studies.

Panel Data Model Specification

Panel data regression models are specified using variables with two subscripts, a firm level i, and a time indicator t. There is a choice of levels of restriction to impose on the equation, commonly giving three alternatives:

Model 1) Pooled OLS, where

$$Y_{it} = \alpha + \beta X_{it} + u_{it}, \qquad i = 1,...,N, \; t = 1,...,T, \; \alpha,\beta = \alpha_{it},\beta_{it}$$

$$(1)$$

which is to assume that both the intercepts and slope coefficients are the same for all the firms.

Model 2) Fixed Effects Model (FEM), where

$$Y_{it} = \alpha_{it} + \beta X_{it} + u_{it}, \qquad i = 1,...,N, \; t = 1,...,T, \; \alpha_{it},\beta = \alpha_{it},\beta_{it}$$

$$(2)$$

which assumes that the individual firm effects are captured as deterministic differences in the intercept term, but the slope coefficients are the same, that is, the firm effects are parametric shifts in the regression. This is

---

[4] The random coefficient model does allow parameter variation across firms, but also requires much more firm-level information about specific inputs than is available in this dataset.

equivalent to using least squares with dummy variables (LSDV) to take account of the different intercepts, or to mean-differencing the data to remove the intercepts entirely.

Model 3) Random Effects Model (REM), is preferred when it is more appropriate to view individual specific constant terms as randomly distributed across cross-sectional units. Thus, the REM allows stochastic firm-specific effects to enter the equation through the error term, as in equation 3), although they are still expressed as an adjustments to the intercept

$$ u_{it} = \mu_i + \epsilon_{it} \ , \ where \ Var(\mu_i) = \sigma_\mu^2 \ , \ Var(\epsilon_{it}) = \sigma_\epsilon^2 \quad (3) $$

Greene (1993) discusses the choice between the FEM and the REM models, including the suggestion that the distinction between fixed and random effect models is an erroneous interpretation. Mundlak (1978) argues that the individual effects should always be treated as random. The fixed effects model is simply analyzed conditionally on the effects present in the observed sample. It can be argued that certain institutional aspects of the data should dictate the choice of model. In support of the REM, the dummy variable approach is costly in terms of degrees of freedom used up. But equally, there is no justification for treating the individual effects as uncorrelated with the other regressors, a necessary assumption in the REM.

Fortunately, two specification tests, the Breusch and Pagan Lagrange multiplier statistic and the Hausman χ^2 statistic can be used. As a general rule, a large value of the Hausman statistic argues in favour of the fixed effects model over the random effects model, and a large value of the LM statistic argues in favour of one of the one factor models against the classical regression with no firm-specific effect.

Diagnostic testing of panel data models is very problematic, largely because of the number of interrelated effects and the difficulty in differentiating between them. Corrections for heteroscedasticity and serial correlation can be done in OLS, using dummy variables (LSDV), although the most efficient set of corrections is offered by Greene's (1992) Time Series, Cross Section (TSCS) programme.

Model 4) The Time Series, Cross Section (TSCS) model is

$$Y_{it} = \alpha_{it} + \beta\ X_{it} + u_{it},\ i = 1,...,N,\ t = 1,...,T,$$

$$where\ \ E[u^2_{it}] = \sigma_{ii},\ \ Cov[u_{it},u_{jt}] = \sigma_{ij},\ \ u_{it} = \rho_i u_{i,t-1} + e_{it}$$

(4)

meaning that the model corrects for group-wise heteroscedasticity, cross-group correlation and within-group correlation. The TSCS procedure uses three-step Generalised Least Squares (GLS) to correct the econometric problems efficiently. Unfortunately, this model does not permit the identification of the individual firm or time effects, and since these are usually important, the TSCS model is frequently rejected. The TSCS results are not reported here, because the firm effects were required and other models that produced these worked perfectly well. Justification for ignoring any unidentified and unresolved problems is given by Chamberlain (1984), who allows for arbitrary serial correlation and heteroscedastic patterns by viewing each time period as an equation, and treating the panel as a multivariate system.

Inter-temporal Consistency

One of the most troublesome aspects of the current dataset, is the choice of accurate deflators to transform the accounting information from current to constant values. While firm specific data is extremely valuable, the level of disaggregation makes the use of an industry level aggregate price deflator inappropriate, unless it can be assumed that the inputs and outputs are homogeneous across all firms. But, clearly, this is not so. Broad industry categories say little about what firms are actually producing. For example, a number of price deflators exist for manufacturing: wood processing, paper, textiles (industrial and clothing), leather, fur etc. But there is no way to match these with the individual enterprises. Equally the expenditure on energy could be on oil, coal, wood, etc. Simply, it is not possible to match actual input items with the appropriate index of price changes.

Continuing with the Cobb-Douglas functional form, a number of ways to deal with inter-temporal comparability were tried. The cross section and time series data is pooled by industry, so 7 years of 117 farms gives an agricultural sample of 819, manufacturing of 301 and services of 283. Model 1, which is simple pooled OLS is estimated for each industry, with four ways of handling the inter-temporal problem.

153

In the first, the value series are deflated with the price indices described in Chapter 4 to give constant values (Model a). In the second, nominal (or current) values are used and dummy variables are included for six of the seven years, to account for inter-temporal changes (Model b); the third model retains the current data and introduces a time trend (Model c) and the fourth makes no adjustment at all to the current values (Model d). If inflation affected all inputs and outputs equally, then the price changes would cancel out in the production equations and model (d) would be adequate. However, if the deflators are accepted, this is not the case. The output deflators rose by about 70% over the period, the deflators for materials, capital and energy all rose by 110% to 120%, but the labour deflator fell by 20%. So, the biggest differences between the nominal and real value regressions should be for labour, where the deflator moves in the opposite direction to the output deflator.

Table 8.1   **Capturing Time Changes in Current Value Data - Agriculture 1985-91**

Regressors	Model a Real values - deflated	Model b Nominal values - dummies	Model c Nominal values - trend	Model d Nominal values
Constant	0.1462 (6.92)	1.2669 (9.21)	1.1412 (8.70)	2.3360 (8.96)
Capital	0.2299 (7.92)	0.1401 (8.46)	0.1363 (8.26)	0.1339 (4.10)
Labour	0.1924 (8.90)	0.3786 (14.86)	0.4097 (16.97)	0.4534 (15.77)
Energy	0.0195 (1.00)	-0.0404 (-0.24)	-0.0294 (-1.83)	-0.0199 (-1.26)
Materials	0.5161 (25.12)	0.4773 (25.38)	0.4827 (26.00)	0.4236 (19.62)
1985 dummy		-0.0189 (-1.08)		
1986 dummy		-0.0014 (-0.08)		
1987 dummy		-0.0129 (-0.75)		
1988 dummy		-0.0098 (-0.59)		
1989 dummy		0.04223 (2.48)		
1990 dummy		0.063 (3.87)		
Time Trend			0.0093 (3.77)	
R^2	0.977	0.984	0.983	0.983

t values given in brackets

The results for agriculture are reported in Table 8.1. The first column, where all the series have been deflated using the price indices, corroborates the single year results of Chapter 5, in that materials has by far the largest and most significant coefficient, but now capital is highly significant and the labour elasticity is far smaller. Energy is again insignificant, even with all the extra power of the pooled sample.

Unfortunately, these results raise a number of problems. With respect to the use of published price deflators, the transformation of current to constant values is unreliable since there is little confidence in this data. Firstly, because any measure of inflation in markets where there is no single price is inevitably flawed, and any attempt to deflate at the product level is almost certainly invalid. Which of many prices is the individual producer facing? Secondly, the non-specific nature of the energy, raw materials and capital inputs, makes the choice of deflators fairly arbitrary. Thirdly, the energy deflator includes electricity, gas, and steam, with an oil index separate.

For these reasons, the alternative ways of dealing with inter-temporal changes are also tried. The use of time dummies instead of deflators does not change the results fundamentally, since materials remains dominant and energy insignificant, while the labour elasticity rises and that for capital falls. The individual year dummies are not significant apart from the positive figures for the last two years, which may, or may not signify a real improvement in the time-related conditions facing producers.

The inclusion of a time trend imposes an increasing monotonic effect which may be inappropriate, and certainly is not supported by the data on price changes published by the Hungarian Central Statistical Office. However, the results are still very similar to the other two models, especially the second, so this crude sensitivity analysis suggests that the deflator problem may not be as critical as was at first supposed. However, there is no way of knowing which is correct, although this is the most methodologically sound so the deflated series are used in the rest of the analysis. Similar results for the manufacturing and service industries are reported in the appendix Tables 8.1A and 8.2A. The next step is to find an acceptable panel model. The time effects retrieved from the panel data models in the remainder of this chapter provide more useful information about changes over the period, although these are not restricted to inflation and interpretation is ambiguous.

Inter-temporal Dynamics

One straightforward application of panel data models is to incorporate a dynamic effect through the cross-section estimates. To achieve this the enterprise data is structured as an ordered panel, and a series of regressions are done for all the years in a moving pair-wise series.[5] The practice of differencing data to reduce the heterogeneity between firms was not done because the variation across firms and across time periods is important in the measurement of individual efficiency differences. The panel data methods which specifically identify the firm and time effects are fundamental in this application.

Table 8.2   Dynamic Effects via Pair-wise Panel Estimation - Agriculture

Year	Constant	Materials	Energy	Labour	Capital	Hausman $\chi^2(4)$	Adj R^2
1985-6	1.187 (9.03)	0.531 (20.54)	0.108 (3.47)	0.350 (11.43)	0.026 (1.18)	4.016 (Pr=0.404)	0.949
1986-7	1.089 (8.28)	0.528 (19.67)	0.074 (2.35)	0.396 (12.78)	0.024 (1.01)	7.65 (Pr=0.105)	0.978
1987-8	1.132 (8.78)	0.504 (18.51)	0.081 (2.38)	0.400 (13.07)	0.033 (1.36)	2.46 (Pr=0.6526)	0.949
1988-9	1.143 (8.20)	0.450 (15.24)	0.108 (2.92)	0.458 (13.17)	0.011 (0.45)	1.03 (Pr=0.9048)	0.942
1989-90	1.182 (7.81)	0.478 (16.65)	0.046 (1.53)	0.446 (11.31)	0.047 (1.88)	1.47 (Pr=0.8319)	0.932
1990-91	1.088 (6.85)	0.454 (18.26)	-0.002 (-0.07)	0.389 (10.07)	0.171 (8.10)	0.87 (Pr=0.9295)	0.903

(critical value χ^2 is 9.49 at 95% confidence)

In agriculture, the seven years reduced to six sub-groups, each of dimension 117 farms by 2 years. The results are reported in Table 8.2.

---

[5] This technique was used by Miroslav Singer at a seminar at London Business School on the transition in the Czech Republic. I thank Ron Smith for explaining the validity of this procedure and the way in which it may be helpful.

In all six pairs, the Hausman test indicated the random effects model was preferred to the fixed effects. (Hausman Ho: $E(u_{it}/X_{it}) = 0$). Low levels of the test, which is $\chi^2(4)$ say that the null hypothesis of no correlation cannot be rejected, therefore rejecting the FEM in favour of the REM (model 3). Since one interesting issue is to detect possible differences across groups it is useful to test the hypothesis that the constant terms are all equal. This is an F test ($F_{n-1,nT-n-K}$), and the hypothesis of equal constant terms was rejected in all six regressions.

These results are interesting, and the models work better than the single year equations. The coefficients on raw materials and on labour do not change a great deal, and are again the most consistently important inputs. But, unlike the results in Chapter 5, energy is significant for all except the last year, although the coefficient falls throughout. The interpretation of the energy coefficient was discussed in Chapter 5, and these results are consistent with the single year cross section estimation. The price index used for the energy series does indicate high levels of inflation, particularly in the last three years of the series, although this is limited to oil, which is the only one available. Capital remains marginal in the early years, but it is highly significant by the last year, when it appears to replace energy.

Table 8.3   Dynamic Effects via Pair-wise Panel Estimation - Manufacturing

Year	Constant	Materials	Energy	Labour	Capital	Hausman $\chi^2(4)$	Adj R^2
1985-6	1.756 (3.16)	0.506 (7.99)	0.013 (0.13)	0.363 (3.34)	0.074 (1.49)	2.277 (Pr=0.685)	0.969
1986-7	3.463 (5.15)	0.382 (8.54)	-0.231 (-1.93)	0.576 (4.91)	0.043 (1.06)	11.23 (Pr=0.024)	0.991
1987-8	2.017 (5.77)	0.484 (14.00)	-0.090 (-1.88)	0.468 (7.24)	0.053 (2.58)	5.49 (Pr=0.004)	0.994
1988-9	3.078 (3.34)	0.286 (5.85)	-0.371 (-3.85)	0.803 (6.37)	0.070 (1.63)	8.40 (Pr=0.005)	0.988
1989-90	2.432 (4.38)	0.391 (9.69)	-0.379 (-5.11)	0.690 (6.78)	0.137 (4.28)	2.849 (Pr=0.0014)	0.992
1990-91	0.929 (1.95)	0.507 (9.85)	-0.013 (-0.14)	0.497 (5.99)	0.033 (0.66)	2.696 (Pr=0.260)	0.982

A similar series of regressions on the other two sectors are less informative. For the manufacturing industry, the coefficient on materials changes very little and that on labour increases overall, while energy continues to be negative (see Table 8.3).

Table 8.4   **Dynamic Effects via Pair-wise Panel Estimation - Services**

Year	Constant	Materials	Energy	Labour	Capital	Hausman $\chi^2(4)$	Adj R^2
1985-6	1.070 (3.18)	0.267 (6.14)	-0.090 (-1.89)	0.790 (8.59)	0.042 (1.19)	7.5909 (Pr=0.108)	0.984
1986-7	0.295 (0.26)	0.385 (3.51)	0.005 (0.05)	0.783 (3.53)	-0.027 (-0.32)	3.5382 (Pr=0.472)	0.980
1987-8	0.619 (1.63)	0.216 (4.97)	-0.045 (-0.98)	0.821 (8.50)	0.084 (2.68)	9.923 (Pr=0.0418)	0.992
1988-9	0.723 (2.65)	0.253 (7.23)	-0.030 (-0.85)	0.766 (10.51)	0.085 (3.24)	6.339 (Pr=0.1752)	0.996
1989-90	0.585 (2.51)	0.288 (8.84)	-0.187 (-2.95)	0.896 (13.69)	0.047 (2.56)	8.223 (Pr=0.0837)	0.997
1990-91	0.687 (2.32)	0.275 (7.73)	-0.097 (-1.60)	0.833 (9.89)	0.043 (1.87)	6.693 (Pr=0.1530)	0.995

The service sector results in Table 8.4 show how labour's share dominates productivity. Raw materials are also significant in each pair of years, which is different from the single cross sections. Also unlike the results in Chapter 5, capital contributes a small influence but a significant one. These more robust results are undoubtedly due to the greater degrees of freedom when the size of the sample is increased, in the above cases doubled, and the use of panel data estimation. Other similar trials using five sets of three years, four sets of four years, etc, contributed no additional information and are not reported.

Error Component Regressions

This chapter began with a discussion of the value of panel data estimation. One of the characteristics included in this discussion is the ability of such models to provide individual firm and time effects. In any study measuring the technical efficiency of specific firms, identifying individual effects is interesting. Equally, in a situation of relative ignorance about changing prices, or the real impact of institutional reform during a period of transition, specific time effects are valuable information. Two error component regression models have been developed to exploit panel data. These are considered as follows.

One-factor error component regression

In this model, μ_i denotes the time-invariant, individual specific effects, which in this case could account for the unobservable entrepreneurial or managerial skills of the decision makers, while v_{it} is the random disturbance term, varying between firms and over time. The form of the estimating equation for the one-factor error component is

$$Y_{it} = \alpha + \beta X_{it} + u_{it}, \ i = 1,...,N; \ t \ 1,...,T$$
$$where \ u_{it} = \mu_i + v_{it}$$
(5)

The firm effect is presented as a constant term, with associated standard error. This positive or negative term is in addition to the average intercept and the two are combined to form an adjusted constant. This term can be interpreted as a measure of the technological endowment available to that firm. Another useful application is to identify all firms for which this adjustment is insignificant. The firms in this group can then be considered to be not significantly different from the average firm. The residual group are different from the average and may provide useful indicators of best or worst practice, perhaps in their input mix or scale of production. Thus, if the successes can be identified, policies can be formulated to ensure that other firms emulate the characteristics of the successes. Finally, the firm effect can be used in forecasting, to predict future productivity growth, although this is not possible with only seven years of data.

Two-factor error component regression

An alternative specification introduces time effects as well as individual firm effects, creating a two element adjustment to the intercept. The form of the estimating equation for this two-factor error component is

$$Y_{it} = \alpha + \beta X_{it} + u_{it}, \ i = 1,...,N; \ t \ 1,...,T$$
$$where \ u_{it} = \mu_i + \lambda_t + v_{it}$$
(6)

159

In this model, as well as μ_i time-invariant, individual effects, and the random disturbance term ν_{it}, λ_t denotes the unobservable time effect, and accounts for any time-specific effect not otherwise included in the regression.

Results

From the error component regression is it clear that there is more to the year by year changes in the value data than can be explained by the available (or selected) price deflators. Table 8.5 shows the results of the re-estimation using the real values (Model a) and the nominal values (Model d), including the time effects generated by the error component model. This model is the first case in which it is possible to claim that a behavioral hypothesis is incorporated in the model. As was discussed in Chapter 5, Schmidt (1988) has shown that the estimating equations for the FEM transformation are exactly the equations derived from the cost minimization problem, when the functional form is the Cobb-Douglas.

The time effects from the deflated value data are different from zero, although they are considerably smaller than those associated with the nominal series, with exception of period 7. The inference is again that the deflation has worked well enough, although period differences still exist which have not properly accounted for. The results for the real values (Model a) using the price deflators and the nominal values (Model d) are reported in Table 8.5 for all three sectors. Since the time effects are collinear with the both the time dummies and the trend, including these as regressors is invalid, so these models are ignored.

The hope was that it would be possible to construct deflators from the time effects series, but the estimates have too little variation and include negatives. Thus, the attempt to construct deflators from the data and use them to deflate the variables for the index number analysis of the next chapter was abandoned.

Most notable in Table 8.5 is the difference between the time effects from the deflated data and that of the nominal data. That there are non-zero period effects at all for the real value equations indicates either the inadequacy of the deflators to take account of price increases, or the fact that other things are going on that have not been captured in the model. The existence of these pre-transition instability factors is confirmed, but their nature not so clear.

160

Table 8.5   **Panel Data Estimation including Time Effects**

Regressors	Agriculture		Manufacturing		Services	
	Real values	Nominal values	Real values	Nominal values	Real values	Nominal values
Constant	1.1297 (4.95)	2.5721 (6.65)	2.0523 (8.18)	3.0685 (7.88)	0.4899 (3.44)	0.1493 (0.55)
Capital	0.2379 (7.82)	0.0775 (2.35)	0.03416 (1.37)	0.0239 (0.96)	0.0273 (1.36)	0.0273 (1.36)
Labour	0.2037 (6.98)	0.3624 (11.39)	0.5110 (8.34)	0.5900 (9.04)	0.9180 (18.03)	0.9180 (18.03)
Energy	0.1963 (0.09)	-0.0316 (-1.67)	-0.1508 (-3.56)	-0.0222 (-0.47)	-0.0376 (-1.36)	-0.0376 (-1.36)
Materials	0.5333 (21.89)	0.4627 (20.27)	0.4044 (14.88)	0.4164 (15.34)	0.2191 (6.92)	0.2191 (6.92)
Time Effects						
Period 1	0.00838	-0.04693	0.15501	-0.03968	0.23357	0.01990
Period 2	-0.00153	-0.02493	0.23084	0.06532	0.15814	-0.05495
Period 3	-0.01257	-0.02720	0.09733	-0.01336	0.19671	0.01585
Period 4	-0.00055	-0.01560	0.05336	-0.00683	0.13565	0.04102
Period 5	0.02256	0.04171	0.01495	0.03892	0.00078	0.00680
Period 6	-0.04922	0.06788	-0.17219	-0.00559	-0.19068	0.00753
Period 7	0.03293	0.00508	-0.37930	-0.03877	-0.53418	-0.03615
R^2	0.977	0.984	0.982	0.982	0.992	0.992
Hausman	27.99 (FEM)	40.13 (FEM)	52.31 (FEM)	49.01 (FEM)	20.84 (FEM)	14.78 (FEM)
Log-likelihood	523.522	675.064	119.759	124.970	115.276	115.276

t values given in brackets: level of significance is 95%

Although accepting there is a real possibility that the choice of specific deflator was incorrect in the first place, it appears that the deflator was reasonably appropriate in the early part of the series, but became less so towards the end. For example, in agriculture, from 1985 to 1988 (periods 1 to 4) the time effect on the real values is greater than that on the nominal values. Since the period effects act simply as another additive constant, this shifts the intercept by the given amount. For 1989 and 1990 the greater effect is on the nominal values and then reverses again in 1991. This pattern is repeated almost identically for the manufacturing and service industries.

It is reasonable to conclude that the price indices published by the Hungarian Central Statistical Office do not adequately account for changes over the period, but that this does not have large effects on the model. This inaccuracy is reflected in all three industries studied, although the price index for energy was common to each. But other aspects of reform do appear to have had an impact on production, as is to be expected.

Table 8.5 shows that the fixed effects model is chosen over the random effects alternative (by the Hausman test), in all three pairs of estimations. Again, this confirms the intuition that there are non-random differences between the enterprises. The non-zero time effects from the two-factor error component model is an indication of changes over the period that may not be solely the fault of inaccurate reporting, but also of other changes taking place prior to the transition later to occur in the CEE states as a whole.

Table 8.6   Firm Level Effects- Two-factor Error Component Model
- Constant Values

	Agriculture	Manufacturing	Services
Mean	1.779	1.955	2.327
Standard Deviation	0.158	0.178	0.157
Minimum	1.318	1.507	2.022
Maximum	2.176	2.334	2.611

The firm effects are the important additional information in this model. All the firm level effects are significant with aggregate descriptive statistics by industry group shown in Table 8.6 and the individual values in the Appendix, Table A8.2. The values are difficult to interpret. As discussed earlier, the firm effects are a measure of how firm i differs from the average firms in the sample. They simply adjust the intercept. But to account for this it is necessary to find out considerably more about the firm than is in apparent in this data. Managerial ability, or an adjustment to the base level of technology would explain differences, but many other explanations can be offered as well. Certainly the relative sizes of the

162

means of the firm effect terms does not imply that services are superior to manufacturing and manufacturing is superior to agriculture, because there are too many inter-industry differences not accounted for.

One claim that could be made is that services and agricultural firms are, on average, more homogeneous than manufacturing.[6] The standard deviation for services and agricultural firms is lower than that for manufacturing. This can just be that the weather is a great equaliser, in the case of agriculture, or else the technology is less sophisticated and therefore variation in skill level is less important, in the case of services.

As a technique the approach reported above is valuable and again allows the identification of the firm with the highest positive additional intercept as having an advantage of some kind in production. What it does not do is provide a measure of technical efficiency directly through the firm effect intercepts, but the general procedure inspires a higher level of confidence in the parameter estimates.

The real value results are probably the best that can be achieved for these data and are the preferred elasticity estimates. They are reasonably consistent with expectations. In agriculture, materials are most important, followed by both labour and capital, but energy is not significant. In manufacturing, labour is even more important than materials, while capital is barely significant and energy is not a constraint on output. In services, labour is dominant, materials less important, capital of marginal value and energy negative and significant at low confidence levels.

Summary

Panel data methods may provide a better model of the production relationship simply because more data is available, there are more degrees of freedom and therefore more efficiency in the estimation, but they do not automatically contribute to efficiency measurement in this situation, due to the poorly deflated series. Retrieving the residuals from the two-factor error component model and transforming them to efficiency effects using the Timmer procedure in Chapter 6 is only meaningful if price changes

---

[6] But see the argument in the last chapter that the differences in agriculture are probably greater, as agriculture includes a range of enterprises as diffuse as market gardens, grain farms and intensive animal units. In the CEE countries, the agricultural units also tend to be agribusiness conglomerates, rather than just farms.

have been sufficiently small so that the year by year changes can be disregarded, and all the variation in the value series arises from changes in quantity rather than price. With the current data, the Timmer efficiencies are hardly worth recalculating, since the Chapter 6 results are more problem-free.

This chapter has endeavoured to improve the estimation of the production function, and hence the measures of technical efficiency generated from it, by using the full power of the panel of data. To do this the problem of price deflation had to be faced. Some transformation of the data was necessary to change the current value data into quantities so that the time series dimension could be exploited. The price indices did not perform particularly well, not necessarily because there were faults in the indices from the Hungarian Finance Ministry, but because a lack of detail on specific enterprise activities made the match of index to variable very difficult.

Furthermore, the enterprises had obviously been subject to a number of effects during this relatively short period. The prices of inputs facing the producers has risen, except that of labour, and the value of output has also risen, although to a varying degree, depending on the final market, that is, whether it is for domestic use or export. Deregulation was beginning to occur in a number of sectors, and producers faced with increasing competition, price supports or subsidies remained available in some sectors and not others, all of which could be responsible for a time effect. These effects are accounted for by deflating, not deflating, with a time trend, or period dummy variables and the results of this crude sensitivity analysis suggest that the main results of the model survive unscathed.

The next step was to use panel data techniques to find good models and retrieve the time and enterprise effects directly from the estimation. This is consistent with the view that even if the series had been properly converted to constant prices and quantities, there is every reason to expect that there may still be a further time effect during a period immediately prior to reform and transition. It can also be assumed that the enterprises are not homogeneous even within an industry. These models were defined and discussed.

The time effects make a valiant attempt to provide a proxy for inflation. From Table 8.5, the correlation between the period effects in the nominal values equations and the reported price indices are 0.4, for agriculture, 0.3 for manufacturing and 0.1 for services. In all cases there is zero or negative correlation between the period effects in the real value equations and the reported price indices. The trade-off between using period effects as an adjustment for current values compared with highly dubious price indices for some variables is not known.

The group effects from the panel data models are represented by a positive and significant adjustment to the constant term. These were surprisingly alike for all enterprises, ranging from 1.3 to 2.6. Two possible explanations can be proposed. This can be an indication that the regression is mis-specified and the fact that each enterprise exhibits such a similar effect can be due to an omitted variable. Equally, it could be consistent measurement error across all enterprises. As discussed before, the most worrying variable throughout is capital, notably a common situation in developing country empirical econometrics and one that can easily occur in transition economies too. Tybout (1992) comments that *curiously, the technical efficiency literature has recognised measurement error in output but has generally ignored measurement error in capital, which is likely to be much larger* (p 27). This is particularly worrying in the present study since as well as making the standard production parameter estimates inconsistent, it distorts the error terms upon which technical efficiency measurement is based.

Short and Long Run Elasticities

A final note is needed on the issue of short and long run elasticities, that was raised in section a) vi. The Between estimates, run as OLS on the mean values for each agricultural enterprise over the seven years gave elasticities of 0.516 for materials, 0.019 for energy (not significant), 0.23 for capital (significant) and 0.19 for labour. The Within estimates for the FEM gave a materials coefficient of 0.49, 0.11 for energy (significant), 0.02 for capital (not significant) and 0.29 for labour. Not too much should be made of these differences, but it does seem reasonable that in the short run energy is significant and capital is not, while in the long run the reverse is true. This long run, short run issue may explain why either capital or energy was often significant, but seldom both together. The results for manufacturing and services add little and are not reported.

165

Conclusion

The panel models give the best estimates possible and confirm the single year results of Chapter 5. In both the sequential, year-on-year models and the one and two factor error component models, the results are reasonably consistent. Materials and labour are the important inputs and in services labour is dominant, as might be expected. Capital is important in agriculture and marginal in the other industries, but energy does not appear to constrain production, except in agriculture. Unlike the last chapter, which contributed largely by showing up the insurmountable weaknesses of the dataset, this chapter successfully overcomes the missing data problems. Such is the power of the added cross-sectional variance and the extra degrees of freedom.

Thus, on the basis of these good econometric tests of the data, it is possible to proceed to the construction of total factor productivity indices. This index number approach does not test the validity of the data, so the econometric verification is useful. However, the indices do offer the most comprehensible and complete review of what these data show. Particularly, the Malmquist index imposes no functional form or assumption of perfect competition. It decomposes into pure technical efficiency, scale efficiency and technological progress and it does allow the industries to be pooled, unlike the econometrics.

Table A8.1:   **Capturing Time Changes in Current Value Data - Manufacturing and Services**

Manufacturing	Model 1	Model 2	Model 3	Model 4
Regressors	Real values - deflators	Nominal values - dummies	Nominal values - trend	Nominal values
Constant		1.7915 (7.87)	1.8518 (8.51)	
Capital	0.1125 (3.78)	0.1340 (8.62)	0.1389 (9.14)	0.0278 (1.11)
Labour	0.0.0145 (0.27)	0.4875 (11.38)	0.4776 (11.61)	0.5831 (8.98)
Energy	0.0447 (0.93)	-0.1429 (-3.99)	-0.1408 (-4.03)	-0.2252 (-4.72)
Materials	0.5547 (18.78)	0.4488 (20.22)	0.4516 (20.59)	0.4135 (15.29)
1985 dummy		0.0135 (0.35)		
1986 dummy		0.0997 (2.62)		
1987 dummy		0.0113 (0.30)		
1988 dummy		0.0534 (1.40)		
1989 dummy		0.0944 (2.47)		
1990 dummy		0.0237 (0.62)		
Time Trend			-0.0040 (-0.78)	
R^2	0.973	0.983	0.982	0.982
Log-likelihood	49.543	124.362	117.167	116.936

Table A8.1: continued

Services	Model 1	Model 2	Model 3	Model 4
Regressors	Real values - deflators	Nominal values - dummies	Nominal values - trend	Nominal values
Constant		0.6056 (3.47)	0.7345 (4.40)	
Capital	0.0938 (2.99)	0.0498 (3.32)	0.0512 (3.52)	0.0261 (1.31)
Labour	0.3983 (6.19)	0.8451 (19.26)	0.8261 (19.44)	0.9090 (18.08)
Energy	0.1139 (2.77)	-0.0695 (-2.83)	-0.0755 (-3.16)	-0.0386 (-1.41)
Materials	0.4531 (9.84)	0.2387 (11.20)	0.2527 (12.47)	0.2298 (7.31)
1985 dummy		0.0551 (1.37)		
1986 dummy		-0.0176 (-0.44)		
1987 dummy		0.0530 (1.32)		
1988 dummy		0.0677 (1.68)		
1989 dummy		0.0379 (0.94)		
1990 dummy		0.0484 (1.20)		
Time Trend			-0.0018 (-0.33)	
R^2	0.979	0.992	0.992	0.992
Log-likelihood	12.453	114.655	109.772	109.691

t values given in brackets: level of significance is 95%

Table A8.2 Individual Firm Effects - Total Sample

Firm	Effect	SE	Firm	Effect	SE	Firm	Effect	SE	Firm	Effect	SE
1	1.822	0.125	49	1.700	0.107	96	2.016	0.119	143	1.676	0.103
2	1.822	0.116	50	1.657	0.107	97	1.831	0.118	144	1.851	0.114
3	1.874	0.118	51	1.564	0.103	98	1.713	0.112	145	1.890	0.102
4	1.933	0.120	52	2.176	0.145	99	1.894	0.113	146	1.981	0.116
5	2.045	0.123	53	1.826	0.121	100	1.806	0.117	147	1.716	0.101
6	1.942	0.132	54	1.910	0.120	101	1.779	0.111	148	2.235	0.104
7	1.840	0.124	55	1.589	0.109	102	1.724	0.112	149	2.334	0.109
8	1.872	0.124	56	1.542	0.110	103	1.939	0.120	150	1.937	0.100
9	1.809	0.121	57	1.622	0.104	104	1.761	0.116	151	2.042	0.115
10	1.782	0.120	58	1.668	0.116	105	1.667	0.114	152	1.765	0.103
11	1.935	0.119	59	1.430	0.100	106	1.754	0.113	153	1.925	0.108
12	2.056	0.125	60	1.708	0.107	107	1.670	0.103	154	2.179	0.111
13	1.946	0.124	61	1.906	0.115	108	1.875	0.112	155	1.972	0.106
14	1.902	0.121	62	2.062	0.131	109	1.887	0.127	156	2.005	0.104
15	2.059	0.097	63	1.695	0.111	110	1.960	0.119	157	2.468	0.114
16	1.861	0.109	64	1.781	0.112	111	1.889	0.126	158	2.194	0.105
17	1.829	0.113	65	1.659	0.108	112	1.896	0.112	159	1.818	0.137
18	1.642	0.128	66	1.631	0.112	113	1.639	0.093	160	1.955	0.125
19	1.898	0.115	67	1.599	0.103	114	2.003	0.100	161	2.046	0.113
20	1.836	0.117	68	1.678	0.100	115	1.670	0.103	162	2.022	0.129
21	1.924	0.120	69	1.682	0.109	116	1.421	0.097	163	2.427	0.127
22	1.775	0.105	70	1.339	0.099	117	2.009	0.110	164	2.410	0.138
23	1.848	0.126	71	1.733	0.117	118	2.064	0.133	165	2.139	0.103
24	1.717	0.113	72	1.823	0.111	119	1.960	0.127	166	2.457	0.094
25	1.780	0.121	73	1.808	0.117	120	2.036	0.138	167	2.648	0.095
26	1.829	0.110	74	1.727	0.102	121	2.189	0.134	168	2.218	0.094
27	1.675	0.095	75	2.079	0.112	122	1.834	0.131	169	2.287	0.088
28	1.612	0.097	76	1.846	0.104	123	1.507	0.124	170	2.330	0.087
29	1.918	0.117	77	1.820	0.100	124	1.997	0.121	171	2.361	0.084
30	1.765	0.111	78	1.926	0.115	125	1.893	0.128	172	2.355	0.092
31	1.831	0.109	79	1.777	0.113	126	1.818	0.133	173	2.611	0.104
32	1.795	0.113	80	1.698	0.110	127	1.918	0.135	174	2.398	0.091
33	1.636	0.108	81	1.646	0.102	128	2.103	0.139	175	2.359	0.091
34	1.896	0.115	82	1.747	0.098	129	1.968	0.133	176	2.147	0.090
35	1.857	0.107	83	1.485	0.107	130	2.106	0.133	177	2.341	0.084
36	1.794	0.109	84	1.654	0.104	131	1.902	0.130	178	2.143	0.084
37	1.719	0.108	85	1.609	0.106	132	2.091	0.125	179	2.415	0.087
38	1.740	0.109	86	1.811	0.107	133	2.080	0.133	180	2.408	0.085
39	1.473	0.097	87	1.821	0.116	134	1.914	0.123	181	2.433	0.088
40	1.318	0.102	88	1.782	0.113	135	1.801	0.118	182	2.286	0.085
41	1.820	0.102	89	1.850	0.118	136	1.903	0.114	183	2.146	0.086
42	1.377	0.106	90	1.631	0.102	137	1.799	0.119	184	2.119	0.084
43	1.734	0.107	91	1.681	0.104	138	1.874	0.122	185	2.521	0.094
44	1.939	0.111	92	1.956	0.112	139	1.743	0.113	186	2.428	0.082

Table A8.2 continued

45	1.949	0.112	93	1.887	0.123	140	1.841	0.105	187	2.283	0.087
46	1.635	0.101	94	1.526	0.111	141	2.000	0.131	188	2.227	0.083
47	1.725	0.107	95	1.923	0.109	142	1.780	0.104	189	2.527	0.094
48	1.878	0.108									

PART III:
THE INDEX NUMBER APPROACH TO PRODUCTIVITY, EFFICIENCY AND TECHNICAL CHANGE; AN APPLICATION TO STRUCTURAL TRANSFORMATION

Introduction

Many of the preceding chapters have addressed methods of determining a production relationship from incomplete data. This has involved investigating a number of approaches to estimation, linear programming and the construction of performance indices in order to improve on the established measurement procedures currently undertaken to assess the beginnings of reform and transition of the countries of Central and Eastern Europe to market economies.

The first chapter of Part III resorts to accounting techniques to construct TFP indices, giving possibility the most defensible results, to complete the study. Again, both parametric and nonparametric approaches are used to ensure that meaningful results are extracted from the inadequate data. Thus, the Tornqvist-Theil approximation of the Divisia index is used first and the results are checked by also calculating the Malmquist index. The TFP is decomposed into technological change, pure technical efficiency and scale efficiency, providing a much clearer picture of the performance of the individual enterprises and the shortcomings that can be addressed by focused restructuring, the reallocation of resources and carefully targeted investment. This completes the analysis of Hungarian industries.

But Chapter 10 goes further, with an application to validate these measurement approaches and extend their use into policy. This shows that the normal process of structural transformation, from agriculture, to industry, to services appears to have been prematurely enforced in the CEE countries, so that the reforms lead to a reversal, in which agriculture may be the leading sector.

9 Examining Changes Over Time Using Parametric and Nonparametric TFP Indices

Introduction

The objective of this chapter is to extend the single period technical efficiency measurement to include a time dimension. This is achieved through the construction of parametric and nonparametric TFP indices, which are explained in some detail, by examining the separate components and then compared to ensure that the results are consistent. There are no statistical tests in the index number approach, to ensure validity of the results, so the econometric testing of the data in the last chapter is an important unpinning for this section. The next chapter extends the analysis by separating the change in technical efficiency for each firm from shifts in the frontier itself. This is an important distinction since if the frontier shifts because of a change in the available technology, there is productivity growth and not simply an increase in technical efficiency.

Previous chapters have considered the measurement of technical efficiency to be based on the distance between the individual firm and the production frontier, where the frontier represents the best practice firms in the sample. In Chapter 5, cross-sectional efficiency measures were developed from a number of models, some estimated and some programmed. Then in Chapter 8, the use of panel data estimation resulted in an improvement on the single year models, adding further time effects to the price index adjustment and also generating a firm level effect. But, thus far, the measures of technical efficiency have been based on discrete observations rather than continuous variables, and an index to evaluate the level of technical efficiency over time has not been developed.

Turning to the issue of differentiating changes in technical efficiency from technical change, this is essential for identifying sectoral progress or regress, and the individual firms' reaction to it. It is also useful to know which firms can keep up, which are responsible for defining the new frontier and also something about the nature of the frontier, particularly whether there is a bias toward new factor combinations, or not. Unfortunately, not all the approaches used in earlier chapters are suitable for these tasks. The econometrics is limited to simple functions, although as in Chapter 5, it was possible to construct frontiers rather than just average production relationships. The Tornqvist-Theil accounting method is valuable in the construction of TFP indices. It includes the attributes of a less restrictive functional form, since it corresponds exactly to the translog, which is a flexible functional form and a second order approximation of any unknown production function. In addition, the input indices are used to show how factor use has varied over time. But, the Tornqvist-Theil index is not suitable for the separation of the efficiency and technical change effects. It is an average measure, an aggregate rather than a frontier. Nor is it easy to differentiate between technical change and returns to scale in either the econometric approach or the Tornqvist-Theil accounting approach.

The conclusion must be that the second objective can only be achieved at all easily using nonparametric methods. Fortunately, the Malmquist index is defined as the product of technical change and changes in technical efficiency, and therefore such a decomposition is easy. It does not require price data and imposes no functional form so pooling is admissible even when the econometrics does not. Furthermore, the indices are multilateral, meaning that the industries are compared cross-sectionally and over time. The starting values are the relative efficiency levels of the firms, or the industries in the first year. Thus, this chapter both constructs a number of indices of technical efficiency for each firm and then separates the effects of technical change and efficiency change. The different firm-level technical efficiency indices are very similar, which is gratifying as the derivation of consistent and reliable performance measures are very much at the centre of this study. Industry comparisons of technical change show that, on average, the agricultural enterprises have suffered technological regress. That is, the isoquant has shifted outwards from the origin in the input-based approach used here, or equivalently, the total physical product function has shifted downwards over time. But the regress in agriculture is less than either manufacturing or services, although the service sector firms have the highest levels of technical efficiency during the early years of the sample period.

An Index of Total Factor Productivity

An accounting-based TFP index is constructed to measure the change in technical efficiency for each firm. Then, these are aggregated to give industry-level indices. Following the discussion of production and efficiency measurement in Chapter 3, the total factor productivity index is derived from the technical production relationship between inputs and output. The Tornqvist-Theil is a discrete approximation of the Divisia input index and the expression used to construct the inputs is

$$\hat{x} = \frac{1}{2}\sum_i (C_{it} + C_{it-1}) \ln\left(\frac{X_{it}}{X_{it-1}}\right) \tag{1}$$

This is simply the logarithm of the ratio of two successive input quantities weighted by a moving average of the share of the input in total cost. Since the data available is in values, the cost shares of the inputs were used, and each firms' individual factor proportions are used for the weights in constructing the input index. This is preferable to retrieving the coefficients from the estimating equations, as this procedure imposes constant shares across the whole sample. The outputs do not need to be aggregated and the TFP is the ratio of the exponent of the output index divided by the exponent of the input index, see Chapter 3.

Once constructed, the index is chained to allow the value in each period to be incorporated into the cumulative output index, that is, each value is calculated relative to the previous observation, rather than relative to a single base year, so that, beginning from the base value of 100

$$Y_t^c = (Y_t)(Y_{t-1}^c) \tag{2}$$

and in the next period

$$Y_{t+1}^c = (Y_{t+1})(Y_t^c) \tag{3}$$

where Y_t is the value before chaining and Y_t^c is the chained index. The indices are now cumulative and based at 100 to make inter-industry comparisons simple.

Table 9.1   Mean Output, Input and Total Productivity Indices

Year	Output	Materials	Energy	Labour[1]	Labour[2]	Capital	TFP[1]	TFP[2]
				Agriculture				
1985	100.000	100.000	100.000	100.000	100.000	100.000	100.000	100.000
1986	100.360	106.283	92.947	98.942	95.932	97.066	99.479	100.047
1987	101.072	108.726	91.729	105.787	94.054	96.019	99.135	100.841
1988	104.120	103.657	93.723	122.055	89.052	97.067	101.417	106.117
1989	92.346	90.034	88.715	133.687	81.888	84.500	99.022	106.592
1990	75.494	80.910	81.592	154.312	72.499	71.329	88.268	98.922
1991	66.801	51.064	68.304	145.633	53.607	52.309	105.257	122.294
				Manufacturing				
1985	100.000	100.000	100.000	100.000	100.000	100.000	100.000	100.000
1986	105.159	95.153	94.635	98.069	96.604	110.905	104.483	106.975
1987	86.584	85.010	89.786	93.518	95.609	110.317	93.905	94.835
1988	78.076	73.168	65.015	87.384	90.904	85.097	94.943	94.814
1989	68.523	60.014	60.815	83.329	88.988	77.634	91.710	91.588
1990	62.365	60.846	60.719	99.240	97.241	74.333	88.168	89.916
1991	47.781	43.724	45.481	112.397	98.398	53.885	84.133	87.367
				Services				
1985	100.000	100.000	100.000	100.000	100.000	100.000	100.000	100.000
1986	92.408	86.760	92.643	102.423	105.042	110.571	91.302	89.098
1987	102.151	98.318	88.678	106.198	100.017	108.160	95.473	94.697
1988	85.145	85.575	67.271	95.671	100.898	89.479	93.650	89.916
1989	75.502	79.847	81.515	99.457	94.892	94.342	79.960	77.262
1990	69.095	70.189	71.088	114.935	108.086	73.243	73.891	74.420
1991	49.857	51.931	50.913	124.615	96.192	64.182	55.133	59.983

* Labour[1] = wages, resulting in TFP[1]. Labour[2] = number of employees, resulting in TFP[2].

177

One small digression here provided some interesting results. The labour variable was the least controversial in that it was not in value units, but represented the number of employees, and was even divided into blue and white collar workers. So even though the economic implications of a particular size of workforce did not enable anything to be claimed about productivity, it was at least an understandable data series. But as this variable was not significant in any of the regressions, whereas the wage bill was, the latter was used. But since the index replies on accounting techniques, with no estimated coefficients and associated standard errors, there is no constraint on the choice of input variables. Therefore, at the same time as retaining the input data to be consistent with the estimation and programming models in previous chapters, an alternative labour variable was used in a second index, although the cost shares continue to use the value data. These two specifications of the labour input give quite different results, as will be discussed later in this chapter.

Table 9.1 shows the geometric means of the TFP index for the three industries, with the original and alternative labour variable inputs. The firm level results are available from the author. The data used to construct these indices are all in constant values and so all suffer from inadequate adjustment factors, but there is no reason to suppose that any single deflator is worse than the others. A straightforward interpretation follows.

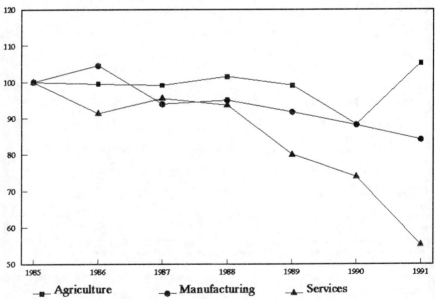

Figure 9.1   Total Factor Productivity Indices (Labour = wages)

TFP for agriculture is higher than for the other two industries, for all years, especially the last one, with the only exception being manufacturing in 1986. This is shown in Figure 9.1, with the wage bill representing the labour input.[1] So even if some especially favourable conditions existed for agriculture in 1991, perhaps particularly good weather or the existence of price supports, there is still a trend to this series which supports the view that, unlike the manufacturing and services industries, the real value of output with respect to inputs is not falling in this sector.[2] This is contrary to the TFP results for manufacturing and services which both decline, very substantially in the case of services.

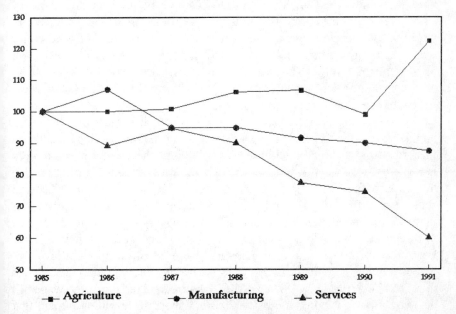

Figure 9.2　　**Total Factor Productivity Indices (Labour = number of employees)**

---

[1] Note that all three series begin at an arbitrary value of 100, and therefore this does not really allow cross-sectional comparisons, although it makes the growth rates of the index easier to visualise. This is done in the next chapter, which uses the multilateral property of the Malmquist TFP index.

[2] See below, where the individual indices are investigated: it seems that the rapid decline in blue collar labour is responsible for the turn-around in agriculture, not good weather.

A similar outcome results when using the alternative labour series, which is in terms of numbers of employees rather than wages, as is shown in Figure 9.2. The trend in TFP, regardless of how labour is measured, is pleasingly consistent but also interesting when considered in more detail. Comparing the two TFP's shows that the lack of quality adjustment in the number of employees series gives higher TFP's, as indeed it should and that this effect is especially strong in agriculture. Since there is information on labour, this is investigated next.

It is known that wages have lagged behind other prices although there is no information on hours worked or differential wage rates between blue and white collar labour. From the data on the number and status of employees, it is clear that the split between blue collar and white collar workers has changed, but not very much. The proportion of blue collar workers in agriculture fell from 84% in 1985 to 82% in 1991; in manufacturing, from 26% to 24%; and in services, from 43% to 38%, with agriculture the only industry with a majority of blue collar workers over white.

Referring back to Table 7.1 in Chapter 7, it is clear that the mean number of employees has almost halved in agriculture, fallen slightly in manufacturing and increased in services, although the number of employees is a quality unadjusted labour series. But the split of the wage bill between blue and white collar labour is not given in the company financial statements. The only information available on the different wage rates is in the national statistics, which claims that managers salaries have risen two to three times as much as those of manual workers, although neither have kept up with inflation rates in general. More detail on the skill levels of labour would be particularly useful as where the labour force is reduced it may well be replaced by higher skilled labourers. Therefore, the wage bill data could be considered a quality adjusted labour series, an argument that can be extended to claim that wage data gives a labour-quality adjusted TFP.

While these results may initially be counter-intuitive, again with reference to Table 7.1, it is clear that, as far as a technical relationship between inputs and outputs is concerned, which is what is being measured here, there is a much greater fall in the value of output in manufacturing and services than in agriculture. This is especially true for the last two years of the series. In 1991, the mean output fell in agriculture to 86% of the previous year, in manufacturing to 71% and in services to 67%, making the average fall in the real value of output in the services industry far greater than in the other industries. But, at the same time, the mean number of employees in 1991 was 75% of the previous year in agriculture, 93% in manufacturing and 83% in services.

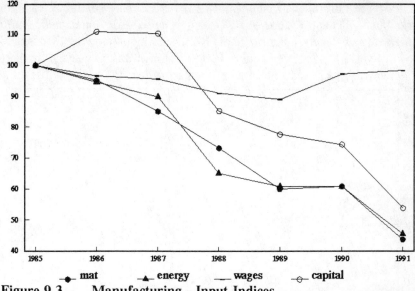

Figure 9.3   **Manufacturing - Input Indices**

However, this is still fairly tenuous and economic rigour is still not possible. If indeed large amounts of unskilled or under-utilised labour were being replaced by small amounts of quality labour, it is reasonable to suppose that higher quality, or newer, capital equipment would be introduced to complement this improved work force. However, referring to the cross section results in Table 5.3, the coefficient on capital does rise in agriculture although this is not the case in manufacturing or services and unfortunately no evidence of the purchase of new capital exists in the data. Regrettably, there is little evidence at the aggregate level that this rational response to the need for more productive labour is occurring. Kornai (1994) notes a reluctance on the part of managers to bring themselves to undertake a radical reduction of their excess labour, with a resulting deterioration of labour productivity, with high levels of underemployment still existing in the enterprises.[3]

---

[3] He also claims that once the state-owned enterprises are privatized, the situation changes and the first thing the new owners do is dismiss the workers they judge to be superfluous (p 50). Unfortunately, this is not

The labour issue is now discussed at the industry level, as it transpires that the three are quite different. Here manufacturing and services are discussed first, followed by the more extreme case of agriculture. Thus, Figure 9.3 shows the individual input indices for manufacturing, where labour (wages) is the only input showing evidence of growth by 1991. This can simply be the result of a random year as there is no evidence of a trend throughout the period for this input.

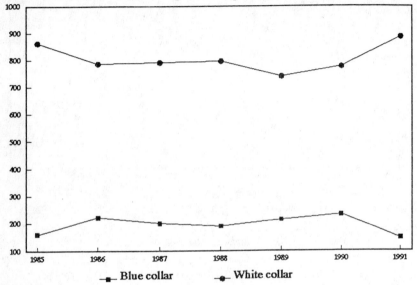

Figure 9.4   Labour in Manufacturing

What is known from the data (Table 7.1) is that while the total number of employees has not changed much, during the last two years there is a shift from blue collar to white collar labour, in a workforce that is predominantly white collar already (see Figure 9.4). Again, following the quality adjusted labour argument presented above, the wage-determined labour variable does rise faster than the number of employees based series (columns 5 and 6, Table 9.1). Unfortunately, while the switch from blue to white collar labour costs more, it also has a detrimental effect on TFP. The capital input series indicates a decrease in the use of capital equipment, indicating that the quality adjusted labour (either managerial or simply

borne out by the data in these industries, although maybe his comments refer to a more recent period than 1991.

182

skilled rather than non-skilled) was not matched by the necessary introduction of higher grade capital.

The substitution of labour for capital between 1987 and 1988 is most marked in manufacturing although as will be seen below, this is reflected to a lesser extent in services. This would be a very interesting result, were it not for the dubious nature of the capital series throughout. Theoretically, this can be interpreted as a move from State subsidises to a real price for capital, and subsequent rationing. At this time, manufacturing enterprises in particular will be restructuring prior to privatisation, if they appear sufficiently attractive for reform of this kind. This trend did then continue for the remainder of the period.

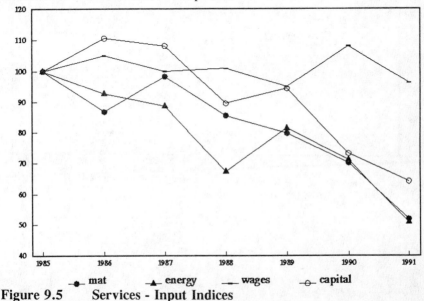

Figure 9.5   Services - Input Indices

The service sector input indices are similar to those in manufacturing, and are shown in Figure 9.5. The mean number of employees has risen from 1985, falling off in the last year (Table 7.1). Again, the major share of the workforce is white collar, although this group declined more than the blue collar workers in 1991, as Figure 9.6 shows.

The wage input index still rises above the number of employees input index, despite the higher reduction in white collar workers. This can be accounted for by the large differential in wages for the managers compared with the unskilled labour. Unfortunately, increased wages do not ensure an improved labour force and the TFP continues to fall. Clearly, improvements in the quality of labour may not have an immediate effect, but this does raise governance issues that would be interesting to track, were there an extension to the series. Finally, the substitution of labour for capital again becomes apparent between 1987 and 1988, reflecting the changes in manufacturing.

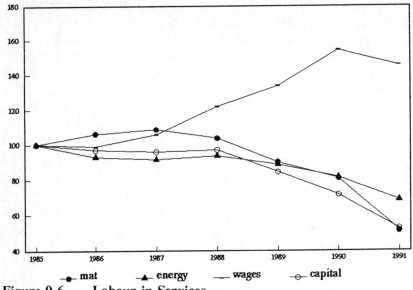

Figure 9.6   Labour in Services

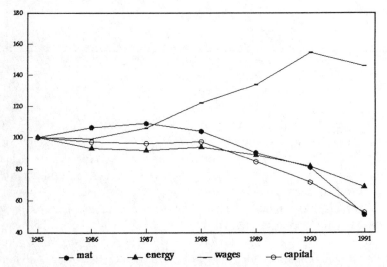

Figure 9.7   Agriculture - Input Indices

For the agriculture sector (see Figure 9.7), labour has the highest growth rate, when measured in wages, as Table 9.1 shows. Indeed, the wage series increases by 45%, whereas the number of employees is reduced to a little more than half its starting value. Thus, the value of resources allocated to labour has risen rapidly, compared with that of other inputs and what remains seems to be highly productive. This is shown in Table 7.1.Mean labour productivity has more than doubled, whereas it has fallen in both the other industries. The majority of labour in this industry is unskilled, and the reduction in the total number of employees is mainly taken from that group (see Figure 9.8). Note too that the decline accelerates in 1991, which is the year that TFP recovers. Thus, the turn-around in the agricultural TFP seems to be driven by the cumulative effect of the rapid shedding of blue collar labour, which accelerated in 1991, rather than by good weather. This decline in labour is what makes agriculture different from the other two industries. Thus, it is not surprising that the wage bill index behaves so differently from the employees index.

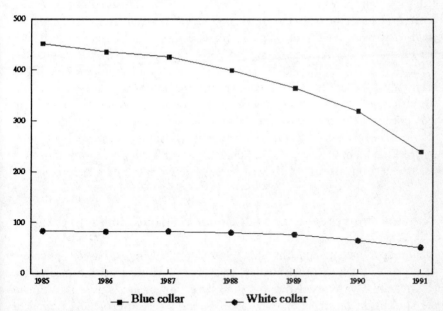

Figure 9.8   Labour in Agriculture

There are a number of possible ancillary reasons for the TFP recovery, although none can be authenticated with the current data. These include the introduction of non-pecuniary incentives, or a move from totally low skilled agriculture to more specialist products, perhaps as a response to increasing consumer demand for more variety. Agricultural output, unlike manufacturing or services, does not necessarily imply the use more capital, as the growth in areas such as herbs and horticulture has shown.

The input variable for which specific information on its nature, price and usage is most elusive is energy. This factor of production was available all over Eastern and Central Europe, pre-reform, at greatly subsidised cost to enterprises, although not to households, and was mostly traded from the FSU in exchange for the low quality output of the other states. One of the results of transition and the end of rationing is that enterprises and households now compete in the same market, although enterprises still have a softer budget constraint than consumers, so firms retain their comparative advantage. Aslund (1994) claims that for this reason, energy intensity has increased sharply for the early years of the transition, and this will continue until the enterprises also face a hard budget constraint. Aslund (p 28) also claims that for countries such as Hungary, with a reasonably strict monetary policy, this trend has reversed, whereas those with soft monetary policies and subsidized energy prices, such as Russia, have seen huge increases in the energy intensity of their production. This position is supported by the data in Table 9.1, but it is difficult to interpret these deflated values correctly. What is clear is that in each industry there is a decline in expenditures on energy, after adjustment for inflation. By 1997, this may be related to the current fall in output, but it is not possible to identify such a relationship in the data used here.

The impact of technological change, leading to the necessity of a more skilled labour force, cannot be determined by these accounting-based performance measures. This will be considered in the next section.

Technical Progress and the Multilateral Malmquist Index

The nonparametric analysis in the earlier chapters is based on cross-sectional estimation of efficiency measures, relative to the best-practice frontier for each year. Now, the time series dimension is used to estimate the shifting of the frontier over time, giving a measure of pure technical progress. Thus, inter-temporal and inter-firm distance functions form the Malmquist TFP index.

The Malmquist index also allows the separation of efficiency change and technical progress. Following Fare et al (1992a, 1994), the Malmquist

TFP index is defined, for firm i and year t+1, in terms of distance functions as

$$M_i^{t+1}(y_i^{t+1},x_i^{t+1},y_i^t,x_i^t)=\frac{D^{t+1}(y_i^{t+1},x_i^{t+1})}{D^t(y_i^t,x_i^t)}\left[\frac{D^t(y_i^t,x_i^t)}{D^{t+1}(y_i^t,x_i^t)}\frac{D^t(y_i^{t+1},x_i^{t+1})}{D^{t+1}(y_i^{t+1},x_i^{t+1})}\right]^{1/2} \quad (4)$$

The first ratio on the right hand side is the efficiency measure for year t+1 relative to that for year t. The distance functions were stated in Chapter 3 and applying these programmes to the data for the next year gives the distance function for year t+1. The other four distance functions define the shift of the technical progress frontier. Two of these terms are identical to the efficiency measures just described. The value of the inter-temporal distance functions are explained by Figure 9.9, repeated from Chapter 3, which shows the way in which the Malmquist index is constructed, from the input requirement sets, factor ratios and isoquants for years t and t+1.

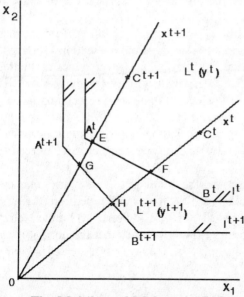

Figure 9.9   The Multilateral Malmquist Index

The base-year frontier, I^t, is defined by two hypothetical efficient firms, with observations A^t and B^t, and the efficiency of a third firm, at C^t, is calculated relative to this frontier. Thus, $D^t(y^t,x^t)$ is equal to OC^t/OF, on the initial vector x^t. In the next year, the frontier has moved to I^{t+1} and firm C now has an input ratio x^{t+1} and is at C^{t+1}.

The efficiency measure is now OC^{t+1}/OG and the efficiency term in (4) is measured by these ratios shown in equation (5).

$$M_i^{t+1}(y_i^{t+1},x_i^{t+1},y_i^t,x_i^t) = \frac{OC^{t+1}/OG}{OC^t/OF}\left[\frac{OH}{OF}\frac{OG}{OE}\right]^{1/2} \qquad (5)$$

The first technical progress term is already defined above and is divided by $D^{t+1}(y^t,x^t)$, which is equal to OC^t/OH, giving the ratio OH/OF in (5). The Figure shows that this is the shift of the frontier measured at the factor ratio x^t. Following the same reasoning, the last term in equation (4) is measured by OG/OE in the Figure and this is the shift of the frontier measured at the factor ratio of the second period, x^{t+1}. The technical progress element of the Malmquist TFP index is the geometric mean of the two alternative measures.

The product of the efficiency terms and the measure of technical progress is a Malmquist TFP index. This can be compared with geometric indices constructed using conventional accounting techniques, such as the Tornqvist-Theil approximation in the previous section. Basing the chained indices on the first year (1985) efficiency levels gives multilateral indices, that allow for inter-spatial and inter-temporal comparisons. This follows Jorgensen and Nishimizu (1978), on inter-country comparisons, which was refined by Caves, Christensen and Diewert (1982) and has now developed into a considerable literature, including empirical applications to Yugoslavia (Nishimizu and Page, 1982) and European agriculture (Bureau, Butault and Barkaoui, 1992).

In the next section, the Malmquist TFP's are compared with the Tornqvist-Theil indices. To avoid too much repetition, the decomposition into efficiency and technical change is deferred to the next chapter, where it is embodied in a study of the possibility that the normal progress of the structural transformation may be temporarily reversed in the transitional economies.

Comparative Performance Indicators

Chapter 2 discussed the importance of measuring productivity and technical efficiency, but also the variability in the performance indicators available. This study has focused on enterprise level performance and claims these to be superior to those at a higher level of aggregation. But even at the firm level, differences persist. A number of approaches have been used to measure productivity, all coming from the basic theoretical perspective of a technical production relationship and using econometric models, programming models and index number techniques.

A degree of confidence is achieved on the basis of the convergence of results. The techniques support each other, despite considerable problems with the data and are complementary in the sense of producing different information. Finally, the two index number approaches are compared to show that both tell the same story. Table 9.2 reports the two indices for the three sectors, all based to 100 for comparability, although it is recognised that forcing the base year to be equal does obscure the different starting points which are also important.

Table 9.2   Comparative Performance Indices

Year	Agriculture Malmquist	Agriculture Tornqvist	Manufacturing Malmquist	Manufacturing Tornqvist	Services Malmquist	Services Tornqvist
1985	100.000	100.000	100.000	100.000	100.000	100.000
1986	100.999	99.479	107.401	104.483	92.484	91.302
1987	96.387	99.135	96.533	93.905	98.356	95.473
1988	95.145	101.417	100.433	94.943	92.720	93.650
1989	89.864	99.022	93.383	91.710	82.699	79.960
1990	76.882	88.268	84.926	88.168	77.522	73.891
1991	86.890	105.257	74.812	84.133	61.923	55.133

Although there are some differences between the indices over the period, the overall trend is very similar. In the agricultural industry, the Malmquist index is lower than the Tornqvist throughout, excepting the first year. Figure 9.10 shows a divergence between the two measures from 1986 onwards, with the difference between them increasing over time, although there is a sharp fall to a trough in 1990 and a rise in 1991, which both capture.

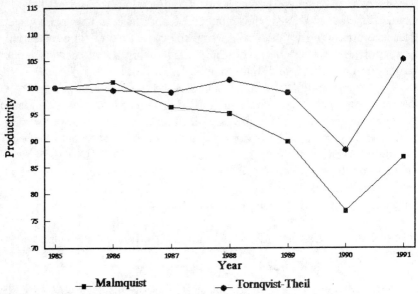

Figure 9.10   Performance Indices - Agriculture

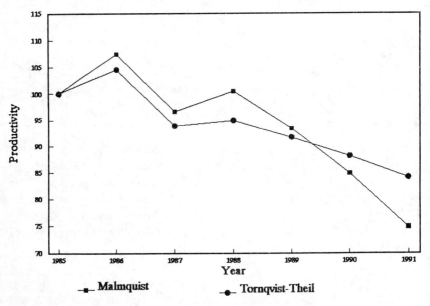

Figure 9.11   Performance Indices - Manufacturing

The Malmquist and Tornqvist results for the manufacturing sector track each other more closely, with the Malmquist higher until 1989. From that year, the two series diverge while continuing to fall sharply. This is shown in Figure 9.11, which demonstrates that both series have the same turning points. It is also reassuring that they cross over, rather than one or the other consistently being an over or under-estimate, which is a common outcome. For both agriculture and industry, the Malmquist index appears to be more sensitive to changing performance, and may thus be a better predictor, but there is no basis for deciding which is more likely to be the correct measure.

Finally, the indices for the service industries move very closely together and again have all the same turning points. This may be due to a greater degree of homogeneity with respect to the production technology in this sector. But certainly the fall over this period is almost 50%, and is agreed by both measures. Note too that in this case the Malmquist is less sensitive to declining productivity. This is shown in Figure 9.12. In all, the two TFP's are almost entirely in agreement, which is often not the case. They are also supported by the econometric estimates of the last chapter, where the tests established that the data were well-behaved.

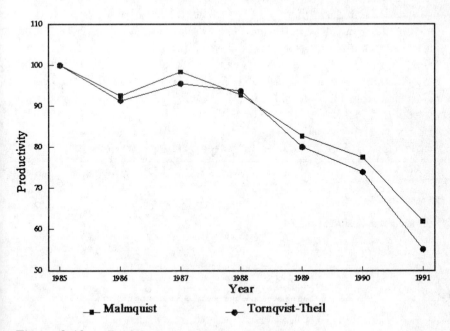

Figure 9.12   Performance Indices - Services

191

Comparing the three industries, the most obvious difference is that whereas industry and services continue to decline, there is a substantial recovery in the agricultural sector in the final year. One good year in agriculture is not the greatest evidence that the sector is on the mend, since it could just be a matter of excellent weather. However, there is nothing in the literature to suggest that this was the case in 1991 and the recovery appears to be genuine. It is entirely plausible that agriculture could be the first industry to recover and this has connotations for policy. The next chapter pursues this issue, by comparing relative efficiency in the three industries.

The consensus view is that the post-socialist countries have undergone a deep recession in the 1990's. This is different from the usual business cycle experienced by established capitalist countries and seems to be peculiar to those undergoing transformation. Economic indicators of aggregate measures of economic performance for Hungary have declined and only in the last couple of years have begun to recover. Hare and Hughes (1991) calculated a number of profitability indicators based on domestic resource costs and social profit rates, which showed a wide range of profitability in some areas of industry in terms of world market prices. At a national level, over two thirds of industrial production was modestly profitable, and less than 10% extremely unprofitable. In another assessment of industrial performance at the national aggregate level, Kornai (1994) reports the index of gross industrial production that begins a sharp decline from 1989 and at the branch level (ie 2 digit industrial classification), Hitchins et al (1995) show a decline since the mid 1980's, using data from the National Bank of Hungary. Data from this last study are reported in Table 9.3.

Table 9.3   Key Economic Indicators: Hungary, 1988 - 1992

	1988	1989	1990	1991	1992
Total GDP	-0.1	0.7	-3.5	-11.9	-4.5
Production indices (real annual growth %)					
Agriculture	-0.4	-6.2	-9.2	-15.7	-22.7
Industry	-0.5	-2.1	-10.1	-16.6	-17.2
Gross Real Earnings (% change)	-4.9	0.9	-3.7	-8.0	1.4

Source: National Bank of Hungary (taken from Hitchins et al, 1995, p.159)

For each of the measurement approaches to firm level productivity, the results produced here support the published ones, with the exception of the TFP and Malmquist results for 1991 in the agriculture industry. A detailed examination of the individual enterprises shows there to be more precise information, as one would expect for a higher level of disaggregation.

Conclusion

Measurement over time imparts considerably more information than can be gained from a single year. If series can be constructed in such a way that two entities can be compared over the same period, relative performance measures can add information that is easy to assimilate, relative to much of the econometric output. Indices do precisely this and in this chapter two sets of indices are derived. The first is an accounting approach, in which the cost shares are used as weights to construct input indices and Tornqvist-Theil TFP indices. This is a well-tested approach and can be used with some confidence. The results show that TFP has fallen in all three industries, with services suffering the worst decline followed by industry and then agriculture. Furthermore, agriculture appears to recover in the last year, whereas the other two sectors do not.

The second approach is the Malmquist productivity index where the panel data enabled the construction of a multi-lateral TFP measures. Comparing the two sets of results showed them to give consistent results. The TFP indices are very similar for the two approaches, which is gratifying, as the derivation of consistent and reliable performance measures are very much at the centre of this study.

The Malmquist results confirm that TFP has fallen in all three industries, with services suffering the worst decline followed by industry and then agriculture. Again, agriculture appears to recover in the last year, whereas the other two sectors do not. A supporting issue is factor substitution, where the overall picture is of the labour input declining least rapidly, so that on a per unit of output basis, labour has been substituted for capital. Also, white collar labour has been substituted for blue collar. A fall in the total number of employees at the same time as the wage bill increased, characterises agriculture. By contrast, in manufacturing, employment and wages are practically constant and in services both employment and wages rise.

193

These firm level results are supported by the national aggregates. The transformational recession in Hungary, as in the other transition countries, does exist. Some authors question the full extent of the fall in productivity levels (but none have so far noted an agricultural recovery). Part is not real, but *mere statistical illusion* (Aslund (1994, p 31) as enterprises move from over-reporting to achieve plan to under-reporting to avoid tax. There is some basis to the argument that this is more prelevant in some industries than others. For example, it may be easier to under-report output in services because of their intangible nature of their products. But equally, agricultural output has frequently been used to pay workers in kind, so could also be understated. What is clear is that neither the national aggregate productivity statistics, nor the firm-level measurement will show any improvement in quality.

10 Decomposing Productivity into Efficiency and Technical Change: Leading Sectors and the Transformation[1]

Introduction

The stages of growth and structural transformation literatures suggest that during the development process agriculture declines in importance relative to industry and later the service sector. However, in Central and Eastern Europe, industrialization was a central feature of development plans and the relative decline of agriculture was forced prematurely by policy.[2]

This chapter completes the intra- and inter-industry results from earlier chapters. It extends the analysis by separating the change in technical efficiency for each firm from shifts in the frontier itself. This is an important distinction since if the frontier shifts because of a change in the available technology, there is productivity growth and not simply an increase in technical efficiency. But, these results are reported in the course of testing the following hypothesis. The strategy of forced growth under socialism gave rise to a production structure unadjusted to user requirements, including domestic consumption, but utilization of a narrow range of products was imposed on buyers by central allocation and shortages. If the natural process of the structural transformation is disrupted by a policy of enforced and premature industrialization, then when that policy changes, the relative importance of the sectors may revert back to that existing before state intervention. Only after a period of adjustment does the natural ordering of development re-establish itself.

---

[1] This chapter is an expanded version of Piesse and Thirtle (1997).

[2] In the next section this proposition is supported by data.

The results do support this hypothesis, but somewhat precariously, since the data series is so short and it is really only the last year that agricultural recovery occurs. Unfortunately, further analysis using longer time series for these enterprises is unlikely to be available, although aggregate industry level data for a larger sample of countries may provide more substantial corroboration.

Reversing the Course of the Structural Transformation in Hungary

In this illustration, the sample enterprises represent the primary, secondary and tertiary sectors. The results of the measurement of technical efficiency in Chapter 6 suggest that in 1985 the average efficiency of the service sector firms was highest, followed by manufacturing and then agriculture. The scale of the enterprise had an impact on this, but as was shown in Chapter 7, the relative levels of technical efficiency did not change when size was taken into account. Then, as the transition progressed and the reform of enterprises intensified, Chapter 9 showed that productivity declined the most in the service sector (37%), by 35% in manufacturing and the lowest in agriculture (21%), possibly reversing the earlier ordering.[3] Thus by the end of period, agriculture is the most productive sector in the Hungary economy and this could well imply that at, least during the transition, agriculture should be supported in its expansion rather than pushed to contract, contrary to the normal dynamics of the structural transformation.

This suggests that liberalization and reliance on market forces may temporarily reverse the normal direction of structural change in the transitional economies as they correct for the bias introduced by earlier policy. This signals that while the reforms are necessary to restructure and reform all aspects of the economy, re-industrialization should not be forced too soon.

---

[3] This is only a possibility because the Tornqvist indices start from the arbitrary value of 100 and the Malmquist was similarly reported to allow maximum comparability. The Malmquist is actually multilateral, starting from the initial year efficiencies, so it will be shown below that agriculture does actually overtake the other sectors.

New Evidence on Old Questions

The superiority of industry over agriculture was suggested by Friedrich List (1841) and played a continuing role in the *theories of economic stages* developed by the German Historical School.[4] The stages approach enjoyed a resurgence when Rostow (1971) popularised the notion of *leading sectors* driven by new technologies. List's three stages of agriculture, manufacturing and commerce, resemble the concept of primary, secondary and tertiary sectors, developed by A G B Fisher in the 1930's and verified by Colin Clark (1940). Clark formalised the relationship between economic progress (the growth of real incomes) and the increase in the proportion of the labour force engaged in manufacturing and later in services.

In the transformation literature introduced in the previous section, the proportions of employment and output in agriculture decline *relatively*, but since industrialization is accompanied by population growth, it is only when the industrial sector has become large enough to absorb more than the increase in numbers that agriculture begins to decline in *absolute* terms. This is known as the *turning point* and Table 10.1 shows the year the turning point occurred and the percentage share employed in agricultural activity in that year. This information is reported for 29 countries. The order of the countries in the Table is determined by the percentage of the workforce employed in agriculture when the turning point was reached. As can be noted, with the exception of South Africa, which is a special case, being a dual economy that was dominated by the fantastic growth of the mining sector, the other seven countries that head the list were all dominated by the USSR and followed its lead.

The USSR is the most extreme case. In 1926, the beginning of Stalin's First Five Year Plan marked the turning point when the proportion of the working population engaged in agriculture was 86.1% Industrialization began and labour was shifted from agriculture into industry at a time when previously only 14% of the labour force were in non-agricultural employment. At a population growth rate of 2% (Nove, 1969, p.180) this required that industrial employment grew at over 14% per year. This was the practical outcome of the great Soviet development debate, in

---

[4] This literature is summarised by Hoselitz (1960) who says that List's view rested not only on the higher productivity of industry, but also on the *social and cultural features by which industrial and agricultural countries differ* (p.202).

which the proponents of genetic development (stressing current costs, returns and comparative advantage) lost to those who favoured the teleological approach, in which the existing situation was to be ignored and the need to industrialise at all costs was accepted. After changing sides in this debate, Stalin followed Lenin's advice, that the way forward was to concentrate resources on *machines to make machines*.

Table 10.1   The Turning Point: Year, with % of Labour in Agriculture

			then Employed in Agriculture					
Country	Date	%	Country	Date	%	Country	Date	%
USSR	1926	86.1	Japan	1947	52.6	Austria	1939	39.0
Romania	1930	78.7	Spain	1950	48.8	Germany	1907	36.8
Yugoslavia	1948	77.8	Portugal	1950	48.4	Denmark	1930	35.6
Bulgaria	1946	75.3	Italy	1936	48.2	Norway	1931	35.3
South Africa*	1921	69.5	Luxembourg	1967	44.5	USA	1910	31.6
Finland	1940	57.4	Belgium	1866	44.4	Canada	1941	27.2
Poland	1950	57.2	Switzerland	1880	42.4	New Zealand	1936	27.2
Hungary	1949	52.9	France	1921	41.5	Argentina	1947	25.2
			Sweden	1920	40.2	Great Britain	1851	21.9
* S.Africa is not included			Czechoslovakia	1921	40.3	Australia	1933	20.5
in either average below						Netherlands	1947	19.3
Average CEE states 69.3						Average all others		36.7

Source: Adapted by the author from Grigg (1982), Table 11, page 109

The other centrally planned economies followed less extreme paths, although as seen in the Table, between 79% to 53% of their labour force is still accounted for by the agricultural sector. This group reached their individual turning points with, on average, almost double the share of the working population in agriculture of that recorded for the other countries (almost 70% as against under 37%). In all the centrally planned economies, the turning point was a matter of policy rather than market forces and industry was supported at the expense of agriculture.

The reform of the CEE countries and the re-establishment of a market economy has led to the introduction of a programme of de-industrialization and restructuring of the existing enterprises. The choice of sectors to receive early attention and support is best informed by a consensus on their relative efficiency, to ensure a successful response to reform. But little attention has been paid to this important issue. Lavigne (1995, p 185) notes that

> For the countries in transition, there was initially no scheme for organising the decline of whole sectors, for promoting small and medium enterprises, for encouraging R&D and modernization, or for *picking winners* for future growth.

Unfortunately, this task is now made more difficult as the data on the relative size of sectors in the transitional economies are not believable. For instance, Table 10.2 lists the shares of agriculture, industry and services in GDP for six such economies, reported by the European Bank. In Hungary, the service sector share is larger than that of the United Kingdom, which is highly unlikely, and from 1988 to 1989 the shares change at a rate that would have impressed Stalin! Furthermore, these European Bank statistics have little in common with the World Bank data, in which the share of Hungarian agriculture stays at around 16% and contrasts with the apparent success of the agricultural sector.[5]

Recent data (Papp, 1995) suggests that while agriculture contributed 6.5% to GDP in 1994, agri-food products accounted for over 20% of total exports but only 7% of imports. For Hungary, agriculture is clearly a leading export sector, and it is one of the few countries able to export grain profitably. From the point of view of this theory, perhaps the most interesting aspects of Table 10.2 are the data for Bulgaria and Romania, where the structural transformation has gone into reverse, and agriculture's

---

[5] The fact that these are ridiculous, and conflict with data from other sources simply reinforces the theory of inadequate and inconsistent data - a major theme throughout this study. Fortunately, these data are not crucial to the analysis in this Chapter.

share has risen relative to industry (or industry fallen relative to agriculture).[6]

Table 10.2   Sectoral Shares of GDP in Transitional Economies (%)

Country	Sector	1988	1989	1990	1991	1992	1993
Bulgaria	Agriculture	11	11	18	15	16	13
	Industry	61	59	51	48	43	42.3
	Services	28	30	31	37	46	44.7
Czech	Agriculture	6	6.3	8.4	6	5.7	6.2
Republic	Industry	61	58.7	57.6	-	45	39.8
	Services	33	35	34	-	49.3	54
Hungary	Agriculture	16	9.7	9.6	8.6	7.3	6.4
	Industry	34	30.1	28.8	25.5	26.4	25.2
	Services	50	60.2	61.6	65.9	66.3	68.4
Poland	Agriculture	13.1	7.8	8.4	9.3	8.3	7.1
	Industry	58	49.5	43.6	39.2	39.6	37.8
	Services	28.9	42.7	48	51.5	52.1	55.1
Romania	Agriculture	13.5	13.9	18	18.5	21.1	21
	Industry	53.7	52.8	48.2	43.6	44.3	41
	Services	32.8	33.3	33.8	37.9	34.6	38
Slovak	Agriculture	6.2	6.3	8.2	5.8	6.1	6.6
Republic	Industry	60.8	59.6	61.6	63.9	38	36.7
	Services	33	34.1	30.2	30.3	55.9	56.7

Source: Selected statistics provided by the European Bank in: Economics of Transition, several issues

---

[6] It has been suggested that the post 1990 downturn in the share of agriculture in Bulgaria is due to a combination of the trading difficulties encountered in circumventing the Balkan blockade. Another factor is the still unresolved land privatisation programme, which has left large amounts of unclaimed produce rotting in the fields.

Colin Clarke's hypothesis can be stated in terms of the effects on GDP per capita of sectoral shares, measured either in terms of employment or value added. Regressing GDP per capita on value added in industry and in services, from 1970-90, for the 115 countries in the World Bank World Tables (1992) shows that there is a relationship. The first set of results in Table 10.3 show that the effects of the shares of industry and services are positive and significant and that the intercept dummy for the ex-command economies is negative and significant. This confirms the expected view that for this group, relative to the other countries, GDP per capita is below the levels expected for the shares of industry and services. However, this table also shows that only 28% of the variance is explained and it is not clear that pooling is justified as the coefficients are considerably different.

Table 10.3   Effect of Sectoral Shares on GDP per Capital, 1970-90

Variable	Industry's Share in Value Added	Services' Share in Value Added	Command Economy Dummy
Coefficient	14199	12907	-1535
t-statistic	(23.58)	(19.67)	(-3.84)

Pooled OLS, Former Command Economies: Dependent variable is Log GDP per capita: Adj R^2 = 0.92

Variable	Industry's Share in Value Added	Services' Share in Value Added	Constant
Coefficient	8.77	9.96	-0.34
t-statistic	(27.34)	(23.48)	(-1.44)

Pooled OLS, Market Economies: Dependent variable is Log GDP per capita: Adj R^2 = 0.64

Variable	Industry's Share in Value Added	Services' Share in Value Added	Constant
Coefficient	6.74	6.76	1.61
t-statistic	(47.24)	(43.64)	(17.88)

Note: This is for 115 Countries Pooled OLS, All Countries: Dependent variable is GDP per capita: Adj R^2 = 0.28

Source: World Bank World Tables, 1992

The rest of Table 10.3 shows that if the logarithm of GDP per capita is used as the dependent variable and the sample is split, the shares explain over 90% of the variance for the ex-command economies and 64% for the rest, which are a very heterogeneous group. These results are a rough indication only and further work is required to extent this to a wider sample of countries.

The Malmquist Index: Comparative Sector Performance in Hungary

The results of the industry comparisons are presented in two parts. First, the within industry measures are constructed with the samples restricted to single sectors. This means that the frontier is comprised of the best practice enterprises in the single industry. Then, the between industry measures include the best firms in the sample as a whole and the frontier may consist of a mixture of enterprises from all three industries, although in fact this is not the case for this sample.

Intra-sector technical progress and the multilateral Malmquist index

It has already been noted that a limitation of the cross-sectional analysis is that the year by year efficiency measures do not take into consideration shifts in the frontier itself. If a individual firm is on the frontier in one period but not the next, this could be due to the introduction of a new technology in the industry which moves the frontier closer to the origin, but to which the firm in question is not able to respond, although continues to practice without diminishing its level of efficiency. However, another firms may be able to take advantage of the new technology, and so overtake their peers. Equally, if there is regression in the industry, the frontier may move to the right, again changing the relative performance of individual enterprises. Therefore the decomposition of inter-temporal changes in performance into efficiency change and technical progress is required.

Table 10.4 reports the mean levels of the changes in the Malmquist TFP measures, technical efficiency and the technical progress for the three industries, in the form of chained indices. The model used is the simplest case, which assumes constant returns to scale.[7] The first third of the table shows that the Malmquist index declines over the sample period for all three industries, although for different reasons. The fall in the Malmquist index is the smallest for agriculture, at 13%, while for manufacturing, it fell by 25% and services by 38%.

---

[7] An alternative VRS model follows shortly.

Table 10.4   Multilateral Technical and Efficiency Change and the Malmquist Indices - Intra Sector

	Malmquist Index			Efficiency Change Index			Technical Change Index		
	Agricult	Man	Services	Agricult	Man	Services	Agricult	Man	Services
1985	83.430	85.526	82.102	83.430	85.526	82.102	100.000	100.000	100.000
1986	84.263	91.856	75.932	79.266	83.391	81.703	106.304	110.150	92.937
1987	80.416	82.561	80.752	77.963	81.137	89.650	103.146	116.488	90.076
1988	79.379	85.896	76.125	77.956	79.542	93.923	101.826	107.457	81.051
1989	74.974	79.867	67.898	58.396	77.514	90.800	128.387	95.725	74.777
1990	64.142	72.634	63.648	74.881	76.060	92.525	85.659	82.933	68.790
1991	72.492	63.984	50.841	74.979	74.327	89.042	96.684	72.698	57.097

The next two columns give some indication of the reasons for this decline in productivity. There is negative TFP growth in the agricultural sector, where the decline over the period is 13%. However the Malmquist confirms the Tornqvist-Theil result that there is a recovery in the last year, when TFP actually increases by 13%, relative to 1990. The decline in TFP is mainly due to a fall in the level of technical efficiency in these firms, which decreased from 83% to 74%, that is, they changed from being 17% inefficient to 26%. The frontier for this industry has shifted further from the origin by 1991, denoting technological regress, but only of 3.5%, with a strong recovery in the last year. For most of the period various degrees of progress can be seen, even if this proceeds in a rather unsteady manner.

Behind these results is the rapid decline in the last two years of the capital input index, and the accelerated fall in blue collar employment, which were shown in Chapter 9. The efficiency index could be further decomposed into pure technical efficiency and scale efficiency, but these results were already considered in Chapter 7, where the main outcome was the discovery that having no information on the nature of the different enterprises made the whole exercise unsatisfactory. To repeat it here would simple obscure what can be determined from these data.

The other two sectors have quite different patterns of performance. TFP in manufacturing is two points higher than for agriculture in the first year, but by 1991 it is more than eight points lower, which is a total decline of 25%. Thus, the decline is almost twice that for agriculture and there is no sign of recovery by the end of the period. Efficiency in manufacturing falls by 13% over the seven years with a consistently downward trend. However, it is the worsening state of technology that accounts for the greater part of the reduced levels of productivity. Technological change is negative from 1988 onwards, and by 1991 has moved backwards 27% relative to the beginning of the period. This is very different from the almost insignificant level of regress in agriculture and suggests that serious attention to technology generation is needed in manufacturing.

The development of the services sector is the hardest to understand. The Malmquist begins at a level lower than for either agriculture or manufacturing, and declines at a faster rate. The construction of the Malmquist index, and the associated decomposition, provides valuable insights into the nature of the difficulties in this industry. The level of efficiency is higher than in the other industries and it increases rather than declining. This is confirmed by the cross-sectional measurement of technical efficiency in Chapter 6. It is an industry with a high proportion of white to blue collar workers, and the average wage is high, as is to be expected with professionally qualified employees and skilled worker in industries like computers.

The underlying cause of the fall in productivity, which is 38%, is the decrease in the level of technology in this industry. The total regression of the technological frontier over the period is 43% and the decline is monotonic, with no sign even of a slowing of the rate of decline. If the data were for a later period, it would be reasonable to assume that this sector was experiencing rapid technological obsolescence. However, it is fairly early in the transition and such an explanation is not really appropriate. Again, interpretation is limited by the lack of information on the firms involved.

Technological regression at this rate would have a very different explanation in say the computer industry, than in the provision of financial services, such as banking or insurance. Interpreting the Malmquist results for the latter type of enterprise is difficult even when there is good information on the firms involved, as has been shown by Piesse and Townsend (1995) who applied this type of analysis to UK building societies.

Another possible interpretation is that while the white collar skilled labour needed by these firms is becoming increasingly scarce (see Figures 5 and 6, in Chapter 9, which show a decline in the wage bill and in actual numbers) in firms where the technology is embodied in human, rather than physical capital. The regression results of Chapters 5 and 8 all show that labour is by far the most important input in services, so a labour-based explanation is most plausible. Capital appeared to be only marginal to the industry and is thus unlikely to explain much. Energy was totally insignificant, leaving only materials, which could mean a great variety of diverse inputs in this case. However, if materials are becoming increasingly scarce and the small firms in the service industries are at the end of the queue, behind manufacturing, the wrong factor proportions between capital and labour may be part of the problem. Thus, ensuring a more equal treatment of industries may be needed as a part of the reform process. Finally, it may be that compared with the other industries, services had a higher initial level of technology and therefore had further to fall.

The cross-industry reduction in the technical change element of the Malmquist index is clearly of concern and not easy to explain at the aggregate level. To say that more investment in research and development is needed to reverse this trend of technical regression is rather glib, and more needs to be known about the nature of R&D in these industries and these enterprises.

In terms of a more general discussion, and to explain why the technological frontier is regressing, it is useful to consider a number of possible scenarios. These can be divided into four main groups. The first is related to technological obsolescence, which was mentioned above. Past research and development investments become redundant as the established technology is overtaken by a completely new process. Alternatively, the technology depreciates and becomes obsolete. Thus, the growth in the net stock of research and development is not equal to the current level of the resources invested in its growth.

The second group is concerned with economic obsolescence. Investment may have been directed towards the development of physical plant and equipment or skills that are no longer required, following changes in consumer demand. For example, a situation where there is continued development in a process to manufacture a now unwanted product is easy to imagine in the transition economies. There is nothing in this study about consumer demand, but markets were developing around the period of this sample and marketing and promotion still in their infancy. Also in this category is technological regress due to movements in relative factor prices. When energy was subsidised, energy intensive processes were developed which would be abandoned in favour of a cheaper factor of production, maybe labour, when subsidies were discontinued.

The third group is where technological regress is due to mismanagement of research and development activity. Inadequate co-ordination of multi-stage projects, with unequal lags associated with various aspects of the new technology which delay completion and implementation

205

will cause a negative growth rate. Specifically, the lag between pure and applied research may be equivalent to good research and poor development. Finally, and possibly of interest in the agricultural industry, is biological obsolescence. The development of a new pesticide will move the frontier positively, but only while the product is effective. As soon as the pests become immune to this, the frontier will regress and remain so until a new treatment is discovered (see Blakeslee, 1987).

There is no way to know which of these, if any, are appropriate in this pre-transition period in Hungary. But, for whatever reason, the technical change element of the Malmquist index indicates a major shift in the production possibility frontier away from the origin in both manufacturing and services. Without this information, the annual changes in efficiency levels are almost meaningless and give a distorted picture of what is happening. The next section which considers inter-industry comparisons may confirm or refute this idea.

Inter-sector technical progress and the multilateral Malmquist index

Thus far, the sectors have been considered independently. This has allowed peer comparisons within sectors and assumed that inherent characteristics, such as industry structure, availability of raw materials and the quality of labour to be homogeneous across all firms. It also allows factors such as the weather in agriculture, the standard of capital equipment in manufacturing or the acceptance of an emerging demand for services to affect all firms to a similar degree.

Since this analysis is confined to the nonparametric frontier construction, pooling is valid. Putting the three industries together allows the construction of productivity indices for the three industries together and provides an indication of their relative productivities, seen particularly in their re-positioning over the period. Table 10.5 reports indices of the mean technical progress and technical efficiency changes and the Malmquist indices for all the firms in the sample. The aggregate results are reported for two different Malmquist indices. The right hand side of the Table shows the constant returns to scale (CRS) version. Imposing an additional constraint (see section D of Chapter 7) give the alternative variable returns to scale (VRS) Malmquist index, which is reported on the left side of the Table.

206

Table 10.5   Multilateral Technical and Efficiency Change and the Malmquist Indices - Inter Sector

	Variable Returns to Scale			Constant Returns to Scale		
	Technical Change Index - Sector Mean					
	Agriculture	Manufacturing	Services	Agriculture	Manufacturing	Services
1985	100.000	100.000	100.000	100.000	100.000	100.000
1986	105.139	103.474	103.675	106.966	103.637	101.111
1987	113.110	111.919	95.760	106.175	100.771	101.337
1988	98.891	104.901	88.472	100.359	96.305	91.330
1989	120.894	100.109	77.793	125.271	96.292	124.528
1990	75.557	81.878	68.968	74.574	72.875	64.746
1991	82.332	74.511	59.833	90.746	70.090	70.115

	Efficiency Change Index - Sector Mean					
	Agriculture	Manufacture	Services	Agriculture	Manufacturing	Services
1985	76.990	79.953	83.079	77.887	76.285	82.403
1986	72.032	79.854	78.510	71.732	78.501	80.218
1987	65.610	65.843	87.354	70.368	68.902	77.223
1988	72.880	74.896	91.009	73.723	74.410	87.728
1989	54.619	74.784	86.670	53.863	69.458	54.558
1990	72.622	78.660	91.849	73.703	77.959	93.339
1991	73.738	76.256	86.551	65.791	68.368	76.485

Malmquist Index - Sector Mean

	Agriculture	Manufacturing	Services	Agriculture	Manufacturing	Services
1985	76.990	79.953	83.079	77.887	76.285	82.403
1986	75.734	82.628	81.395	76.729	81.356	81.110
1987	74.211	73.691	83.650	74.713	69.433	78.255
1988	72.072	78.566	80.518	73.987	71.661	80.122
1989	66.032	74.865	67.424	67.475	66.883	67.939
1990	54.871	64.406	63.346	54.964	56.812	60.434
1991	60.710	56.819	51.786	59.702	47.919	53.627

The terminology in the programming literature is counter-intuitive for those used to econometric estimation. As Figure 7.1 showed, the CRS total product curve is linear. Imposing an addition constraint (Chapter 7, section D) envelopes the data more closely so that firms that are the wrong size are put on the frontier. Thus, the VRS version of the Malmquist is odd, in that it is constructed as the product of technical change and pure technical efficiency. It is net of the scale efficiencies and so is actually a hypothetical index which shows what TFP would be if all the firms were the right size, and could indicate a restructuring policy.

The first part of the Table reports the technology indices. Since the inter-industry results indicated a fall from the initial level of technology in all three cases, it is not surprising that there is still regression for all three industries when the technical frontier is estimated from the pooled sample. Again reflecting the single industry results, the VRS output shows that services exhibit the greatest fall in the level of technology, with the average 1991 level of technology only 60% of that in 1985. This is followed by manufacturing, followed by agriculture.

Clearly, the characteristics of best practice for all industries is different, and there is no assumption of homogeneous technology in production. In addition, the means are the average of enterprises in a single industry, and it is only the frontier that is defined by a group taken from the entire sample. More enterprises are now included in the frontier, and this has the effect of not just shifting the frontier closer to the origin, but also altering its shape (see the figures in Chapter 6). This means that the lack of investment in new technology is not neutral between the sectors. Manufacturing experiences a lower level of technical change in the variable returns to scale model, unlike the other two industries where the reverse is true.

Moving to the index of efficiency change, agriculture and manufacturing enterprises have lower levels of change in efficiency in the pooled sample than they did in the industry-specific analysis. The only positive growth is in efficiency in services, and this falls to only half the reported value in the individual sector analysis when included as part of the pooled sample. Where scale economies are incorporated into the efficiency measurement, even this becomes negative, although it clear that this index of scale adjusted efficiency change is very unstable in this sector.

The resulting Malmquist index combines these two effects. The higher levels of technical efficiency in the service industry helps to reduce the effects of a failure to maintain an adequate increase in technological innovation but all three industries are at a lower level of productivity by the end of the series than at the beginning. Restructuring, the introduction of competition and a poor mix (and/or quality) of inputs has had a negative effect on productivity levels in all three industries. This is noted at the national level, where the volume of investment has declined by 1992 to 27% below its peak level in 1987, resulting in technical backwardness (Central Statistical Office of Hungary, quoted in Kornai, 1994).

When the scale effect is included, in the CRS results shown on the right, the agricultural sector regress is slightly less pronounced, and is only one third of that in the other two sectors. This reflects the results shown in, where agriculture was found to have decreasing scale efficiency over the period. The VRS index is slightly odd, in that it shows what productivity would have been if the farms had been the right size. But, the results indicate that this biases the technical change series, with the decrease in scale efficiency being added to the technological regress. This result may be important, as it is not clear how the VRS index should be used and arguments in the literature continue. Thus, it is the CRS results that are preferred here and these can be compared with Table 9.2 in order to see the effects of pooling the sample.

The CRS results for technical change show that in the pooled sample agriculture and manufacturing regress more than in the single industry model, but the regression for services is lessened. However, this is partially offset by the efficiency changes, which remain the same for agriculture and manufacturing, but now show an erratic decline for services, rather than the efficiency gains of the single sector model.

Since the Malmquist TFP is the product of technical change and efficiency, the results are already predictable. Agriculture shows the smallest decline of 23%, while for manufacturing the figure is 37% and for services 35%. The equivalent figures for the single sectors model were 13%, 25% and 38%, so services looks less disastrous in the pooled model, but manufacturing falls to almost the same extent. These figures are the best comparisons that can be made, but all the approaches give basically consistent results. The most interesting of these is that agriculture appears to have turned the corner in the last year and becomes the most productive industry.

The lesson here is that the efficiency terms alone are thoroughly misleading for inter-temporal comparisons as efficiency change and movement of the frontier are opposite sides of the same coin. To look at one without the other makes little sense, and in the end it is TFP that matters. The TFP index is generally far more stable and trustworthy, while its two components move around much more, but mostly cancel out. Essentially, not much is made of the VRS results, because they give similar TFP's and are less straightforward.

Leading Sectors and Structural Transformation

The Malmquist TFP indices reported in tables 10.4 and 10.5 are multilateral and allow inter-industry and inter-temporal comparisons of TFP. The indices are now applied to the problem raised in the introduction to this illustration. That is, following the relaxation of enforced industrialization by the State, does the relative performance of the sectors revert back to the pre-command economy position before growth and structural transformation can begin again? Since the results were discussed in detail in earlier chapters, and obviously do not change, these will not repeated here. Rather a summary of the major findings is supported by

210

diagrams and followed by an interpretation to illustrate the value of these kinds of measurement methods.

First the within industry analysis, that was reported in Table 10.4. The number of frontier firms in the three sectors is nearly the same, despite the different sized groups (see Table 6.2). Table 10.4 shows that the agricultural enterprises begin by achieving the same level of productivity as the other sectors, although performance levels over time are more volatile, presumably due to the uncertain nature of external factors, such as the weather. However, Table 10.5 showed that farm size appears to be a continuing problem. Manufacturing, in general, does not seem to be affected in this period by privatisation policy, and a large proportion of the operations are still too big. Service firms are smaller, and more efficient, whether the total or the technical efficiency measure is used.

The shift from blue to white collar workers, and the increasing gap between the wages of these two groups is evidence of a structure of incentives directed to the managers or skilled labour group, although there is little evidence of a similar policy for the blue collar workers. Unfortunately, there is little improvement in efficiency in this sample period, although it will inevitably be some time before this effect is clear.

Technical progress, efficiency change and the Malmquist index

Table 10.4 presented the Malmquist indices for the within industry productivity. This measures the relative performance of the sectors and is shown in Figure 10.1.

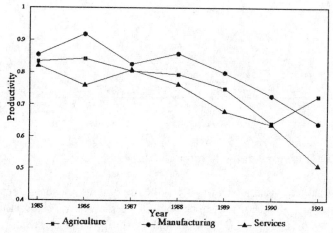

Figure 10.1   Malmquist Index - Intra Sectors

Similarly, Table 10.5 presented the between-industry productivities. This measures the absolute performance of the sectors and is shown in Figure 10.2. Both the un-pooled and the pooled multi-lateral TFP indices clearly show the although there is continued decline in manufacturing and services, agriculture recovers in the last year. The cause of the recovery is not good weather, but the accelerated decline of blue collar labour. Unlike the other two sectors, agriculture has shed a huge amount of labour and is the only sector with rising labour productivity.

The pooled model reported in Figure 10.2 is preferred for inter-industry comparisons as the frontier is defined by the most efficient farms from all three sectors. In this case, services began with the highest mean absolute level of TFP, followed by manufacturing and then agriculture. All sectors had declining TFP indices, due mainly to technological regress, although they were also inefficient in varying degrees. However, by the end of the period, agriculture had the highest productivity of the three sectors, due to the turn-around in the final year.

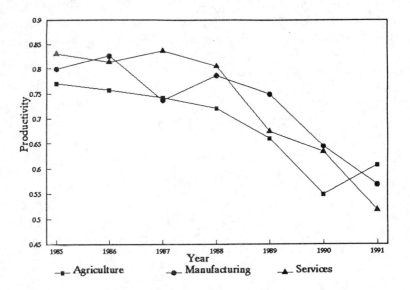

Figure 10.2   Malmquist Index - Inter Sectors

Thus, it appears that agriculture may be the potential leading sector at this stage in the transition, and may gain in output share, rather than continuing the relative decline that is normal in the process of structural transformation.

212

Conclusion

This chapter completes the analysis of the efficiency in Hungary by decomposing the Malmquist productivity index, where the panel data enabled the construction of a multi-lateral TFP measure to compare the sectors. More importantly, it allows the separation of changes in technical efficiency for each firm from shifts in the frontier itself. This is an important distinction since if the frontier shifts because of a change in the available technology, there is technical change and not simply an increase in efficiency. It is also useful to know which firms can keep up, which are responsible for defining the new frontier and also something about the nature of the frontier, particularly whether there is a bias toward a new factor combination or not.

Of these two components, technical regress is mainly responsible for the transitional recession, suggesting that industrial policy should concentrate on stopping the technological backsliding which has occurred. There is as much as a 30% regression of technology in industry and services, while in agriculture it is only about 10% (see Table 10.5). Efficiency levels have fallen much less, with only the 16% decline in agriculture being greater than the losses due to technical regress. The decline in efficiency was only 10% in manufacturing and 7% in services, so for these sectors the technological regress dominates.

But, the efficiency levels started at only around 80%, according to these pooled data, so the gains that can be made from efficiency increases are very substantial. Whereas the single year frontier analysis of Chapter 7 showed final year efficiencies of 76% for agriculture, 89% for industry and 91% for services, the equivalent figures from the pooled model are 66%, 68% and 76% (Table 10.5). In other words, agriculture and manufacturing could have a one third increase in output by becoming 100% efficient and services could increase output by one quarter. So, there are also large gains to getting the system working better, independently of technological change.

The Malmquist decomposition is embedded in a comparison of sectoral productivities which shows that the normal direction of the process of structural transformation may be reversed in the transition. Whereas agriculture should decline in relative importance, it appears to have become the most productive sector and may expand, reversing the normal direction

213

of the process of structural transformation, at least for some period during the transition.[8]

There are obvious limitation to this analysis. Firstly with respect to the Malmquist index, application of the index to firms operating at non-constant returns to scale needs to be interpreted with caution. Grifell-Tatje and Lovell (1995) show that the Malmquist index overstates productivity change when input growth occurs in the presence of decreasing returns to scale and understates productivity growth when input growth occurs in the presence of increasing returns. However, in this application, these biases do not present a problem, but confirm the basic hypothesis. If variable returns to scale are allowed for, the productivity of agriculture, a sector increasingly subject to scale economies, would be higher than reported. Conversely, as a sector experiencing diseconomies of scale, manufacturing would be operating at lower levels than those defined by the Malmquist index.

Fischer et al's (1996) note on informational bias favours the sector still under public control and is the second limitation. Unprivatised enterprises may have to distort the data to appear attractive, and thus be considered suitable for privatisation. In addition, the practice of record keeping and accounting for firms' activities will be more complete in the declining state sector than in the growing private sector.

Finally, the data series is very short for any test of sectoral growth, and may not even cover the beginning of the transition in many countries. But within the constraints of the data inadequacies which complicate the evaluation of a structural transformation, the Malmquist decomposition allows the causes of productivity change to be separately considered and this leads to a better understanding of the forces driving the growth process. It also emphasises the implications of government intervention which distorts the natural progression from primary to secondary and then to tertiary sector development, which is now showing signs of the beginning of a reversal in the new market environment. The early gains in the agricultural sector from increasing recourse to the market are being made as the large scale enterprises are being divided into smaller, more profitable operations, while industry is now in decline, mainly due to a lack of

---

[8] The reversal can only be temporary, since the long run relative decline of agriculture is driven by the dominant demand side issue of relatively low elasticities of demand, whereas here the reversal is based on the supply side notion of a leading sector.

investment in technology rather than poor management practice or unskilled or unmotivated labour. In policy terms, new technology needs to be made available to all the firms, to reverse the technological regress of the last few years, to rejuvenate manufacturing and to build a service sector that is able to contribute to the implementation of the transition programme.

Conclusion

Summary and Major Findings

This is a study of efficiency and productivity, using firm level data for the Hungarian economy for 1985-1991, which covers the beginnings of the transitional period. The study was in a real sense driven by the availability of these data and the alarming disparities in the national income accounts for the CEE countries. Thus, the study tries to identify problem areas in which empirical results are needed just to know what is happening and maybe to help in policy formulation, both to encourage the promotion and to smooth the difficulties of the transition process. The output is really two inter-connected sets of information. The first is an ongoing assessment of what the data can produce and what would have been necessary in order for it to do the job properly. The second is a series of results on efficiency and productivity leading up to, and for the early years of the transition, rather than for the Hungarian economy per see, which are used to formulate limited policy conclusions.

Part I provides the background, sets out the relevant theory and describes the data. Chapter 1 begins by explaining why valid measures of efficiency in production are important in the context of transitional economies and outlines the contribution of the book. Chapter 2 reviews the transition literature to provide a framework for the subsequent analysis. The approach to performance measurement leans heavily on established methodologies in the production economics literature, and the basic theory behind these approaches is outlined in Chapter 3. An analysis of the emergence of an information-based accounting system from the pre-reform socialist reporting procedures is discussed in Chapter 4. This chapter also

216

describes the available data in detail, discusses the reconciliation of the accounting definitions, and provides a rationale for the series used and the choice of the industrial sectors and enterprises that have been included in the analysis that follows.

Part II is the kernel of the study, as it is the estimation and results section. Chapter 5 begins the process by first determining that state of the arts techniques are not compatible with these rather limited data. Dual approaches and flexible functional forms are eschewed in favour of simple and even archaic techniques which work. Thus, the Cobb-Douglas, fitted to cross-sectional data for agriculture, manufacturing and services is the vehicle used for checking the consistency of the data, which was found to be surprisingly well-behaved. Output elasticities of the firms are estimated and the changing relative importance of inputs in the industries is considered, as well as the effect of new forms of ownership on the individual enterprises.

The main result of this chapter is that all the regressions showed that raw materials and labour were the most important inputs, while capital was marginal (significant in agriculture and industry by the end of the period) and energy was not a constraint on production. Energy was not significant for the state enterprises in agriculture, while it was for the private farms. Thus, the implication is that energy has a positive shadow price to private farm managers, but not to State enterprise managers. Labour is underemployed, or inefficient, or both, in the State owned enterprises in agriculture, with little obvious attempt to reverse this. Indeed, the elasticities become increasingly insignificant. Conversely, for the private sector farms, the labour elasticities are large and highly significant.

Chapter 6 resorts to more recent alternatives for measuring efficiency at the firm level. Two econometric and one programming model are presented and the outcomes compared. There is a wide dispersion of efficiency scores, with the lowest firms at around one third efficient, which suggests that large gains are possible if policies can correct these practices. This is the type of information that could well be used to ensure the reforms are achieving the desired objectives, but little can be said here, due to the lack of detailed information accompanying the data. The second set of results compares the three industries. The main finding is that the econometric estimates suggest that the service sector is more efficient than manufacturing and that agriculture is the least efficient. The real problem is that although the efficiency scores are all that can be observed in a single year, over time they depend on the movement of the frontier and should not be studied independently of technical change. Thus, later chapters show that the efficiency measures alone are usually misleading. Finally, the variables that were most frequently slack in the programming models were energy and capital, which corroborates the results of Chapter 5.

Chapter 7 extends the analysis by separating pure technical efficiency and scale efficiency, so as to consider the effect of firm size during the reform process. The importance of enterprise size is central to the privatisation programme, and the programming models allow the separation of pure technical and scale efficiency. The results show high levels of pure technical efficiency, particularly in the services sector where for several years, nearly 50% are on the technical efficiency frontier, although only one third are the right size. The econometric results for agriculture show that there is clear evidence of increasing returns (firms too small) but not of firms being too large, which is something of a surprise since the agricultural units are all relatively large. Furthermore, the nonparametric models show that restructuring has had poor results in that efficiency has declined by about 10%. The cause is simply that the smaller units are less efficient and size has fallen considerably. A further surprise is that in the cross section, it is not scale efficiency that makes the smaller firms worse, but pure technical efficiency. For some reason, large firms are more technically efficient. A final puzzle is that in 1985, more than half the enterprises were too large, but by 1991, the same proportion were too small, with no increase in the number that are the right size. One assumption must be that the wrong enterprises are being reduced in size, but the lack of information on the types of agricultural enterprises makes the data practically worthless for the purpose of determining farm size, when agriculture appeared to be by far the most interesting of the industries in the sample.

The attempts to compare across years using annual cross sectional regressions fared fairly well, but the nonparametric efficiencies without considering technical change are likely to be misleading, as they are frequently simultaneous. Thus, it is essential to achieve inter-temporal comparability, to include technical change and move on to TFP measurement. Fairly naive methods are used to check on the deflators, which were all fairly suspect but were used throughout the time series analysis.

To exploit the panel to the full extent, less restrictive specialised estimation techniques are used. Pooling combines the explanatory power of the cross-sectional and time-series variances and give massive degrees of freedom. The models included a sequential, year-on year technique, specially appropriate for messy CEE data and one and two-factor error components models. The behavioral assumption of cost minimisation can even be claimed to be incorporated in some of these panel models. The results corroborate those from the simple models in Chapter 5, but with far greater power and finesse. Firm and time effects are both found to be important, and hard to interpret. In the short run energy matters and capital does not, while in the long run, the reverse is true. Labour and materials are always important, but labour is the dominant input in the service industries.

Part III begins with Chapter 9, where TFP indices are constructed to compare productivity measures within and between the sectors. Measurement over time imparts considerably more information than can be gained from a single year. Two sets of indices are derived. The first is an accounting approach, in which the cost shares are used as weights to construct input indices and Tornqvist-Theil TFP indices. This is a well-tested approach and can be used with some confidence. The results show that TFP has fallen in all three industries, with services suffering the worst decline followed by manufacturing and then agriculture. Furthermore, agriculture appears to recover in the last year, whereas the other two sectors do not. The cause appears to be an acceleration in the long-continuing process of reducing blue collar employment. It is this cumulative reduction in labour that causes the recovery, rather than especially good weather.

The second approach is the Malmquist productivity index, which leads to multi-lateral TFP measures. Comparing the two sets of results showed them to give consistent results. The TFP indices are very similar for the two approaches, which is gratifying, as the derivation of consistent and reliable performance measures are very much at the centre of this study. The Malmquist results confirm that TFP has fallen in all three industries, with services suffering the worst decline followed by manufacturing and then agriculture. Again, agriculture appears to recover in the last year, whereas the other two sectors do not.

Chapter 10 completes the intra- and inter-industry results. It extends the analysis by separating the change in technical efficiency for each firm from shifts in the frontier itself. This is an important distinction since if the frontier shifts closer to the origin because of a change in the available technology, there is productivity growth and not simply an increase in technical efficiency.

Of these two components, this analysis indicates that technical regress is largely responsible for the transitional recession, suggesting that industrial policy should be concentrate on stopping the technological backsliding which has occurred. There is as much as a 30% regression of technology in industry and services, while in agriculture it is only about 10% (see Table 10.5). Efficiency levels have fallen much less, with only the 16% decline in agriculture being greater than the losses due to technical regress. Thus, the most acute problem with agriculture is the decline in scale efficiency identified in Table 7.3. The decline in efficiency was only 10% in manufacturing and 7% in services, so for these sectors the technological regress dominates.

But, the efficiency levels started at only around 80%, according to these pooled data, so the gains that can be made from efficiency increases are very substantial. Whereas the single year frontier analysis of Chapter 7 showed 1991 efficiencies of 76% for agriculture, 89% for industry and 91% for services, the equivalent figures from the pooled model are 66%, 68% and 76%. In other words, agriculture and manufacturing could have a one third increase in output by becoming 100% efficient and services could increase output by one quarter. So, there are also large gains to getting the system working better, independently of technological change.

These results are reported in the course of testing the following hypothesis, addressed in the application in Chapter 10. The strategy of forced growth under socialism gave rise to a production structure unadjusted to user requirements, including domestic consumption, but utilization of a narrow range of products was imposed on buyers by central allocation and shortages. If the natural process of the structural transformation is disrupted by a policy of enforced and premature industrialization, then when that policy changes, the relative importance of the sectors may revert back to that existing before state intervention. Only after a period of adjustment does the natural ordering of development re-establish itself. Thus, the agricultural productivity recovery result is put in an historical context. Agriculture could be the leading sector to help Hungary through the transition. Whereas agriculture should decline in relative importance, it appears to have become the most productive sector and may expand, reversing the normal direction of the process of structural transformation, at least for some period during the transition. Certainly, comments by the Gyorgy Rasko, Secretary of State for Agriculture, confirm the importance of agricultural exports in the past, and expressed the wish that this should continue. He stated

.. the agricultural and food exports of Hungary have a pivotal role in our integration, firstly with the European Economic Area, given that Hungary is a European country, as well as with the world economy. Further, it should be

220

stressed that the future development of the Hungarian economy and the success of the country's integration into the European Economic Area will continue to rely heavily on the performance of its agricultural exports (Rasko, 1993).[1]

Throughout this summary there have been two strands to the discussion; the first is what has actually been discovered about Hungary and the transition process more generally; the second is an assessment of the limitations of the data and the reliability of the results. Having outlined the major findings, the study concludes by placing these in the context of the recent literature. This shows that these data do corroborate the recent history and experience.

Concluding Remarks

This study is an analysis of financial accounting data for a large number of Hungarian firms from 1985 to 1991, with relevance to other reforming or transitional market economies. Three main objectives have been achieved. The first was a reconciliation of accounting definitions and concepts which enabled the utilization of company balance sheet and income statement data recorded under the rules of the socialist reporting system with the decision-useful information required for modelling firm performance. This necessary aspect of the book was motivated by a recognition of the importance of information at the level of the individual consumer or producer and the difficulties associated with the development, implementation and evaluation of policy reform initiatives, in the absence of such data.

The second aim was to quantify the efficiency of the firms using information from the financial statements. This involved two approaches to productivity measurement, panel data econometrics and programming techniques. These were used to construct measures of efficiency in production for three industrial sectors, disaggregated to the level of the

---

[1] This could be rather unfortunate in the current policy context if the present arrangements for EC membership explicitly exclude trade in agricultural products from the former socialist countries, as protection against incumbent agricultural producers.

221

firm. The two methods chosen were appropriate as they either do not require fully efficient price information or the assumption of profit maximising behaviour, respectively. High levels of complementary between the results from each method added validity to the performance measurement obtained.

Initial cross section estimation showed a radical shift in the use of inputs over the period, as unseen relative factor real price changes resulted in a reallocation of resources. Labour was the most important and energy the least important input in all three industries. Firm ownership did not appear to affect the choice of production technology, implying equal access to factors and no evidence of dual pricing of resources. However, the scale of production was found to be significant. High levels of technical efficiency was evident, for example, in the services sector nearly one third of the firms were operating at full efficiency with respect to skills and competence, but were not on the frontier due to the size of the operation. This is an important issue for the privatisation of enterprises and the separation of large firms into smaller operations is counter-productive if the new units are too small.

Finally, this study has contributed to policy relating to industrial transformation. The use of the Malmquist index, at this level of disaggregation, allowed the specific nature of productivity change to be identified and a distinction made between a lack of growth due to technological regress and that resulting from managerial incompetence, obsolete capital or a lack of skilled labour. In all three sectors, technical change dominated although to varying degrees, suggesting that industrial policy should be concentrated on the level of research and development and the acquisition of technology which was found to be in deficit throughout this study. This has been shown to have negative effects on productivity and growth, although this should be read within the context of the discussion of technological regress earlier in this chapter.

An example illustrated the application of this analysis to policy which considered the distorting effects of past interventionist industrial policy. The policy conclusion is that future support for industrial transformation based on the new institutions and markets should identify common areas of neglect and reverse these, allowing for a market-based reallocation of factors of production across the economy as a whole.

To relate these results briefly to the burgeoning literature on the progress of the transformation is not easy. There is now disappointment that the fall in GDP has been so great, but the transition is an economic transformation, not a prescription for instant growth, as stated repeatedly by Vaclav Klaus (1993). It is the long-term performance in terms of economic growth, stability and consumer welfare that matters. Given the poverty of the production statistics and the tendency that they get even worse during the transition, with biases changing over time, any evaluation is dangerous. False accounting has led to statistical revisions that are sometimes startling. For example, Bulgaria has recently reduced the decline in GDP in 1992 by over 13 percentage points. Still, there are differences too large to be disputed. Poland, the Czech Republic, Hungary and Slovenia have experienced total official GDP reductions of about 20%, although it is likely that little further decline is to be expected.

Thus, Aslund (1994) argues that the fall in national income in the transitional economies has been great everywhere but the declines have varied considerably. A number of comments can be made on this. Firstly, part of it is not real, but merely a statistical illusion. In the old system, over-reporting for the purposes of achieving plan targets was notorious. Now state enterprises and especially new private firms try to evade tax through under-reporting of their production. The easing of restrictions has given evident new life to the informal sector, which represents real production, but is by definition not included in GDP. Much of the prior production represented value detraction, but this did not show up. Equally, nor will quality changes now.

Similarly, the abolition of prior shortages and forced substitution do not show up in statistics. An example of the extent of the mis-counting is given in Aslund (1994, p 31). The decline in Polish GDP was reported as 20% in 1990 and 1991, but recent adjustment have officially reassessed it at only 5-10%, implying that any decline in the standard of living is bound to be much less than first thought, if there is any fall at all. There has been a reallocation of resources from defense and investment to consumption, and consumer welfare also rises as the efficiency of the market increases and forced substitution and rationing by queuing decline.

Secondly, part of the fall in GDP prior to the reforms occurred because of shortages. People reduced their work because they could not purchase anything with their money. Enterprises had to cut back production because of the input constraints on labour (employees absent as they took time out to queue for goods) and on raw materials. Thirdly, GDP has contracted due to the real fall in output, although this is appropriate if the output was not acceptable, and many manufactured goods are unsalable, for example, canned fish and armaments.

But also, some of the more desirable branches of industry, such as food processing and light manufacturing suffered serious declines. This can be explained in part to the fall in spending power due to unemployment, but also many enterprises in these industrial sectors had long suffered from under-investment. These were in such poor shape that they lost out to competitors in the private sector or to domestic production, as the increases in leisure time resulted in households producing their own clothes and performing their own property maintenance. Also, firms in these sectors tended to be small and became subject to the hard budget constraint before the large enterprises.

Thus, the transition of enterprises in practice, from a supply driven structure to a market demand-led economy presents an opportunity to investigate the changes in the approach to productivity. To monitor the progress of the reform programmes it is necessary to develop a robust system of measurement that can truly identify trends in growth and in progression that are sufficiently credible to be included in policy formulation. This is a daunting task and these Hungarian data are certainly not up to it. Clearly, major obstacles to proper measurement remain.

But, there is no doubt that the recession is causing very serious damage. Hungary is suffering from a variety of problems including technical backwardness, widespread poverty due to unemployment and inflation, incomplete institutional reform and lack of infrastructure. Kornai (1994) argues that the private sector is the force on which Hungary can most reply for overcoming the recession, but the reductions in income noted in this study mean that now insufficient demand is holding back private sector development rather than supply constraints. It has been suggested that there are two ways out of the recession. Backwards, by the restoration of the old structure with subsidies, support for inefficient exports, subsidies for state-owned firms to protect jobs and support to ensure the survival of inefficient organisations. Or forwards, which means the elimination of loss-making enterprises and a concerted effort to ensure that the private sector expands, with new jobs being created and reinforced by clear incentives and evidence of the necessary structural adjustment.

It is practically an act of faith that privatisation is so widely considered to be the main means of overcoming the recession and inducing growth. In the long term, efficiency and thereby growth may be increased by the spread of private ownership, and the privatisation of assets previously owned by the state, along with the enforcement of financial discipline in all sectors. But, in the short term, unemployment is increased and demand is thereby reduced and, as has been shown, the post-socialist transformation results in a reduction in aggregate production. Investment led growth is viewed as the ideal solution, but this is a medium or long-term phenomenon. Before privatisation takes place, the state must ensure that assets reach the new owners in the best possible condition. Conservation and careful maintenance of assets is required, but many firms need reorganisation and thus usually entails investment. Thus, managers are being given greater incentives to assess, repair and invest, so that the privatised assets are valuable, rather than being in poor condition. All of these developments require decent measurement and accounting, or the process cannot work, so this book returns to its starting point.

Finally, it does seem that policies which force one industrial sector to advance at the expense of another have proved to be unsuccessful and in some cases damaging. Historically, all of the CEE economies pursued highly interventionist policies resulting in the misallocation of resources between sectors. Future support for the industrial transformation, based on a neutral approach, should identify common areas of neglect and reverse them, allowing the economy as a whole to realise the benefits. Research and development and the acquisition of technology has been found to be in deficit throughout this study, with negative effects on productivity and growth. The highest returns should flow from expenditures with public good characteristics and those that increase the likelihood of spillovers from innovative firms to others, as well as between sectors.

Thus, the transformation literature has assimilated the basic tenets of endogenous growth theory, but many of the theories of economic growth were developed in a context of western countries and markets and may not be easily transferred to transitional economies. For example, it is not clear what rate of growth can be expected after four decades of distorted industrial policy and restricted markets. But, the developing high levels of human capital in the CEE countries provides a good basis for optimism and the cumulative nature of growth of technical knowledge will assist the catching up process. There was every indication that Hungary was moving along a traditional path of economic development prior to 1945 (see Hitchens et al, 1995, ch 8). The results of this study suggest that the Hungarian economy may be moving back towards this earlier growth path, with agriculture recovering first, although a painful period of adjustment is necessary to reverse the negative effects of central planning from 1945-89.

Bibliography

Adams W and Brock W (1986), *The Bigness Complex*, Pantheon, New York.

Aghion P and Blanchard O (1994), On the Speed of Transition in Central Europe, *NBER Macroeconomic Annual*, **9**, 283-320.

Aigner D, Lovell C A K and Schmidt P (1977), Formulation and Estimation of Stochastic Frontier Models, *Journal of Econometrics*, **6**, 21-37.

Alexander and Archer (1992), *The European Accounting Guide*, Academic Press, London.

Anderson J, Pray C and Spiridonova S (1996), *The Other X percent of the Global Agricultural Knowledge System: The Past and Future of the Former Soviet Union Agricultural Research System*, presented at Development Studies Association Conference, University of Reading, 1996.

Aslund A (1994), Lessons of the First Four Years of Systemic Change in Eastern Europe, *Journal of Comparative Economics*, **19**, 22-38.

Bailey D (1988), *Accounting in Socialist Countries*, Routledge.

Balcerowicz L (1995), *Socialism, Capitalism, Transformation*, Central European University Press, Budapest.

Baltagi B (1995), *Econometric Analysis of Panel Data*, Wiley, Chichester.

Baltagi B and Griffin J (1984), Short and Long Run Effects in Pooled Models, *International Economic Review*, **25**, 631-45.

Barros A (1993), *Some Implications of New Growth Theory for Economic Development*, paper presented at the ESRC Development Economics Study Group, LSE, February.

Bator F M (1957), The Simple Analytics of Welfare Maximization, *American Economic Review*, **47**, 22-59.

226

Baumol W (1958), On the Theory of Oligopoly, *Economica*, **24**.

Beckford G (1972), Strategies for agricultural development: comment, *Research Institute Studies in Agricultural Economics, Trade, and Development*, **9:2**, 149-54.

Ben-Ner A and Neuberger E (1992), The feasibility of planned market systems: the Yugoslav visible hand and negotiated planning, *Journal of Comparative Economics*, **14**, 768-790.

Berman K and Berman M (1989), An empirical test of the theory of the labour-managed firm, *Journal of Comparative Economics*, **13**, 281-300.

Berndt E R and Christensen L R (1973), The Translog Production Function and the Substitution of Equipment, Structures and Labour in US Manufacturing, 1926-68, *Journal of Econometrics*, **1:1**.

Berndt E R and Khaled M S (1979), Parametric Productivity Measurement and Choice among Flexible Functional Forms, *Journal of Political Economy*, **87:6**, 1220-1245.

Binswanger H, Deininger K and Feder G (1995), Power, Distortions and Reform in Agricultural Land Markets, in *Handbook of Development Economics, Vol III*, Berman and Srinivasan (eds), North Holland, Amsterdam.

Blakeslee R (1987), Measuring the Requirements and Benefits of Productivity Maintenance Research, Miscellaneous Publication, 52-1987, University of Minnesota.

Blanchard O (1996), Theoretical Aspects of Transition, *American Economic Review*, **86:2**, 117-122, Papers and Proceedings, May.

Bolton P and Roland G (1992), Privatisation in Central and Eastern Europe, *Economic Policy*, **15**, 276-309.

Boyd M L (1987), The performance of private and co-operative socialist organisation: postwar Yugoslav agriculture, *Review of Economics and Statistics*, **69:2**, 205-14.

Boyd M L (1991), *Organisation, Performance and System Choice*, Westview Press.

Brada J (1996), Privatisation is Transition - or is it? Journal of Economic Perspectives, **10:2**, 67-86.

Brada F and King A (1993), Is private farming more efficient than socialized agriculture?, *Economica*, **60**, 41-56.

Brada J, Singh I and Torok A (1994), *Firms Afloat and Firms Adrift: Hungarian Industry and the Economic Transition*, M E Sharpe, London.

Bratowski A (1993), the Shock of Transformation or the Transformation of the Shock? The Big Bang in Poland and Official Statistics, *Communist Economics and Economic Transformation*, **1**.

Brewster J M (1950), The Machine Process in Agriculture and Industry, *Journal of Farm Economics*, 32, 69-81.

Bromwich M (1992), *Financial Reporting, Information and Capital Markets*, Pitman, London.

Brooks K (1991), Decollectivization and the Agricultural Transition in East-Central Europe, *Transactional Law and Contemporary Problems*, **1:2**, 508-37.

Bureau J C, Butault J P and Barkaoui A (1992), Productivity Gaps Between European and United States Agriculture, in S Narayayanam and King J (eds) *Measuring Agricultural Productivity and Related Data for Regional, National and International Comparisons*, Agriculture Canada, Ottawa.

Capalbo S, Denny M, Hoque A and Overton C (1991), *Methodologies for Comparisons of Agricultural Output, Input and Productivity*, USDA, Economic Research Service, Washington DC.

Charap J and Zemplinerova A (1993), *Restructuring in the Czech Economy*, EBRD Working Paper no.2, London.

Caudill S, Ford J and Gropper D (1995), Frontier Estimation and Firm-specific Inefficiency Measures in the Presence of Heteroscedasticity, *Journal of Business and Economic Statistics*, **13:1**, 105-111.

Caves D W, Christensen L R and Diewert W E (1982), Multilateral Comparisons of Output, Input and Productivity, *Economic Journal* **92**, 73-86.

Chamberlain G (1984), Panel Data, in Griliches and Intrilligator, eds, *Handbook of Econometrics*, North-Holland, Amsterdam.

Chambers R G (1988), *Applied Production Analysis: A Dual Approach*, Cambridge University Press, Cambridge.

Charnes A, Cooper W and Sueyoshi T (1988), A Goal Programming/Constrained Regression Review of the Bell System Breakup, *Management Science*, **34**, 1-26.

Christensen L R (1975), Concepts and Measurement of Agricultural Productivity, *American Journal of Agricultural Economics*, **57:5**, 910-15.

Clark C (1940), *The Conditions of Economic Progress*, Macmillan, London.

Clarke R (1989), *Hungary: The 2nd Decade of Economic Reform*, Longman, London.

Coase R H (1937), The nature of the firm, *Economica*, **4**, 386-405.

Corbett J and Mayer C (1991), *Financial Reform in Eastern Europe: Progress with the Wrong Model*, CEPR Discussion Paper, no 603, London.

Cowling K (1990), A New Industrial Strategy: Preparing Europe for the Turn of the Century, *International Journal of Industrial Organisation*, **8**, 165-183.

Deininger K (1993), *Cooperatives and the Breakup of Large Mechanised Farms*, World Bank Discussion Paper, **218**, World Bank, Washington, DC.

Diewert W E (1982), Duality Approaches to Microeconomic Theory, in Arrow and Intrilligator (eds), *Handbook of Mathematical Economics*, Vol II, North-Holland, Amsterdam.

Diewert W E (1986), *Index Numbers*, Discussion Paper No 86-33, Department of Economics, University of British Columbia, Vancouver.

Estrin S (1989), Some reflections on self-management, social choice, and reform in Eastern Europe, *Journal of Comparative Economics*, **15**, 349-66.

Estrin S, Gelb A and Singh I (1995), Shocks and Adjustments by Firms in Transition: A Comparative Study, *Journal of Comparative Economics*, **21**, 131-58.

Fare R and Grosskopf S (1992), Malmquist Indices and Fisher Ideal Indexes, *Economic Journal*, **102:410**, 158-60.

Fare R, Grosskopf S, Lindgren B and Roos P (1992), Productivity Changes in Swedish Pharmacies 1980-1989: A Nonparametric Malmquist Approach, *Journal of Productivity Analysis*, **3**, 85-101.

Fare R, Grosskopf S and Lovell C A K (1983), The Structure of Technical Efficiency, *Scandinavian Journal of Economics*, **85**, 181-90.

Fare R, Grosskopf S and Lovell C A K (1985), *The Measurement of Efficiency of Production*, Kluwer-Nijhoff, Boston.

Fare R, Grosskopf S, Norris M and Zhang Z (1994), Productivity Growth, Technical Progress and Efficiency Change in Industrialised Countries, *American Economic Review*, **84**, 66-83.

Farrell M (1957), The Measurement of Productive Efficiency, *Journal of the Royal Statistical Society*, Series A (General), **120**, 253-81.

Ferrier D and Lovell C (1990), Measuring Cost Efficiency in Banking: Econometric and Linear Programming Evidence, *Journal of Econometrics*, **46**, 229-45.

Fischer S and Gelb A (1991), The Process of Socialist Economic Transformation, *Journal of Economic Perspectives*, **5:4**, 91-105.

Fischer S, Sahay R and Vegh C (1996), Economies in Transition: The Beginnings of Growth, *American Economic Review*, **86:2**, 229-233, Papers and Proceedings, May.

Geroski P and Jacquemin A (1985), Corporate Competitiveness in Europe, *Economic Policy*, **1**, 170-218.

Good D (1994), The Economic Lag of Central and Eastern Europe: Income Estimates for the Hapsburg Successor States, 1870-1910, *Journal of Economic History*, **54:4**, 869-91.

Grabowski R (1988), The theory of induced institutional innovation: a critique, *World Development*, **16**, 385-394.

Greene W (1980), Maximum Likelihood Estimates of Econometric Frontier Functions, *Journal of Econometrics*, **13**, 27-56.

Greene W (1991), *The Econometric Approach to Efficiency Measurement*, Stern School of Business, New York University, Mimeo.

Greene W (1993), *Econometric Analysis*, 2nd ed, Macmillan, New York.
Grifell-Tatje E and Lovell C A K (1995), A Note on the Malmquist Productivity Index, *Economic Letters* **47**, 169-75.

Griffin K (1974), *The Political Economy of Agrarian Change: An Essay on the Green Revolution*, Harvard University Press, Cambridge.

Grigg D (1982), *The Dynamics of Agricultural Change*, Hutchinson, London.

Griliches Z (1986), Economic Data Issues, Chapter 25 in the *Handbook of Econometrics, Volume 3,* Griliches and Intrilligator (eds), Amsterdam, North Holland.

Griliches Z (1994), Productivity, R&D and the data Constraint, *American Economic Review*, **84:1**, 1-23.

Grossman G (1990), Promoting New Industrial Activities: A Survey of Recent Arguments and Evidence, *OECD Economic Studies*, 87-125.

Grossman S and Hart O (1986), The costs and benefits of ownership: A theory of vertical and lateral integration, *Journal of Political Economy*, **94**, 691-719.

Hayami Y and Ruttan V (1985), *Agricultural Development: An International Perspective*, Johns Hopkins, Baltimore.

Hienonyri O (1990), *Economic Policies for the New Hungary: Proposals for a Coherent Approach*, Battelle Press.

Hill B E and Ingersent K A (1982), *An Economic Analysis of Agriculture*, 2nd Edition, Heinemann, London.

Hitchens D, Birnie J, Hamar J, Wagner K and Zemplinerova A (1995), *Competitiveness of Industry in the Czech Republic and Hungary*, Avebury, Aldershot.

Hofler R A and Payne J E (1993), Efficiency in Socialist versus Private Agricultural Production: The Case of Yugoslavia, *Review of Economics and Statistics*, **73**, 153-157.

Houthakker H (1965), New Evidence on Demand Elasticities, *Econometrica*, **33**, 277-88.

Hughes G and Hare P (1991), Competitiveness and industrial Restructuring in Czechoslovakia, Hungary and Poland, *European Economy*, Special Edition, no.2, Brussels: Commission of the European Communities.

Jensen M and Meckling W (1976), Theory of the Firm: Managerial Behaviour, Agency Costs and Ownership Structure, *Journal of Financial Economics*, **3**, 305-360.

Johnson N and Ruttan V (1994), Why are Farms so Small? *World Development*, **22:5**, 691-706.

Jondrow J, Lovell C A K, Materov I and Schmidt P (1982), On the Estimation of Technical Inefficiency in the Stochastic Frontier Production Function Model, *Journal of Econometrics*, **19**, 233-238.

Jorgeson DW and Nishimizu M (1978), US and Japanese Economic Growth, 1952-1974: an International Comparison, *Economic Journal* **88**, 707-26.

Kawagoe T and Hayami Y (1985), An Intercountry Comparison of Agricultural Production Efficiency, *American Journal of Agricultural Economics*, **67**, 87-92.

Keating G and Hoffman J (1990), *The Remaking of Europe*, Credit Suisse First Boston, London.

Kirzer I (1979), Comment: X-Inefficiency, Error and the Scope for Entrepreneurship, in M J Rizzo (ed), *Time Uncertainty and Decision*, Lexington.

Klaus V (1994), *Rebirth of a Country: Five Years After*, Ringier, Prague.

Kolanda M and Kubista V (1991), *Costs, Performances and Behaviour of Czechoslovak Manufacturing Enterprises on World Markets*, Institute for Forecasting, Academy of Science Working Paper, Prague.

Kornai J (1993), Transformational Recession: A General Phenomenon Examined through the Example of Hungary's Development, *Economie Applique*, **46:2**, 181-227.

Kornai J (1994), Transformational Recession: The Main Causes, *Journal of Comparative Economics*, **19**, 39-63 .

Kravis I (1976), A Survey of International Comparisons of Productivity, *Economic Journal*, **86**, 1-44.

231

Kravis I, Heston A and Summers R (1978), *International Comparisons of Real Product and Purchasing Power*, United Nations International Comparison Project: Phase II, World Bank, Johns Hopkins University Press, Baltimore.

Kuh E (1959), The Validity of Cross-Sectionally Estimated Behaviour Equations in Time-Series Applications, *Econometrica*, 27, 197-214.

Landesmann M and Szekely I (1995), *Industrial Restructuring and Trade Reorientation in Eastern Europe*, (eds), Cambridge University Press, Cambridge.

Lavigne M (1995), *The Economics of Transition*, Macmillan, London.

LIMDEP Version 60 (1992) *Econometric Software*, Inc Bellport, New York.

Lingard J and Rayner A J (1975), Productivity Growth in Agriculture: A Measurement Framework, *Journal of Agricultural Economics*, 26:1, 87-104.

Lipton M (1989), Agricultural Research and Modern Plant Varieties in Sub-Saharan Africa: Generalizations, Realities and Conclusions, *Journal of International Development*, 1:1, 168-79.

List F (1841), *Das Nationale System der Politishen Oekoenomie*, J G Cotta, Stuttgart.

Lund P (1983), The Use of Alternative Measures of Farm Size in Analysing the Size and Efficiency Relationship, *Journal of Agricultural Economics*, 34:2 187-189.

Magyar Statisztikia Evkonyv (1993),*The Statistical Yearbook of Hungary 1992*, Budapest.

Malmquist S (1953), Index Numbers and Indifference Surfaces, *Trabajos de Estadistica*, 4, 209-42.

Marschak J and Andrews W (1944), Random Simultaneous Equations and the Theory of production, *Econometrica*, 12, 143-205.

McFadden D L (1966), *Cost, Revenue and Profit Functions: A Cursory Review*, Working Paper No.86, University of California at Berkeley.

McKinnon R (1991), *The order of Economic Liberalisation: Financial Control in the Transition to a Market*, Johns Hopkins University Press, Baltimore.

Milgrom P and Roberts J (1989), Bargaining Costs, Influence Costs and the Organisation of Economic Activity, in Alt and Shepsle, (eds) *The Foundations of Political Economy*, Harvard University Press, Cambridge.

Muller J (1974), On Sources of Measured Technical Efficiency: the Impact of Information, *American Journal of Agricultural Economics*, **56**, 730-738.

Mundlak Y (1978), On the Pooling of Time Series and Cross Sectional Data, *Econometrica*, **48**, 69-86.

Murrell P (1991), Can Neoclassical Economics Underpin the Reform of Centrally Planned Economies? *Journal of Economic Perspectives*, **5:4**, 59-76.

Nishimizu M and Page J (1982), Total Factor Productivity Growth, Technological Progress and Technical Efficiency Change: Dimensions of Productivity Change in Yugoslavia, 1965-1978, *Economic Journal* **92**, 920-36.

Nove A (1972), *An Economic History of the USSR*, Pelican, Harmonsworth, Middx.

Olson J, Schmidt P and Waldman D (1980), A Monte Carlo Study of Estimators of Stochastic Frontier Production Functions, *Journal of Econometrics*, **13**, 423-445.

Papp B (1995), A Survey of Hungary, *Business Central Europe*, December, 35-47.

Pasour E (1981), A Further Note on the Measurement of Efficiency and Economies of Farm Size, *Journal of Agricultural Economics*, **32:2**, 132-46.

Peterson W and Kislev Y (1991), *Economies of Scale in Agriculture: A Reexamination of the Evidence*, Staff paper 91-43, Department of Agricultural and Applied Economics, University of Minnesota, St Paul, Minn.

Piesse J (1993), The Transition to a New Accounting System: The Case of Hungary, *Journal of European Business Education*, **2:2**, 19-29.

Piesse J and Thirtle C (1997), Sector Level Efficiency and Productivity Measurement in Hungary, 1985-1991: Reversing the Course of Structural Transformation, *Eastern European Economics*, **35:4**, 5-39.

Piesse J, Thirtle C and Turk J (1996), Efficiency and Ownership in Slovene Dairying: A Comparison of Econometric and Programming Techniques, *Journal of Comparative Economics*, **22**, 1-22.

Piesse J and Thirtle C (1996), The Productivity of Private and Social Farms: Multilateral Malmquist Indices for Slovene Dairying Enterprises, *Journal of Productivity Analysis*, **7**, 447-460.

Piesse J and Townsend R (1995), The Measurement of Productive Efficiency in UK Building Societies, *Applied Financial Economics*, **5:6**, 397-408.

Pinto B and van Wijnbergen S (1994), *Ownership and Corporate Control in Poland: Why State Firms Defied the Odds*, Policy Research Department Working Paper no 1308, World Bank, Washington DC.

Portes R and Spaventa L (1990), *The Impact of Eastern Europe*, Centre for Economic Policy Research, Discussion Paper London.

Prais S and Houthakker H (1955), *The Analysis of Family Budgets*, Cambridge University Press, Cambridge.

Prasnikar J, Svejnar J and Klinedinst M (1992), Structural Adjustment Policies and the Productive Efficiency of Socialist Enterprises, *European Economic Review*, **36**, 179-99.

Rasko G (1993), *Hungarian Experience with Structural Adjustment and Privatization of Agriculture*, Papers of the 9th Farm Management Congress, Budapest, compiled by C Forgacs, Farm Management Development Foundation.

Roland G (1994), *On the Speed and Sequencing of Privatisation and Restructuring*, CEPR Discussion Paper no.942, London.

Rostow W W (1971), *The Stages of Economic Growth*, 2nd ed, Cambridge University Press.

Russell N and Young T (1983), Frontier Production Functions and the Measurement of Technical Efficiency, *Journal of Agricultural Economics*, **34:2**, 139-150.

Sachs J (1993), *Poland's Jump to the Market Economy*, MIT Press, Cambridge.

Sachs J (1996), The Transition at Mid Decade, *American Economic Review*, **86:2**, 128-133, Papers and Proceedings, May.

Salter W (1966), *Productivity and Technical Change*, 2nd Edition, The University Press, Cambridge.

Schmidt P (1988), Estimation of a Fixed-Effect Cobb-Douglas System using Panel Data, *Journal of Econometrics*, **37**, 361-380.

Shepard R (1953), *Cost and Production Functions*, Princeton University Press.

Solow R (1957), Technical Change and the Aggregate Production Function, *Review of Economics and Statistics*, **39:3**, 312-320.

Stiglitz J (1994), *Whither Socialism?* The MIT Press, Cambridge, Mass.

Sunderland A (1980), Capital Transfer Tax and Farming, *Fiscal Studies*, **1**, 51-65.

Svejnar J (1991), Microeconomic Issues in the Transition to a Market Economy, *Journal of Economic Perspectives*, **5:4**, 123-38.

Swain N (1992), *Hungary: the rise and Fall of Feasible Socialism*, VERSO, London.

Thirtle C and Bottomley P (1992), Total factor productivity in UK agriculture, 1967-90, *Journal of Agricultural Economics*, **43:3**, 381-400.

Timmer C (1971), Using a Probabilistic Frontier Production Function to Measure Technical Efficiency, *Journal of Political Economy*, **69**, 776-94.

Tybout J R (1992), Making Noisy Data Sing, *Journal of Econometrics*, **53**, 25-44.

Waldman D (1982), A Stationary Point for the Stochastic Frontier Likelihood, *Journal of Econometrics*, **18**, 275-279.

Walters A A (1963), Production and Cost Functions: An Econometric Survey, *Econometrica*, **31**, 1-66 .

Walters A A (1968), *An Introduction to Econometrics*, Macmillan, London. van Brabant J (1987), *Adjustment, Structural Change and Economic Efficiency*, Cambridge University Press.

Zou L (1992), Ownership Structure and Efficiency: An Incentive Mechanism Approach, *Journal of Comparative Economics*, **16**, 399-432.